2014
To Isabelle
my Favorite Pastry Queen!
Happy Birthday
Love, Kath

Pastry Queen
Parties

Pastry Queen Parties

Rebecca Rather
and Alison Oresman

PHOTOGRAPHY BY
Laurie Smith

Entertaining
Friends and Family,
Texas Style

TEN SPEED PRESS
Berkeley

For my sister, Mary Jane (1956–2007)
RR

For my parents, Patricia and Donald Oresman
AO

Published in the United States by Ten Speed Press,
an imprint of the Crown Publishing Group,
a division of Random House, Inc., New York.
www.crownpublishing.com
www.tenspeed.com

Ten Speed Press and the Ten Speed Press colophon are
registered trademarks of Random House, Inc.

Library of Congress Cataloging-in-Publication Data on
file with publisher

ISBN 978-1-58008-990-6
Printed in China

Design by Toni Tajima
Food and prop styling by Erica McNeish

10 9 8 7 6 5 4 3 2 1
First Edition

Contents

Introduction

WE TEXANS are known for a lot of things, including our knack for entertaining and our penchant for backslapping, happy-talking, generous hospitality. Whether it's a glittering, dress-up soiree; a spur-of-the-moment informal gathering; or an intimate dinner, Texans love to party and they do it with gusto. A Texas native myself, I've created parties in just about every corner of the state, starting with the beach weenie roasts I masterminded as a teen on the Gulf Coast's Bolivar Peninsula, then moving on to pasta and wine parties as a new bride in Houston's River Oaks neighborhood, black-tie bashes for the likes of Audrey Hepburn and Sarah Ferguson, Duchess of York, as a Houston-based caterer, and finally, informal garden-to-table feasts in my current hometown of Fredericksburg, smack in the heart of the Texas Hill Country. These days I'm in the business of entertaining daily at my nine-year-old Rather Sweet Bakery & Café, where we serve up breakfast and lunch as well as plenty of cakes, pastries, brownies, and pies for snacking in between.

As far as I know, it's darn near impossible to grow up Texan without succumbing to the urge to entertain. I figure my lifelong passion for parties stems from my genetic makeup as well as my Lone Star State upbringing. Hey, friendship is our state motto. And what's a party but a pack of friends—old, new, and just-about-to-be friends—eating and drinking together?

A Texan's natural conviviality and our state's natural bounty combine to make fertile ground for food-centered entertaining. We feast on homegrown tomatoes for at least half of the year, oranges and grapefruit in winter, peaches and berries in the spring, and pecans and persimmons in the fall. The Gulf Coast is a cornucopia of high-quality seafood. Numerous cattle ranches, excellent pork, Texas lamb, and an abundance of wild game mean meat is almost always featured prominently on the menu.

During hunting season, dove, duck, venison, quail, and wild boar show up at many local dinner parties. Everybody wins—the wives are dropped off to shop in town and the guys head for the countryside, dogs and shotguns in tow, and return home with enough wild game to feed family and friends. (Or at least that's the way it was in the old days. I know plenty of sharp-shooting women whose husbands wouldn't dare leave them behind to go hunting.)

Hill Country ranch parties are epidemic in mid-April when San Antonio billionaire Red McCombs holds his annual Texas longhorn cattle auction at his Johnson City RM Ranch. Weekend ranchers come in from all over the country to buy the horned cows, which are more ornamental than edible. Barbecue—ribs,

brisket, pork, and even *cabrito* (goat)—is often featured, along with corn on the cob (perhaps flavored with poblano chile butter), beans, and make-ahead salads.

When the question of parties arises here, Texans tend to respond with, "Why not?"

Yvonne Bowden, a particularly creative friend, recently hosted a poolside spaghetti party with a twist—no utensils allowed. She supplied disposable plastic gloves in a chi-chi shade of lavender, and we dug in with our hands. Soon a few guests strayed well beyond eating with their gloved hands, and some major league meatball pitching ensued. Yvonne vowed to serve spaghetti with ground meat sauce next time.

Texas parties often revolve around games. Skeet shooting get-togethers are common for men and women, and ranch bocce, played free-style winding up and down the hilly terrain, is a favorite among ranch owners in the Hill Country. It should come as no surprise that many

Texas parties have a casual feel, and cowboy boots are often the footwear of choice, even during the heat of the summer.

Even Kay Oxford, my dear Houston friend and veteran entertainer who keeps her formal dining room table set and "camera ready" at all times, says that no matter how fancy the food, she usually invites her guests to show up in casual attire.

I caught the entertaining bug from my mother, who continued to trump up excuses to party long after she became ill with kidney disease. Her penchant for all things Mexican meant that her parties were often Mexican-themed, perfect for our south-of-the-border-style home. She'd serve easy-to-prepare Tex-Mex creations on her festive Mexican pottery, and always offered guests a generous flow of drinks and laughter. She often entertained in one of her many colorful, hand-embroidered Mexican dresses, and I remember her greeting guests with such radiant happiness that I vowed right

then to follow in her party-throwing footsteps when I was old enough to have a home of my own.

As soon as I married—more than a few parties ago—I hosted informal dinners in our Houston dining room. I'd throw open the door to the yard outside and we'd feast on wine and pasta. The parties were a success, but my marriage wasn't, and I soon needed to find a job to support my baby daughter, Frances, and myself. The parties continued, but, as a caterer, I helped others throw theirs. For a celebration honoring Sarah Ferguson, Duchess of York, I created 650 individual, white butter cakes filled with lemon curd and iced them in a pale yellow that matched her evening dress.

You won't find that recipe in this book, because I've written *Pastry Queen Parties* for home cooks like you. I doubt you throw parties for a living, but you may live to throw parties, and staying up all night to ice 650 of anything is not likely to make it onto your already packed "to-do" list. On the other hand, how about whipping up a batch of Lemon-Chip Cookies (page 205) or Black-and-White Bars (page 208), both of which can be made ahead for a soignée little cocktail party this weekend? If you don't have a matching cocktail dress, so much the better. Matchy-matchy is so 1980s.

Entertaining has always excited and inspired me. After my first book, *The Pastry Queen*, came out in 2004, *More* magazine invited me to create a backyard party for a multi-page spread. At the time, it struck me that I found it easier doing that than dreaming up a new soup of the day for my bakery. From that moment on I decided to do a book about entertaining, and I wanted it to include foods from all of my favorite Texas places. The state of Texas is bigger than many European countries and our food covers a lot of ground. Our culinary history is as rich and varied as the people who have settled here: Germans and Czechs in the Texas Hill Country; Cajun, Creole, and southern traditions concentrated in East Texas, Alsatians in the Rio Grande valley, and, of course, the strong Mexican influence that emanates from San Antonio.

I've lived in or near all of the places included in this book's six chapters, and each region holds a special meaning for me. Once you've cooked your way through this book, I'm betting you'll feel the same way.

NOTE: A number of the recipes in *Pastry Queen Parties* are what I call "Party Express" dishes: they can be whipped up in 60 minutes or less. You'll recognize them by the 🏃 following the yield line.

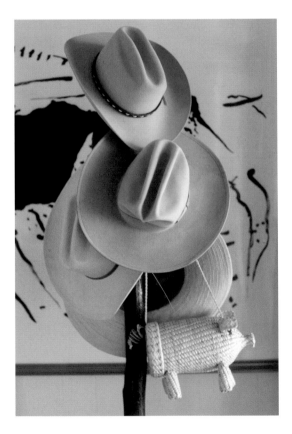

CHAPTER ONE

HILL COUNTRY GARDEN PARTY

HILL COUNTRY FOLKS will seize upon the smallest of excuses to throw a party. Take Wurstfest, a ten-day salute to sausage held every October in the Hill Country town of New Braunfels. It starts when the town's dignitaries stand on stage and simultaneously bite on a long strand of linked sausage.

Or the annual weekend party hosted at the Johnson City ranch of Texas tycoon Red McCombs, who built a fortune investing in oil, automobiles, and airwaves. It starts with a barbecue and ends with a lively auction of Texas longhorns, an impressive-looking but unpractical breed that has become a status symbol for wealthy weekend ranchers.

Then there's Camey Stewart, who lives on a gorgeous spread just outside of Fredericksburg. Her annual Bluebonnet Bash to celebrate the splendid blossoming of the state flower every spring has grown into what must be one of the area's biggest potlucks. She sets up an outdoor table that stretches as far as the eye can see. Camey provides the meat, and guests—almost 200 showed up last year—bring a side dish and a chair.

For many in the Hill Country, parties are an inevitable part of the landscape, much like the swelling hills, breathtaking vistas, and stands of old oaks that define the area. Perhaps our hearty appetite for entertaining grows out of the isolation of spread-out country living, where the closest neighbor often is far from shouting distance away. Maybe it's just that we are a hospitable lot—thriving on connections, a fine story well told, and good food shared. Whatever it is, my Hill Country compatriots party often, and I'm always impressed with the sense of fun and creativity that they bring to the table.

Bobby Watson, who sells commercial kitchen equipment for a living, built his ranch home outside of Fredericksburg with parties in mind. "We wanted a great big kitchen with a bedroom attached," he says. Bobby and his wife, Linda, stage an annual Fourth of July celebration that starts July 3 with a well-stocked bar and a passel of friends to help decorate a float for the annual Fredericksburg Independence Day Parade. The party continues the next day when thirty-five or so of their closest friends squeeze onto the brightly festooned float and parade through the center of town,

Bloody Marys and beers in hand. Then it's back to the Watson house for a down-home lunch with barbecue, pork and beans, coleslaw, and potato salad. It doesn't end there. After a nap and a swim, they head out to the fairgrounds for the fireworks display, grills, folding tables and chairs, tablecloths, and candles in tow. There, they enjoy an all-American cookout, with hot dogs, hamburgers, peach cobbler, and chocolate cake.

Local ranchers aren't the only ones drawn into the Hill Country partying spirit. Art teacher Paige Conn, who lives near the center of Fredericksburg, joined a monthly supper club with twelve friends, and the results have been hilarious. Themes have ranged from Barbie and Ken, with Paige and husband, Blaine, showing up as Mermaid Barbie and Captain Ken; Survivor, with outdoor games in the couple's backyard; and a Pure Polyester Party, where guests came in vintage 1970s clothing. "We dress up, we have drinks and appetizers, and the evening takes its course," says Paige. The couples take turns hosting, and the hosts are in charge of the food.

The Hill Country's mild year-round temperatures mean that outdoor parties aren't just for spring and summer. Even in the middle of December, evenings can be warm enough for alfresco entertaining.

Navajo Grill chef-owner Josh Raymer recalls the two-wheeled progressive dinners he organized as a young bachelor. They started with bicycle barhopping and continued as he and his friends pedaled from one house to the next, feasting on a single course at each stop. Unlike much of the surrounding Hill Country, Fredericksburg's flat terrain and relatively small size make it ideal for bicycle entertaining.

Mary and Marshall Cunningham host casual dinner parties just about every week at their Wild Rock Ranch, and they head out to friends' homes for dinner almost as often.

"This is one of the friendliest areas I've ever seen," says Mary, who grew up in Louisiana and moved to Texas with her family seven years ago. In the Hill Country, regular entertaining begets even more.

"At every party you get to meet new people, and then you want them to meet some people that you already know, and it goes round and round," she says. The parties are always casual, with guests likely to show up in jeans and boots, and everyone pitching in with cooking and cleanup. The food is simple at the Cunninghams', often grilled game and something from the garden. Mary asks what her friends have growing and tells them to bring whatever they have. Food is served buffet style and leftovers go straight to the animals (they have a menagerie that includes pigs and donkeys), so there's not a lot of cleanup.

About four times a year, the Cunninghams throw big parties, with live music—they always hire local bands—and dancing on a stage glittering with lights hung from cedar poles. For parties big or small, Mary doesn't bother with a lot of extra decorating when she entertains.

"In the spring we have the wildflowers, in summertime flowers are everywhere and we have a million stars in the sky. When the whole sky is lit up there's not a lot of need for decorating."

Mini Okra Pancakes

After handing guests a drink, I often like to offer them a special morsel of food to perk up their taste buds and to make everyone feel at home. My friend and Austin farmer extraordinaire Carol Anne Sayle shared this recipe, and it warmed my southern gal's heart. (For skeptics, these little pancakes do not suffer from the slime factor some associate with okra.)

I served these at my annual garden party for chefs and friends, and people couldn't get enough. The trick is to serve them hot off the griddle, so make sure you have someone to fry them in a skillet, and someone else to pass them around while they're still hot. For this kind of job, I often enlist a shy guest or two. It keeps them busy, and frees them from the stress of having to make small talk. I've found that people will eat as many of these as they can get, but one or two per person is plenty and when they're gone, they're gone. (The recipe doubles easily if you're serving a crowd, though.)

I have added a little touch of my own to Carol Anne's recipe. My garden was producing way more jalapeños than I could manage, so I decided to pickle them. I tossed a few chopped, pickled chiles into Carol Anne's pancakes and loved the result. You can leave them out if you like.

Serves 8 as an appetizer; about twenty-four 2-inch pancakes

¾ cup cornmeal (preferably stone-ground)

¼ cup all-purpose flour

1 teaspoon baking powder

¾ teaspoon kosher salt

¼ teaspoon freshly ground black pepper

¼ teaspoon cayenne pepper (optional)

2 large eggs, lightly beaten

1 cup buttermilk, plus more if needed

¼ cup olive oil

2 tablespoons Dijon mustard

2 cups fresh okra, stemmed and sliced into ¼-inch pieces, or 1 (8-ounce) package frozen sliced okra, thawed

¼ cup drained, chopped pickled jalapeño chiles (page 254, or use a store-bought version)

2 small onions, cut into ¼-inch dice

4 cloves garlic, minced

Mix the cornmeal, flour, baking powder, ½ teaspoon of the salt, and black pepper together in a bowl, along with the cayenne pepper if desired. In a large bowl, whisk together the eggs, the 1 cup buttermilk, 2 tablespoons of the olive oil, and the mustard. Sprinkle the chopped okra evenly with the remaining ¼ teaspoon salt. Add the okra, pickled jalapeños, onions, and garlic to the egg mixture and stir until combined. Add the cornmeal mixture and stir lightly until just combined. The dough should resemble a thin pancake batter. If it seems too thick, add 1 or 2 tablespoons of buttermilk.

Add the remaining 2 tablespoons olive oil to a large skillet set over medium heat. When the oil begins to shimmer, drop in 2 heaping tablespoons batter per pancake, leaving room between pancakes so they don't touch. Cook the pancakes, flipping once, until golden brown on both sides and cooked through, about 1½ minutes per side. Serve immediately.

High's Hummus with Pita Crisps

High's Café is located in Comfort, Texas (about twenty-three miles south of Fredericksburg). In addition to their tasty sandwiches and homemade soups, friends Brent and Denise make the best hummus ever. A wonderful informal party appetizer, hummus is easy to make, healthy, and a favorite for kids and adults alike. I serve it with toasted pita wedges and either carrot or celery sticks (or both) for dipping.

Makes about 3 cups

HUMMUS

2 (16-ounce) cans chickpeas (about 4 cups), rinsed and drained

1 tablespoon minced fresh garlic (about 3 medium cloves)

1/2 teaspoon cayenne pepper

1/2 teaspoon ground cumin

1/2 teaspoon Hungarian paprika

2 teaspoons kosher salt

1/4 cup freshly squeezed lemon juice (about 1 large lemon)

2 tablespoons tahini

6 tablespoons extra-virgin olive oil, plus more for drizzling

2 tablespoons chopped fresh Italian parsley leaves, for garnish

Greek olives, for garnish

Chopped fresh tomatoes, for garnish

PITA CRISPS

8 white or whole wheat pita pockets

About 1/4 cup olive oil, for brushing

Kosher salt, for sprinkling

TO MAKE THE HUMMUS: Combine the chickpeas, garlic, cayenne pepper, cumin, paprika, salt, lemon juice, and tahini in the work bowl of a food processor fitted with the metal blade. Add just enough olive oil through the feed tube to get the mixture turning, usually about 2 tablespoons. (Too much oil at the beginning will pre-vent the finer pieces of chickpea from grinding smoothly, creating a coarse blend.) Scrape down the sides. Run the processor until the chickpeas are ground completely. Once the mixture is smooth, slowly add up to 4 tablespoons more olive oil to achieve a silky consistency. The folks at High's say, "Run your machine a long time. We almost whip it." I let the machine run for another 3 minutes or so. Spoon the hummus into a serving bowl; set aside.

TO MAKE THE PITA CRISPS: Preheat the oven to 350°F. With a knife, slit open the pitas along their edges and pull each apart into 2 rounds. With a pastry brush, lightly paint both sides of each pita half with olive oil. Sprinkle both sides with salt and cut each round into 8 wedges. Lay the pita wedges in a single layer on baking sheets. Bake until light golden brown and crisp, about 10 minutes.

To serve, drizzle olive oil over the hummus and sprinkle with chopped parsley. Accompany with pita crisps, Greek olives, and chopped fresh tomatoes.

TIP Tahini is made by pulverizing sesame seeds into a paste with a consistency similar to peanut butter. Many regular grocery stores stock tahini, so ask for help if you can't easily find it yourself, or try stores that specialize in Middle Eastern food.

Sweet-and-Sour Lamb Ribs

Austin chef Jesse Griffiths and his wife, Tamara Mayfield, brought succulent lamb ribs to my Fredericksburg garden party, and everyone devoured them. Jesse cleverly ensures these ribs are party-friendly for guests and hosts alike—the recipe can mostly be done in advance. The ribs are initially simmered on the stove top and then need just a very short turn on a grill before serving. Jesse and Tamara are co-founders of Austin's Dai Due Supper Club; their dinners are movable feasts staged at various local farms, vineyards, hotels, and private homes featuring local, sustainably produced ingredients prepared onsite by Jesse.

If you can't find lamb, pork spareribs or beef shortribs will work equally well. If you use beef ribs, they'll need to simmer for 4 to 5 hours. You can simmer the ribs up to 24 hours in advance, and the glaze will keep for 3 weeks in the refrigerator.

Serves 8 as an appetizer

RIBS

- 1 package (2 racks, 8 ribs each) lamb short ribs
- 1 medium yellow onion
- 2 bay leaves

- Salt and freshly ground black pepper
- 2 tablespoons chopped fresh Italian parsley, for garnish

GLAZE

- 1 cup guajillo honey or your favorite mild honey
- 1 cup cider vinegar
- 2 cloves garlic, minced
- 1 teaspoon chopped fresh rosemary
- 1/2 teaspoon anise seed
- 1/2 teaspoon chili powder

TO PREPARE THE SHORT RIBS: Put the ribs, onion, and bay leaves in a large pot, cover with water, and bring to a boil over high heat. Immediately turn the heat down to a simmer, skim any froth that comes to the surface, and cook the ribs until tender, about 2 hours.

Remove the ribs and refrigerate until ready to use. This can be done a day ahead. Cool the stock to room temperature. This stock can be frozen in ice cube trays, bagged, and used another time.

TO MAKE THE GLAZE: In a bowl, whisk together the honey, cider vinegar, garlic, rosemary, anise seed, and chili powder.

TO COOK THE RIBS: Start a hot fire in in a charcoal grill. Jesse prefers additive-free oak or mesquite lump charcoal, and advises against using charcoal starter, a known pollutant. If you are using a gas grill, set the heat at medium. When the coals are hot, lightly brush the grate with olive oil and grill the ribs for 2 minutes per side. Brush the glaze onto 1 side of the ribs and grill this side for about 30 seconds. Glaze the reverse side of the ribs and grill.

To serve, season the ribs with salt and pepper and sprinkle with chopped parsley. Serve warm or at room temperature.

Rebecca's Table Caprese Salad

Every summer I have out-of-control basil growing in my garden, and it's a serious challenge to come up with ways to use it all. It sometimes seems to grow faster than I can pick it. Then there is my garden arugula and several bountiful bushes of candy-sweet cherry tomatoes of varying colors. This salad guarantees that no cherry tomato or basil leaf goes to waste.

For parties, I take a huge platter-size version of the salad, drizzle the pesto vinaigrette over the fresh mozzarella, and leave a small pitcher of the vinaigrette on the side for those who can never get enough of the deliciously pungent stuff.

Serves 10 to 12

LEMON-PESTO VINAIGRETTE

$1/2$ cup pine nuts

2 cloves garlic, coarsely chopped

4 ounces fresh basil, stemmed (about 4 cups lightly packed leaves)

$1/2$ to 1 teaspoon kosher salt

1 cup plus 3 tablespoons extra-virgin olive oil

1 tablespoon freshly squeezed lemon juice (about $1/2$ medium lemon)

SALAD

2 (8-ounce) packages baby arugula (about 4 cups lightly packed) or other baby greens

2 pounds fresh mozzarella cheese, sliced in $1/4$-inch-thick rounds

2 pints cherry or pear tomatoes, halved (I use a mix of yellow, reds, and oranges, or whatever I have on hand in the garden)

6 to 8 medium-to-large, ripe tomatoes, sliced in $1/4$-inch-thick rounds and lightly sprinkled with kosher or sea salt

TO MAKE THE PESTO VINAIGRETTE: In a large skillet set over medium heat, add the pine nuts and stir until they turn golden brown, about 4 minutes. (Don't leave them unattended, they burn easily.) Remove from the heat and let the nuts cool.

Place the garlic and $1/4$ cup of the toasted nuts in the jar of a blender or work bowl of a food processor fitted with the metal blade and process at medium speed until combined. Add the basil, salt, and $1/2$ cup of the olive oil, and blend for a few minutes until the basil is thoroughly pureed. Add the lemon juice and the remainder of the olive oil and pulse a few times, just until combined. Set aside.

TO COMPOSE THE SALAD: Using a large platter, make a generous bed of arugula in the center, and arrange a line of overlapping mozzarella slices on top of the greens. Arrange overlapping slices of tomatoes on 1 side of the mozzarella and a mound of the halved cherry tomatoes on the other side. Decorate the mozzarella with a generous drizzle of the vinaigrette and pour the rest into a pitcher for serving on the side. Sprinkle the remaining $1/4$ cup of pine nuts on top of the dressed salad just before serving.

TIP Whether serving sliced fresh tomatoes as part of a salad or eating them solo in their natural glory, I always sprinkle them lightly with salt to bring out their flavor.

Party Tips from a Legendary Host

Vernon Frost, once a caterer specializing in parties held at his own elegant home, holds strong opinions about entertaining. And given his status as one of the Hill Country's most accomplished hosts, when he talks parties, I listen. Here are some tips, tricks, and nuggets of wisdom he shared with me one day over iced tea.

- Consider guests first. When you pick a time for the event, think about what your guests will be doing a few hours before, so the timing will be comfortable for them. (Vernon is so organized that when he throws a party he makes sure to build in a short nap just before party time so he's refreshed when guests arrive.)

- If you are considering NOT serving alcoholic drinks, think again. "When Uncle Pete comes from West Texas, you'd better have some bourbon for him," Vernon advises. A well-stocked bar will do, no need to go overboard. "Basic drinks are all I have found necessary," Vernon says, but he often has a pitcher of margaritas on hand as well. "If people get there and there's just a pitcher of sangria—that's not entertaining."

- When guests arrive, greet them, and immediately aim them toward the bar. Vernon says it's gauche to offer guests food as soon as they come in the door.

- Remember to include a few alcohol-absorbing foods, such as deviled eggs, or finger sandwiches.

- Always have music, and if you can afford it, make it live.

- Don't invite guests over unless you are going to feed them well. You certainly can't present them "with just a couple of nothings." Always have at least one anchor food, such as a carved ham. And serve the best quality food and drink you can afford. "I hate it when I go to a party of a wealthy person and they serve Smirnoff vodka," Vernon says.

- Always have an alternative to red meat. These days there is always someone who cannot or will not eat it.

- For large buffet dinners, make sure that people can serve themselves from both sides to cut down on long waits for sustenance.

- For large, elegant, seated dinner parties, use decorative tiles to number each table. Assign guests to tables with cards, which can be handed out as they arrive. Once they find their tables, place cards tell them where to sit.

- Have a Plan B. If you are having an outdoor party make sure there's room inside if the weather turns nasty. Bad weather has never ruined a Vernon Frost production: "The guests get inside, get close together, eat more, drink more, and have more fun."

- Always invite a crowd. (For reasons, see Plan B, above.)

- Keep records, take notes. Vernon has loose-leaf notebooks stuffed with menus and photos of recent and favorite parties; maps of table settings; standing lists of all of his linens, including dimensions of all of his table coverings; and detailed to-do lists starting three days out.

Fresh Corn and Pea Salad

My mother loved fresh peas and she'd routinely prowl local farmers' markets to find them. Purple hull peas were her favorite, but she also had a thing for cream peas, black-eyed peas, or just about any fresh legume that showed up at the farmstand. She'd make us kids shell the peas, and I always suspected it was to keep us out of her hair. I didn't mind, though. For some reason I enjoyed shelling peas. Naturally, I liked eating them better than shelling them and this recipe, which makes enough to feed a crowd, showcases peas and my mother's other summer favorite, fresh corn.

Just like my mother, I find fresh peas at Texas farmers' markets and sometimes even at my regular grocery store. Any fresh southern pea (see Tip) will work, but I especially favor cream peas. Do not use green peas, which will not hold up. I use canned black-eyed peas if I can't get my hands on fresh and the salad still shines.

Serves 10 to 12

1/2 pound thick-sliced applewood-smoked bacon (about 6 slices)

1/2 medium yellow onion, chopped

2 stalks celery, chopped

2 cloves garlic, minced

1 pound fresh cream peas, or 2 (15-ounce) cans black-eyed peas, drained and rinsed

1 red bell pepper, cored, seeded, and cut into medium dice

1 green bell pepper, cored, seeded, and cut into medium dice

4 ears fresh sweet corn, husked and kernels sliced off the cob

1/4 cup red wine vinegar

1/4 cup Champagne vinegar

1/2 cup olive oil

1/2 teaspoon kosher salt

1/4 teaspoon freshly ground black pepper

1/4 cup chopped fresh chives

1/4 cup chopped fresh Italian parsley leaves

In a large skillet, cook the bacon over medium heat until crisp. Drain on paper towels; set aside. Dispose of all but 1 tablespoon bacon fat from the skillet. Cook the onion and celery until the onions are translucent but not browned, about 3 minutes. Stir in the garlic and cook for about 1 minute. Add the fresh peas and enough cool water to cover. Simmer the bean mixture, uncovered, over medium-low heat until the peas are tender, up to 45 minutes. Thoroughly drain off the liquid and pour the pea mixture into a large bowl.

Place the peas in a large bowl along with the cooked onion, celery, and garlic; stir until combined. If you are using canned peas, don't cook them; just rinse and drain. Stir in the red and green bell peppers, and fresh corn.

In a bowl, whisk together the vinegars, olive oil, salt, and pepper until emulsified. Pour into the pea mixture and toss to combine well. Crumble the bacon into bite-size pieces and stir it into the salad with the chopped chives and parsley.

Cover and refrigerate for at least 4 hours so the flavors can blend. Serve cold or at room temperature.

DO IT EARLY

This salad keeps well. It can be made at least 24 hours in advance and holds up to 3 days, making it a slam-dunk dish for a summer party or potluck.

TIP A word about peas: When Southerners talk peas, also known as southern peas or cowpeas, they often are talking about what people in other parts of the country call beans. Most have a small but pronounced eye that marks where the pea was attached to the pod. (Eyeless cream peas are among the exceptions.) For obvious reasons, Southerners also fondly refer to the peas as "shellies," and as a result of the hours I spent as a child shelling them, I can attest to the sad fact that they take a lot longer to liberate from their shells than they do to eat.

Rustic Bread Salad

This hearty salad is packed with so many vegetables that I often serve it as a main course. It's a real lifesaver when guests announce, "Oh, by the way, did I mention I'm a vegetarian?" It welcomes just about any edible treasure from the farmers' market or my garden, from sliced sugar snap peas to colorful nasturtium flowers, slender French green beans to crunchy cucumbers, plus all kinds of peppers. Think seasonally: try fall veggies like roasted acorn squash, steamed broccoli florets, or fall lettuces, or bias-cut and steamed spring asparagus. Any good artisan bread will do, but I prefer a dense white or whole-wheat sourdough; try day-old loaves from your bakery.

Serves 12

SALAD

- $1/4$ to $1/2$ cup pine nuts, for garnish
- 1 whole round loaf day-old rustic bread (about 1 pound)
- 3 tablespoons unsalted butter, melted
- $1/3$ cup extra-virgin olive oil
- $1/2$ teaspoon kosher salt
- 3 ears sweet corn, shucked and steamed in the microwave on high for 3 minutes
- 3 bell peppers (red, yellow, orange, or any combination), cored, seeded, and coarsely chopped
- 1 medium zucchini, cut in $1/8$-inch-thick slices and quartered
- 1 medium yellow squash, cut in $1/8$-inch-thick slices and quartered
- 2 pints assorted cherry tomatoes, halved
- 1 cup loosely packed fresh basil leaves, cut into ribbons
- 2 cups loosely packed baby arugula or other baby greens
- 3 tablespoons loosely packed fresh Italian parsley leaves, chopped
- 1 large heirloom or farmstand tomato, cored, sliced, and cut into bite-size pieces
- Parmesan curls, for garnish (see Tip, page 18)

VINAIGRETTE

- $1/3$ cup red wine vinegar
- 1 tablespoon balsamic vinegar
- 2 tablespoons freshly squeezed lemon juice (about 1 medium lemon)
- 1 tablespoon Dijon mustard
- 2 large cloves garlic, minced
- 2 teaspoons kosher salt
- $1/2$ teaspoon freshly ground black pepper
- $1/2$ cup extra-virgin olive oil

TO MAKE THE BREAD SALAD: Preheat the oven to 350°F. Spread the pine nuts on a baking sheet in a single layer and bake until golden, about 5 minutes. Check frequently to make sure they do not burn. Set aside to cool.

Increase the heat to 400°F. Cut the bread (with crust) into $3/4$-inch cubes. Combine the melted butter, olive oil, and salt in a small bowl. Spread the cubes on a baking sheet in a single layer and toss with the butter mixture to coat evenly. Bake, turning occasionally, until the cubes are browned and crisp, about 30 minutes. Cool the bread thoroughly on the baking sheet.

continued

Cut the corn kernels off the cob, and place in an extra-large serving bowl along with the bell peppers, zucchini, squash, cherry tomatoes, basil, arugula, and parsley. Toss to mix evenly. Add the heirloom tomato pieces and toss gently.

TO MAKE THE VINAIGRETTE: Whisk together the vinegars, lemon juice, mustard, garlic, salt, and pepper. Add the olive oil in a steady stream, whisking constantly until the dressing emulsifies. Pour over the salad and toss to mix.

TO SERVE: Garnish with the Parmesan shavings and toasted pine nuts. Serve the dressed salad immediately.

DO IT EARLY

Cover and refrigerate the salad and dressing separately up to 24 hours in advance. Dress the salad and garnish with Parmesan and pine nuts just before serving.

TIP To make Parmesan curls, scrape a vegetable peeler across the surface of the block of cheese.

Artisan Cheesemaker Chrissy Omo

Chrissy Omo's passion for goat cheese began at age sixteen, when her father's job took the family to Europe. It was love at first taste and Chrissy, whose pet goat had taken second place in a Future Farmers of America competition when she was fifteen, now embarked on a quest to learn to make the stuff. While still a high schooler she worked for two months at Pure Luck Farm and Dairy in Dripping Springs under its award-winning goat-cheese maker Amelia Sweethardt. "Mom wanted me to see what it was really like," says Chrissy.

Mother, father, and daughter agreed to finance the cheese business with savings from Chrissy's college fund. They invested in a small herd of goats and created a dairy on their property. When Chrissy was a senior in high school, she began selling her cheese commercially. CKC Cheese (the initials stand for Chrissy and younger brothers Kenny and Conner) is a family-run operation. Chrissy's mom,

Adriana, is an experienced entrepreneur who handles the finances. Mother and daughter often do the deliveries together, bringing her handcrafted cheeses to customers throughout the Hill Country, including the Fredericksburg farmers' market, as well as to specialty stores in Austin. Chrissy's brothers help out with milking and other chores, but "no one but me touches the cheese," she says.

The goat herd has grown to more than 160 head, and Chrissy produces 300 to 400 pounds of cheese a week, from seasoned feta and baby caprino (a soft, Italian-style cheese that is aged for three weeks) to creamy fresh chèvre. Despite the expanded production, Chrissy continues to juggle her cheesemaking with schoolwork. She's on track to graduate with a degree in international business from Texas State University in San Marcos. "I love making cheese," she says. And I love eating it- especially when it comes from Chrissy's goats.

Roasted Beet Salad with Spicy Maple Pecans and Chrissy's Fresh Chèvre

This elegant appetizer or starter salad for a dinner party celebrates two loves: goat cheese and roasted beets. It takes more time than a simple tossed salad, but all can be done in advance for entertaining. Mixing red beets with golden and candy-striped varieties makes an especially gorgeous presentation. The CKC chèvre that I use is from Chrissy Omo, a local cheesemaking prodigy. (For more about Chrissy, see opposite page.) Although I highly recommend it, CKC cheese is hard to get outside of the Austin– Hill Country area. Support your local cheesemaker by checking out neighborhood farmers' markets.

Serves 8

ROASTED BEETS

6 equal-size medium beets (about
    2 pounds), washed and greens trimmed
    (leave a stubble)

3 cups chicken stock

1 cup dry white wine

1 cup firmly packed golden brown sugar

3 tablespoons balsamic vinegar

1 yellow onion, quartered

1 knob fresh ginger (with peel)

1 teaspoon kosher salt

1 tablespoon olive oil

SPICY MAPLE PECANS

1 tablespoon olive oil

3 tablespoons real maple syrup

3 tablespoons sugar

2 tablespoons balsamic vinegar

$1/2$ teaspoon cayenne pepper

1 cup pecan halves

BEET VINAIGRETTE

6 tablespoons reserved beet braising liquid

1 tablespoon freshly squeezed lemon juice
    (about $1/2$ lemon)

2 tablespoons white wine vinegar

1 tablespoon plus $1 1/2$ teaspoons balsamic
    vinegar

$1 1/2$ teaspoons chopped fresh rosemary leaves

$1 1/2$ teaspoons Dijon mustard

1 teaspoon kosher salt

Freshly ground black pepper

$1/2$ cup extra-virgin olive oil

SALAD

8 cups arugula, butter lettuce, or mixed salad
    greens

1 goat cheese round, about 8 ounces (more if
    you love goat cheese)

TO ROAST THE BEETS: Preheat the oven to 400°F. Set the beets in a roasting pan or ovenproof casserole in a single layer. Pour in the stock, wine,

continued

brown sugar, the 3 tablespoons balsamic vinegar, onion, ginger, salt, and the 1 tablespoon olive oil. Cover the pan tightly with aluminum foil or the casserole lid. Roast the beets until they are tender, about 45 minutes to 1 hour (a sharp knife will pull out easily from the center of a beet). Transfer the beets with tongs to a clean cutting board to cool. Reserve 6 tablespoons of the beet braising liquid for the vinaigrette.

Wearing clean rubber gloves to prevent red fingertips, if desired, cut off the beets' green "stubble" and skinny tails. Hold the beets under cool running water to loosen the skins, then slip off the skins with a little pressure from your fingers. Set the beets aside.

TO MAKE THE PECANS: Line a baking sheet with aluminum foil and grease it with butter or cooking spray. In a frying pan set over medium heat, combine the 1 tablespoon olive oil, maple syrup, sugar, the 2 tablespoons balsamic vinegar, and cayenne pepper. Bring the mixture to a simmer and stir in the pecan halves. Continue stirring until the mixture thickens slightly and coats the pecans, about 10 minutes. Pour the pecans onto the prepared baking sheet, spreading evenly with a spoon. Let cool before breaking them apart.

TO MAKE THE VINAIGRETTE: Whisk together the reserved 6 tablespoons beet braising liquid, lemon juice, white wine and balsamic vinegars, rosemary, mustard, salt, black pepper, and the 1/2 cup olive oil.

TO ASSEMBLE THE SALAD: Cut the beets into bite-size pieces. Toss the beets with the salad greens in a large bowl. Divide the salad evenly among 8 salad plates. Cut the goat cheese into 8 slices and top each salad with a slice. Sprinkle with a few candied pecans and drizzle on the vinaigrette. Serve immediately.

DO IT EARLY

You can roast the beets ahead and refrigerate them with the reserved beet juice in a covered container for up to 2 days. The pecans can be made up to 2 days ahead and stored at room temperature in a tightly covered container. Prepare the vinaigrette up to 3 days in advance, cover, and refrigerate until needed.

TIP When you roast beets, purchase ones that are all about the same size. That way they will be done at the same time.

Watermelon Salads with Tequila-Lime Dressing

My friend Yvonne makes this salad for her summertime pool parties when we crave something cool and light, which is often. She tosses it in a big bowl, we throw something on the grill, and everyone heads for her backyard pool. Sometimes we float in the pool all afternoon, climbing out of the water only when we need a watermelon break. It's a great way to beat the Texas heat.

Using the scooped-out watermelons as serving bowls means this dish performs double duty: satisfying your guests' appetites and adding an eye-catching decorative touch. It's easier than you think and your friends will marvel at your artistic flair.

Serves 12

SALAD

2 individual-size seedless watermelons (about 6 pounds total)

1 small red onion, thinly sliced

1/4 cup loosely packed chopped fresh mint (about 12 large mint leaves), plus a few whole sprigs for garnish

2/3 cup feta cheese (about 3 ounces), crumbled

TEQUILA-LIME DRESSING

6 tablespoons freshly squeezed lime juice (about 3 medium limes)

2 tablespoons tequila

1/4 cup honey

1/2 teaspoon kosher salt

2 tablespoons chopped fresh mint (about 6 large mint leaves)

2 tablespoons red wine vinegar

TO MAKE THE SALAD: Set each watermelon on its side (not the stem end) on a flat surface. Slice off just enough of the tops, cutting only into the rind, to make a stable surface. Flip the melons to rest on their cut sides. With a long,

sharp knife, horizontally slice off about the top one-quarter of each melon and discard. To form the bowls, using a large metal spoon, carefully scoop out the flesh in as large pieces as possible. Cut the flesh into 1 to 1½-inch chunks—you'll have about 10 cups—and put them in a large bowl. (To create a smooth, party-perfect watermelon serving bowl, you'll lose some of the flesh when you scrape out the fruit closest to the rind. Hey, watermelon is good for you, so snack on the bits that aren't pretty enough to go in the salad.) Cover the watermelon bowls with plastic wrap and refrigerate until ready to serve.

Reserve some of the red onion slices for garnish, and add the remaining slices to the watermelon chunks along with the chopped mint leaves. Cover the watermelon-onion mixture and refrigerate until ready to serve.

TO MAKE THE DRESSING: Whisk together the lime juice, tequila, honey, salt, mint, and vinegar. Refrigerate the dressing in a covered bowl or glass jar until ready to serve.

continued

TO SERVE: Add the dressing and the ⅔ cup feta cheese to the watermelon mixture and gently mix until both are evenly distributed. Mound half of the salad into each of the watermelon bowls. Garnish with mint sprigs and a few onion rings.

DO IT EARLY

The salad components—melon bowls and chunks and dressing—can be made ahead, but not assembled, up to 1 day in advance and refrigerated until needed.

TIPS Feta cheese, a pungent, brined cheese that originated in Greece, has become so popular that feta-style cheeses are produced in many countries. I like the traditional Greek style, often made from a blend of milk from sheep and goats. Experiment with several types to find a feta to your liking.

To take the bite out of raw onions, presoak slices in ice water for 30 minutes. Drain and pat dry before using.

Avocado-Cucumber Soup

This cold soup is yet another use for the exploding basil in my garden. I created it for a backyard party that Country Living photographed for a summertime issue. There's something special and a little bit elegant about starting an alfresco party meal with soup. Texas summers are so hot that I always like to offer something refreshing right off the bat. The gorgeous green color of this soup is set off beautifully by stark white serving bowls.

Makes 8 (1-cup) servings

4 ripe avocados, peeled, pitted, and lightly
  mashed (about 3 cups)

3 cucumbers, peeled and coarsely chopped
  (about 4 cups)

2 cloves garlic, coarsely chopped

4 cups buttermilk

^{2}/$_3$ cup sour cream or plain yogurt

3 tablespoons freshly squeezed lemon juice
  (about 1 ^{1}/$_2$ lemons, optional)

1 teaspoon Tabasco sauce

1 tablespoon kosher salt

^{1}/$_2$ cup coarsely chopped red onion

1 cup loosely packed fresh basil leaves,
  chopped

Combine the avocados, cucumbers, and garlic in the work bowl of a food processor fitted with the metal blade and process until smooth. Add the buttermilk, sour cream, lemon juice if you like, Tabasco, and salt. Pulse until incorporated. Add the red onion and basil and pulse 3 to 4 times, so that the onion and basil are evenly mixed in but still visible. Cover and refrigerate for at least 4 hours. Serve chilled.

DO IT EARLY

Beyond the initial 4 hours that the soup must sit, refrigerated, before serving, it can be made up to 24 hours in advance. If it gets too thick, thin it with buttermilk.

TIP If you'd like to shave some fat from this recipe, don't mess with my beloved avocados, which are packed with good-for-you monounsaturated fat. Substitute low-fat versions of the sour cream or yogurt instead. Your taste buds won't miss a thing.

Grilled Quail Salad

Josh Raymer, the creative young chef behind Fredericksburg's Navajo Grill, enjoys a little low-key partying at home on his days off. He and his wife, Julie, often invite friends in for a relaxed evening with simple food, a few good wines or a cooler full of beer, and some good conversation. Josh describes Hill Country parties as generally laid-back—dressing up means stepping into your "nicer" boots. But even the most casual affair on his stone patio includes music—Willy Nelson and the Texas Tornados are favorites. Decoration often consists of little more than bunches of herbs clipped from his carefully tended herb garden and plunked in jars. "We don't do much."

Josh and Julie came to my garden party with their two-year-old son Hank and this equally irresistible salad. Don't let the semi-boneless instructions frighten you. You can order neatly packaged, semi-boned quail from just about any commercial outlet, including Josh's Bandera, Texas, supplier, Diamond H Ranch (www.texasgourmetquail.com). Semi-boned quail means the back, breast, and thigh bones have been removed, leaving the bird's skin and its tiny leg bones intact. This allows the birds to be laid out flat for easy grilling.

Serves 4

MARINADE

- 1 small red onion, diced
- 1 teaspoon ground dried pasilla chile
- 3 cloves garlic, crushed
- 1 large sprig rosemary, leaves stripped and coarsely chopped
- 2 large sprigs thyme, leaves stripped and chopped
- 1 teaspoon freshly ground black pepper
- Zest and juice of 2 limes
- 1 cup extra-virgin olive oil

- 4 semi-boneless quail (back, breast, and thigh bones removed)
- Kosher salt and freshly ground black pepper
- 2 ears fresh corn, unshucked

VINAIGRETTE

- 1 small red onion, finely diced
- 1 teaspoon ground dried pasilla chile
- Zest and juice of 1 large lime
- 1 teaspoon Dijon mustard
- 1/2 cup extra-virgin olive oil
- 1 teaspoon kosher salt
- Freshly ground black pepper
- 1 pint fresh blackberries

- 1 pound arugula or mixed greens of your choice
- 6 ounces fresh goat cheese, cut into bite-size pieces

TO MAKE THE MARINADE: In a large bowl, stir together the red onion, chile, garlic, rosemary, thyme, black pepper, lime zest and juice, and the 1 cup olive oil.

continued

Submerge the quail in the marinade, cover, and refrigerate for at least 2 hours and up to 12 hours. If you are in a rush, marinate the quail for 1 hour at room temperature.

TO GRILL THE CORN AND QUAIL: In a covered grill, prepare a hot fire using hardwood (Josh prefers pecan) or fruitwood. Pull back the husk from the corn, remove the silk, and rewrap the ear with the husk. Arrange the corn around the edges of the fire, close the lid, and let them smoke for about 15 minutes. Transfer them to a plate and cover with a clean dish cloth. Remove the quail from the marinade, drain on paper towels, and season all over with salt and pepper. When the fire has cooked down to hot coals, place the quail over the hottest part of grill, close the lid, and cook them until the quail's interior is reddish pink and the flesh is firm to the touch, about 20 minutes.

TO MAKE THE VINAIGRETTE: In a bowl, whisk together the onion, chile, lime zest and juice, mustard, the ¹/₂ cup olive oil, salt, pepper, and half of the blackberries. Season with more pepper or salt, to taste. Gently stir in the remaining berries.

TO MAKE THE SALAD: Put the greens in a large bowl. Cut the corn kernels from the cobs. Toss the corn and cheese with the greens and vinaigrette. Arrange the quail on top of the salad. Let guests serve themselves, but gently remind them to take just 1 quail per person.

DO IT EARLY

Both the quail and the corn can be grilled at least 24 hours in advance and refrigerated. The vinaigrette can also be made 1 to 2 days ahead and refrigerated. Bring the quail to room temperature before serving.

VARIATION

Grilling corn in its husk gives the kernels a golden color and a deeply sweet flavor. But if you prefer, grill them shucked, about 2 minutes per side, just until the kernels begin to blacken and blister.

Garden Tomato Lasagna with Pesto

Here's a great party dish that feeds a horde and can be made a day ahead and baked at the last minute. It can handle an endless amount of fiddling—from adding more vegetables (I've tucked in layers of sautéed sliced yellow and green zucchini, eggplant, red and green peppers, and mushrooms, to name a few) to tweaks like eliminating all cheese (including in the pesto) for a vegan version created for my lactose-intolerant daughter (see Variation). Buy prepared pesto if you want less prep work.

Serves 8 to 12

3 tablespoons olive oil

1 tablespoon kosher salt

$1/2$ pound dried lasagna noodles

$1/2$ medium yellow onion, chopped

4 small zucchini, thinly sliced (optional)

2 cloves garlic, minced

1 pound bulk Italian sausage (optional)

$1/4$ cup ($1/2$ stick) unsalted butter

2 cups freshly made breadcrumbs (from day-old bread) (see Tip)

3 large eggs

2 (15-ounce) containers part-skim ricotta cheese

1 cup mascarpone cheese

1 teaspoon kosher salt

1 tablespoon minced fresh oregano leaves

$1 1/2$ cups homemade pesto (recipe follows) or purchased

6 to 8 ripe medium farmstand tomatoes, cored and cut in $1/4$-inch-thick slices

Parmesan curls, for garnish (optional)

Coat the bottom of a 9 by 13-inch pan or casserole dish with 1 tablespoon of the olive oil; set aside.

In a large pot, add the salt to 5 to 6 quarts of water, bring it to a boil, and cook the lasagna noodles according to the package directions (see Tip). Drain the noodles and separate them. To keep them from getting tangled, I drape them around the edges of the cooking pot.

Heat the remaining 2 tablespoons of the olive oil in a large sauté pan set over medium heat. Add the onion and zucchini, if using, and sauté until the vegetables have softened, about 5 minutes. Add the garlic and sauté for another minute. Spoon the vegetables into a bowl; set aside.

In the same sauté pan, cook the Italian sausage, if using, until it is no longer pink, breaking up into small pieces as it cooks. Drain off the fat and add the cooked sausage to the vegetables.

In the same sauté pan (no need to wash it), melt the butter over medium heat. Add the breadcrumbs and stir until the butter evenly coats the crumbs. Remove the pan from the heat.

In a bowl, lightly scramble the eggs with a fork. Stir in the ricotta, mascarpone, and oregano; set aside.

To assemble the lasagna, place half the noodles on the bottom of the prepared pan or dish. In this order, add half the pesto, half the sliced tomatoes, half the sautéed vegetables, and half the ricotta mixture. Repeat the layers in the same order using the remaining ingredients, starting with noodles and ending with cheese. Spoon the buttered breadcrumbs over the top.

Preheat the oven to 350°F. Bake the lasagna until it bubbles around the edges and the bread-crumb topping is crisp and golden brown, 35 to 40 minutes. Serve hot from the oven, warm, or even at room temperature.

Pesto

Makes about 2 cups

4 cups lightly packed fresh basil leaves

4 cloves garlic, quartered

1/2 teaspoon kosher salt

1/2 cup pine nuts

1/2 cup extra-virgin olive oil

1 1/2 cups freshly grated Parmesan cheese

Whirl together the basil, garlic, salt, and pine nuts in the jar of a blender or the work bowl of a food processor fitted with the metal blade. With the machine running, if possible, slowly add the olive oil through the feed tube until it is incorporated. Otherwise, add the olive oil with the other ingredients and process until combined. Pour the mixture into a bowl and stir in the Parmesan cheese.

DO IT EARLY

The pesto can be made up to 1 week ahead and refrigerated until ready to use. Assemble the lasagna up to 1 day ahead and refrigerate. Bake the day you plan to serve it.

TIPS When making lasagna, take care to cook the noodles only until just chewy (*al dente*, in Italian). Slight undercooking keeps the noodles from turning mushy when they are baked later.

I prefer homemade breadcrumbs, easily made from the leftover bread I freeze just for this purpose. Toast bread until crisp and lightly browned, then cool to room temperature. Break the toast into pieces with your hands and whirl in a food processor or in a blender. For a more rustic look, simply crumble up the toast with your hands. If that seems like too much work, prepared breadcrumbs from the store work just fine, too.

VARIATION

It's a sad irony that my college-age daughter, Frances, has developed an intolerance to dairy products, ingredients I use constantly in my work as a chef. Luckily, she still likes my food, and I've learned to modify some of my recipes to keep her healthy, including lasagna. For Franny, I make homemade pesto as above but eliminate the Parmesan cheese. I use whatever veggies I have on hand, sauté them as above, and mix them with a 28-ounce can of drained, diced tomatoes. Needless to say, the ricotta layer doesn't make the cut for my daughter's lasagna, and instead of butter, I use an equal amount of olive oil to moisten the breadcrumbs. Franny loved the vegan lasagna hot the first night I made it for her and—ignoring my pleas to let me heat it—she ate it cold straight from the refrigerator the next day.

31

Three Pigs Stuffed Pork Tenderloin with Candied Carrots

Three Pigs is one of my favorite party dishes because it feeds a lot a people without breaking the budget. I make the stuffing one day in advance, refrigerate it, and all that's left is to slather it onto the pork in a thick layer, roll it up, top it with a bacon roof, and put it into the oven. The carrots are a snap as long as you have a mandoline, or a carrot guy or gal (someone whose sole job is to cut the carrots into even slices on the diagonal; I'm just fantasizing here). We had a bread guy when I was the executive pastry chef at Tony's in Houston, and all he did was make bread, all day, every day. Sadly for me, I don't have a carrot boy or girl. When I'm entertaining at home, the work mostly falls to me, so I hook up my iPod, turn up the volume, and slice my own carrots. And unless I'm at work, it's up to me to butterfly the pork loin so that it lies flat for stuffing. If I were you, I'd ask your butcher to do it, specifying that the loin be butterflied twice for stuffing.

Day-old scones make a fabulously rich stuffing, I've discovered. Bake my smoked tomato scones (page 35) for another meal and stow three in the freezer for use whenever you fancy making this dish.

Serves 8 to 10

CANDIED CARROTS

2 bunches whole carrots (about
    20 carrots), peeled and cut on the
    diagonal into 1/4-inch-thick slices

1 cup (2 sticks) unsalted butter

1 cup firmly packed golden brown sugar

1/2 teaspoon kosher salt

Zest of 1 orange

STUFFED PORK

3/4 pound bulk Italian sausage

1/2 medium yellow onion, chopped

2 cloves garlic, minced

2 tablespoons finely chopped fresh sage, plus
    several whole leaves for garnish

1 pound fresh baby spinach

3 Savory Smoked Tomato–Asiago Scones
    (page 35)

4 pounds pork loin roast, butterflied twice for
    stuffing (see headnote)

Kosher salt and freshly ground black pepper

3/4 pound thick-sliced applewood-smoked
    bacon

PORT GRAVY

2 tablespoons unsalted butter

1 small yellow onion, chopped

2 cloves garlic, chopped

1 750 ml bottle port wine (ruby or tawny)

Salt and freshly ground black pepper

3 Granny Smith apples, cored and chopped

TO MAKE THE CARROTS: Preheat the oven to 375°F. Arrange the carrots in a single layer on a large rimmed baking sheet. Melt the butter in a saucepan set over medium heat. Stir in the brown sugar, salt, and orange zest and heat until the mixture is bubbling and the sugar is dissolved, 1 to 2 minutes. Pour the sugar mixture over the

continued

33

carrots, and toss until they are evenly coated. Spread them evenly on the baking sheet. Bake until the carrots are tender and browned around the edges, 20 to 25 minutes. They might look slightly wrinkled.

TO MAKE THE STUFFING: In a large, deep skillet or heatproof casserole set over medium heat, cook the sausage, breaking it up into small chunks with a spatula as it browns. Add the onion and cook until the onion is translucent and the sausage is no longer pink. Add the garlic and chopped sage and stir for 1 minute. Add the spinach, a few handfuls at a time, stirring until the spinach wilts and begins to melt into the sausage mixture (it will all fit!). Remove the pan from the heat. Break the scones into bite-size pieces with your hands, and stir them into the spinach mixture. Set the stuffing aside.

TO COOK THE PORK: Lay out the pork flat on a large piece of waxed paper or a large synthetic cutting board. Sprinkle both sides with salt and pepper. Evenly and completely cover the top of the pork with the stuffing out to the meat's edges. Roll up the pork jelly roll–style and secure it with butcher's string. Put the pork in a large roasting pan, seam side down, and completely cover the top of the pork with overlapping strips of bacon. Roast until an instant-read thermometer inserted in the center of the roast registers 140° to 145°F, about 40 minutes. Let the roast rest at room temperature for at least 10 minutes before slicing and serving.

TO MAKE THE GRAVY: In a large skillet set over medium heat, melt the butter and sauté the onion until it is translucent, about 3 minutes. Add the garlic and sauté for 1 more minute. Pour in the port and bring the mixture to a boil. Reduce the heat, let the mixture come to a slow simmer, and cook for about 10 minutes. Add the apples and cook until the gravy begins to thicken, about 15 minutes more. Remove from the heat and serve warm.

For a spectacular presentation, lay the roast in the middle of a serving platter surrounded with the roasted carrots and garnished with fresh sage leaves.

DO IT EARLY

The glazed, cooked carrots can be covered and refrigerated for up to 24 hours before serving. To warm them, spread them on a baking sheet and heat them in a 300°F oven for about 15 to 20 minutes. If you are not ready to cook the pork loin, the stuffing can be prepared, then covered and refrigerated for 24 hours.

Savory Smoked Tomato-Asiago Scones

My friends Larry Butler and Carol Ann Sayle, owners of Boggy Creek Farm in Austin, sell the most fabulous smoked tomatoes. I've used them to enhance meat dishes and salads. But I'd never tried them in a bread or scone, so I came up with this recipe to showcase them. As soon as the first fragrant scone came out of the oven, I knew I'd be delighted with the result. I even devised a way to use the day-old scones to stuff my Three Pigs pork tenderloin (page 33). As much as I love Larry's smoked tomatoes, I must admit the scones are delicious made with any high-quality sundried tomatoes.

Makes about 25 small scones

1/2 cup pine nuts

3 cloves roasted garlic, mashed (see page 255)

1/2 cup firmly packed smoked tomatoes (see headnote) or sundried tomatoes packed in oil, drained and chopped

3 1/2 cups bleached all-purpose flour

1 1/2 tablespoons baking powder

1 teaspoon salt

1 to 2 teaspoons freshly ground black pepper

3/4 cup (1 1/2 sticks) unsalted butter, chilled and cut into pieces

1 cup grated 5-month-aged Asiago cheese (grated with the large holes)

2 tablespoons thinly sliced green onions (white part only)

1/2 cup heavy whipping cream

1/2 to 3/4 cup buttermilk

Preheat the oven to 400°F. Arrange the pine nuts on a baking sheet in a single layer and bake until golden, about 5 minutes; set aside. (Keep checking; they burn easily.)

In a bowl, stir together the tomatoes and the roasted garlic, making sure the garlic breaks up and is evenly distributed.

In a large bowl, stir together the flour, baking powder, salt, and pepper. Gradually cut in the butter with a pastry blender or 2 knives until the mixture resembles small peas. Stir in the tomato-garlic mixture, pine nuts, grated cheese, green onions, cream, and 1/2 cup of the buttermilk. Using your hands, mix all the ingredients until they are incorporated. If the dough is too dry to hold together, add more buttermilk, 1 tablespoon at a time, until the dough is pliable and can be formed into a ball. Mix as lightly as possible to ensure a light-textured scone.

Transfer the dough to a lightly floured surface. Pat the dough into a rectangle. Using a well-floured rolling pin, roll out the dough to about 3/4 inch thick. With a sharp knife, halve the dough lengthwise into 2 long, rectangular pieces. Cut each piece into 2-inch rectangles, then halve each rectangle on the diagonal to make small scones. Bake on an ungreased baking sheet until the scones are golden and no longer sticky, about 15 minutes.

Fred's Party

WHERE THE HOST WITH THE MOST IS A MYTH

The host of one Fredericksburg's most talked-about social events is a mythical character. But that doesn't stop the 500-plus attendees from pulling out all the stops to prepare for this biannual party. Nor does it detract from its popularity: the soiree for January 2009 was sold out more than a year in advance. Welcome to Fred's Party—a testament to the incredible energy and imagination of Hill Country partygoers.

Members, who pay $350 each for the privilege, invite up to ten guests to the festivities. A theme is chosen for each gala event, held in a decidedly un-chic locale—a barnlike, cement-floored building on the Gillespie County Fairgrounds. Members are responsible for decorating and providing food for their tables and, being Texans, they do it up big.

Fred's Party organizers—there's a six-person steering committee—insist their main goal is to throw a great party, but they've managed to raise more than $100,000 for local charities since the first Fred bash was held in 2001. When guests walk in the door, they are asked to donate what they might "spend for a great night out," says steering committee member Paige Conn. Fred's Party members vote well in advance to select four local nonprofits eligible to receive funds raised at the party. Donations are collected and counted, and the total is announced during the party. Organizers spin a charity Wheel of Fortune. Where the needle stops determines which nonprofit will win 80 percent of the event's take. The other 20 percent is divvied up among the three remaining nonprofits.

For the 2005 movie-themed party, notable efforts included a credible re-creation of the *MASH* officers' club with participants dressed in combat fatigues; an all-white *Indiana Jones*–style tent stocked with whip-cracking Indie wannabes outfitted in leather jackets; a spiffy black vintage car driven into the building in honor of *Driving Miss Daisy*; a colorful blow-up casting couch accompanied by a prominent sign announcing the next audition; and a cozy area outfitted with a large couch, a few easy chairs, TVs, and DVD players, allowing guests to munch on chips while watching movies.

My business partner, Dan Kamp, and I came with an *Airplane* entourage, and we dressed as airline pilot and stewardess, with me pushing a cart well stocked with single-serving bottles of booze.

Some Fred partyers pour just as much energy into the food as they do into designing props and costumes, setting their tables with china and crystal and bringing in elegant food to match; others concentrate on liquid libations and just bring a few appetizers. Bathrooms and the stage are decorated by the organizing committee and dancing to a live band often goes well into the late hours of the evening.

All of this in the name of a guy who is just a figment of someone's imagination. All we know of the man is revealed on the Fred's Party Web site: "Fred, his parties were legendary. His generosity was abundant. His photos are few. He was known as a world traveler. He was known for his dances. He was known for his charitable giving. But most of all he was known for his parties. Fred's party was a night to remember."

And every two years outside of the small Texas town of Fredericksburg, the memory of a Fred who never was lives on.

Belted Galloway
Ice Cream Sandwiches

Eating ice cream sandwiches always brings out the kid in me. Why not spread the joy? At a recent party, more than a few giggles erupted when I handed out overstuffed ice cream sandwiches for dessert. I owe my renewed interest in ice cream sandwiches to a herd of Belted Galloway cows that I often spot as I head home on Route 290 just outside of town. Those dark cows with the big white stripe running right around their middles remind me of great big ice cream sandwiches. I found the perfect recipe for the chocolate cookie part in an old favorite of mine, the Deer Valley Ranch Family Cookbook, *a spiral-bound treasure trove of recipes from the kitchen of a Colorado dude ranch. The soft, slightly cakey cookies are the perfect foil for a creamy vanilla ice cream center. These cookies are also fabulous alone: sometimes I don't quite get around to filling them with ice cream and before I know it they are gone.*

Makes about 40 (3-inch) cookies, enough for about 20 ice cream sandwiches, or 20 (5-inch) cookies, enough for about 10 ice cream sandwiches

COOKIES

- $^3/_4$ cup (1$^1/_2$ sticks) unsalted butter, at room temperature
- 1$^1/_2$ cups firmly packed golden brown sugar
- 1 tablespoon vanilla extract
- 2 large eggs
- 1$^1/_2$ cups all-purpose flour
- $^1/_3$ cup unsweetened dark cocoa (such as Scharffen Berger)
- $^1/_2$ teaspoon kosher salt
- $^1/_2$ teaspoon baking soda
- 1 cup white chocolate chips (optional)

FILLING

- 1 quart high-quality vanilla ice cream

Preheat the oven to 375°F. Lightly coat a baking sheet with cooking spray or butter, or line it with parchment paper or a silicone liner.

TO MAKE THE COOKIES: Using an electric mixer fitted with the paddle attachment, beat the butter, sugar, and vanilla together on medium-high speed until fluffy, about 2 minutes. Add the eggs and beat for another minute. In a bowl, stir together the flour, cocoa, salt, and baking soda until combined. Pour the dry ingredients into the butter mixture and beat on low speed until just incorporated. Cover the dough with plastic wrap and refrigerate for 15 to 30 minutes for easier scooping. Using a 1-inch scoop (for 3-inch cookies) or a 2-inch scoop (for 5-inch cookies), drop mounds of dough about 2 inches apart (the cookies will spread) on the prepared baking sheet. Bake until there is no visible raw dough on top, 7 to 9 minutes (don't overbake). Remove from the oven and cool on the baking sheet for a couple of minutes. With a spatula, transfer them to wire racks to cool completely.

TO ASSEMBLE THE ICE CREAM SANDWICHES: Place the cookies on a work surface, flat side up. Using a 2-inch scoop, drop a rounded scoop of ice cream on half of the cookies. Top with the remaining cookies, flat side down, pressing lightly and stopping just before the ice cream begins to ooze out the sides. Store 2 per bag in waxed paper sandwich bags, fold to close, and freeze until ready to eat.

VARIATION

I'm a purist when it comes to ice cream sandwiches: I like them black and white, just like my favorite cows. Nonetheless, other fillings from mint chocolate chip to butter pecan are fantastic, too. And feel free to experiment with mix-ins: into soft ice cream stir ingredients like toffee bits, toasted nuts, mini M&Ms—whatever your imagination dictates.

Figgy-topped Pound Cakes

My backyard fig tree is not always the most reliable producer, but when I have figs I make this dessert. It pairs an old-fashioned pound cake (recipe courtesy of my great-aunt Emma) with a chunky sauce made with my homegrown Brown Turkey figs. I love this dessert's down-home elegance—a figgy topping poured over individual pound cakes baked in cupcake pans.

You can use any fresh fig that's available—light green, brown, or purple. In Texas you'll most likely find Brown Turkeys, which I've been told were planted throughout the state by early homesteaders. If fresh figs are not available, use Bosc pears or tart apples. If you want a large, belt-busting dessert, use Texas-size cupcake pans. Standard-size cupcake pans will give you double the servings.

Makes 12 Texas or 24 standard servings

POUND CAKE

- 1 cup (2 sticks) unsalted butter
- 2 cups sugar
- 6 large eggs
- 1 teaspoon freshly squeezed lemon juice
- 1 teaspoon vanilla extract
- 2 cups all-purpose flour
- 1/2 teaspoon kosher salt

TOPPING

- 2 cups ruby or tawny port (inexpensive is fine)
- 2 cups sugar
- 1/4 cup freshly squeezed lemon juice (about 1 large lemon)
- Zest strips from 2 fresh lemons
- 1 teaspoon fresh lemon thyme leaves
- 1 cup dried cranberries or sour cherries
- 2 pints fresh figs, stemmed

TO MAKE THE POUND CAKE: Preheat the oven to 350°F.

Using an electric mixer fitted with the paddle attachment, beat the butter and the 2 cups sugar on medium-high speed until fluffy, about 2 minutes. Add the eggs, 1 at a time, beating on medium-high speed after each addition. Beat in the 1 teaspoon lemon juice and vanilla. Add the flour and salt and beat on low speed until thoroughly incorporated. Evenly fill 12 Texas-size muffin tins or 24 standard-size muffin tins. Bake until the muffin tops are golden brown and a toothpick inserted into the center of a cupcake comes out clean, about 1 hour. Let cool in pans 10 minutes, then invert onto a wire rack to cool completely.

TO MAKE THE FIGGY TOPPING: Meanwhile, combine the port, the 2 cups sugar, the 1/4 cup lemon juice, lemon zest, lemon thyme, and dried cranberries in a large saucepan set over high heat. Bring the mixture to a boil, stirring occasionally. Decrease the heat to medium-low so that the mixture simmers. Add the figs and cook until the syrup thickens slightly (just a little thicker than maple syrup), 7 to 10 minutes.

TO SERVE: Arrange the pound cakes on individual plates and spoon on about 3 tablespoons of warm or room temperature port sauce and 2 figs for each Texas-size cake and about half that for the standard-size version.

DO IT EARLY

Both the cakes and the sauce can be made in advance. The sauce will keep for at least 3 days in the refrigerator. The cakes can be baked, cooled, wrapped in plastic wrap, and held at room temperature for up to 1 day, or frozen for up to 3 weeks.

VARIATION

If fresh figs are unavailable, substitute 6 cored tart, firm apples or Bosc pears, quartered and cut into large hunks.

TIP When I want lemon zest I normally turn to my Microplane, a rasp-type grater invented by an imaginative woodworker. It's easy to use and produces a flurry of flavorful, fluffy bits of zest. For making long, curly zest ribbons, perfect for this recipe, I rely on my old-style zester (supplanted by the Microplane in many kitchens). This tool has three round holes that form perfect little zest strips when pulled across the skin of a lemon, lime, or orange.

Plum Tart

This party-perfect showpiece recipe is pure simplicity: fresh plums, flour, sugar, butter, salt, and water. Once it cools, free the tart from its springform pan and you'll have a golden-crusted beauty with a jewel-toned plum center that advertises—in an elegant but low-key way—the wonders of summertime fruit. If you feel your guests need more, serve it with a scoop of vanilla bean ice cream.

Serves 8 to 10

3 cups bleached all-purpose flour

1/4 teaspoon kosher salt

1 teaspoon lemon or orange zest

1/2 cup plus 1 tablespoon sugar

1 1/4 cups (2 1/2 sticks) unsalted butter, chilled and cut into 1/2-inch cubes

1/2 cup ice water, plus a few tablespoons more, if needed

5 medium plums, pitted and cut into 1/4-inch slices

In the bowl of an electric mixer fitted with the paddle attachment, combine the flour, salt, zest, and 1/2 cup sugar on low speed, about 30 seconds. Add the butter to the flour mixture and combine on low speed until the mixture resembles small peas. Add the 1/2 cup ice water, 1/4 cup at a time, mixing on low speed for 15 seconds after each addition; the dough should start to clump together in a ball. If it doesn't, mix about 10 seconds more. If it still looks too dry, add more ice water, 1 tablespoon at a time, until the dough clumps together. Gently mold the dough into a disk, cover tightly in plastic wrap, and refrigerate for at least 1 hour or up to 24 hours.

Preheat the oven to 425°F. Remove the dough from the refrigerator, unwrap it, and place it on a lightly floured work surface. With a lightly floured rolling pin, roll it into a 1/4-inch-thick circle large enough to cover the bottom and sides of a 10-inch springform pan with about 1 1/2 inches of excess all around. To keep the dough from sticking as you roll it, gently lift and rotate it periodically, adding more flour as needed. Carefully drape the dough over the rolling pin and center it over the springform pan. Lightly press the dough into the bottom and up the sides of the pan, letting the excess drape over the pan edge. Arrange the plums on the dough pinwheel style, fully covering the bottom of the pan (you may have more than 1 layer of fruit). Sprinkle the plums evenly with the 1 tablespoon sugar. Gently fold the excess dough over the plums, letting creases in the dough develop naturally to fit the pan and leaving a circle of uncovered fruit in the center of the tart.

Bake the tart until the top crust looks golden brown, 25 to 30 minutes. Let the tart cool for about 30 minutes on a rack, then remove from pan to serve. Serve either warm or at room temperature.

DO IT EARLY

The dough can be prepared up to 24 hours ahead, or you can freeze it for up to 3 weeks.

TIP To reheat the tart, warm it in a preheated 400°F oven for about 10 minutes.

Kimmie Cookies

These light, melt-in-your-mouth cookies are named for my good friend Kim, who started baking them as a child with her Scandinavian grandmother. While Kim makes them with her kids during the Christmas holidays, I think they are great for a spring or summer party. I tint the butter icing a light pink or pale blue. They always disappear quickly: kids love them, adults can't resist them, and I never tire of them.

Makes about 6 dozen cookies

COOKIES

- 2 cups (4 sticks) unsalted butter, at room temperature
- 1 cup sugar for the cookies, plus $^1/_2$ cup sugar for sprinkling (optional)
- 2 teaspoons pure almond extract
- $^1/_2$ teaspoon kosher salt
- 4 cups all-purpose flour

BUTTER FROSTING

- $^1/_3$ cup unsalted butter, at room temperature
- 1 teaspoon vanilla extract
- Pinch of kosher salt
- 4 tablespoons (or more) whole milk, slightly warmed
- 2 cups (or more) powdered sugar
- 2 or 3 drops food coloring of your choice (optional)

TO MAKE THE COOKIES: Preheat the oven to 350°F. Lightly grease 2 baking sheets with cooking spray or butter, or line with parchment paper or silicone liners.

Using an electric mixer fitted with the paddle attachment, beat the butter and the 1 cup sugar on medium-high speed until light and fluffy, about 2 minutes. Beat in the almond extract and salt. Add the flour and beat on low speed just until thoroughly combined. Using your hands, roll the dough into 1-inch balls. Put the $^1/_2$ cup sugar in a shallow bowl and roll each cookie in the sugar to coat, if you like.

Place the cookies about $^1/_2$ inch apart on the prepared baking sheet and flatten by lightly pressing down on the dough with the bottom of a juice glass. (The cookies should be about $^1/_4$ inch thick.) Bake until the bottoms begin to turn golden brown, 10 to 12 minutes. Don't let the tops brown or the cookies will be overdone. Transfer to a wire cooling rack and frost while the cookies are slightly warm.

TO MAKE THE BUTTER FROSTING: In the bowl of an electric mixer fitted with the paddle attachment, beat the $^1/_3$ cup butter, vanilla, salt, and warm milk on low speed until combined. Add the powdered sugar and beat on medium speed until combined. If the icing seems too runny to spread, add a few tablespoons more of powdered sugar. If it seems too thick, add more milk, 1 teaspoon at a time, until it reaches the desired consistency.

continued

DO IT EARLY

Like most cookies, these are at their very best eaten the day they are baked. You can make the dough and stow it in a container in the refrigerator up to 1 week before baking. Make the icing and bake the cookies the day of your party.

TIPS Some people dislike the taste of almond extract, but I have found that even avowed almond-extract haters love these cookies without detecting their almond flavor. The extract lends a subtle depth of flavor, not a pronounced almond taste. Make the cookies once with the extract and see if the naysayers react. If they do—I'd be surprised— you'll have more cookies for yourself. Next time you make them, you can substitute vanilla extract for the almond.

Using a 1-inch-diameter metal ice cream scoop eliminates the drudgery from portioning out cookie dough, and insures that your cookies will be of uniform size and bake at the same rate. The best scoops are lever-activated and push the dough out and onto baking sheets quickly and easily.

Garden Party Cocktails

While most of my friends are foodies, David Alan's central focus is liquid refreshment. A coffee distributor by trade, he devotes most of his free time to the art of the cocktail. He writes a witty, drink-packed blog called Tipsy Texan. I asked him to create a couple of drinks for my backyard garden party. Both are beautiful to look at and delicious enough to be dangerous.

The drinks are tastiest made one at a time and enjoyed immediately. If you are throwing a party with a spouse or partner, suggest they help by manning (or woman-ing) your "bar"—any small to medium table will do—for the first 30 to 45 minutes of the party. The bar action provides a focal point for incoming guests, and it's a great icebreaker. Have all the ingredients and drink-mixing paraphernalia assembled in advance and set them out on your bar just before guests arrive. A large ice bucket, or even two, filled with crushed ice is a must.

Each recipe makes 1 cocktail

Fredericksburg Fizz

1¹/₂ ounces (3 tablespoons) gin

1¹/₂ ounces (3 tablespoons) peach nectar

¹/₂ ounce (1 tablespoon) freshly squeezed lemon juice (about ¹/₂ a medium lemon)

1 large egg white (1 ounce)

¹/₂ ounce (a scant tablespoon simple syrup) (see Tip, page 191)

Crushed ice

In a cocktail shaker, vigorously "dry shake" (in bartender's parlance, shake without ice) the gin, peach nectar, lemon juice, egg white, and simple syrup to emulsify. Add crushed ice and shake athletically for 20 seconds. Strain into a fizz (highball) glass or other decorative glass. Serve immediately.

TIP If you are concerned about consuming raw egg whites, buy already-pasteurized egg whites at your grocery store.

Black Diamond

6 blackberries, thawed if frozen

3 fresh cilantro leaves, stemmed

¹/₂ ounce (a scant tablespoon) simple syrup

1¹/₂ ounces (3 tablespoons) blanco tequila (100 percent de agave)

¹/₂ ounce (1 tablespoon) Pimm's No. 1 Cup

¹/₂ ounce (1 tablespoon) freshly squeezed lime juice (from about ¹/₂ lime)

Crushed ice

Using a small wooden spoon or mallet, muddle (mash together) the blackberries, cilantro leaves, and simple syrup in the bottom of a cocktail shaker. Add the tequila, Pimms No. 1 Cup, lime juice, and crushed ice and shake vigorously. Strain into a chilled cocktail (martini) glass. Serve immediately.

TIP Spicy, citrusy Pimm's No. 1 Cup is a gin-based British liqueur that is the base of Wimbledon's official drink.

CHAPTER TWO

GULF COAST BEACH BASH

WHEN I WAS YOUNG, summertime meant beach time. We'd rent a cottage on the Bolivar Peninsula, a spit twenty-seven miles long that runs along the Texas Gulf Coast and separates Galveston Bay from the Gulf of Mexico. Like many families from nearby Beaumont, we spent as many summer weeks in Bolivar as possible. We'd rent the same place year after year—a light green cottage on stilts with swinging beds that hung from the ceiling on chains. We knew most everyone in the surrounding cabins, which were typically painted in sherbet colors and also sat on stilts. Life on the shores of the Gulf of Mexico always felt like a big party: heck, we were away from home, on vacation from school, surrounded by friends, and at the beach.

As little kids, we embarked on many a shrimping expedition, pulling up all this cool stuff in our nets, always shrimp, but other weird things, too, like squid or eels. It all seemed like valuable treasure to us. Other days we'd aim for crab, tying a chicken neck on a string, dropping it in the water, and waiting for a crab to snatch the bait with its claw. Then we'd scoop it up in our net and throw it into a portable ice chest. We'd cook whatever we caught, and if we came up empty, there was always Milt's seafood, where the bounty of the Gulf Coast—grouper, flounder, redfish, or snapper—lay cool and fresh on a clean bed of ice. Roadside stands offered 'maters and melons—Bolivar-speak for garden-fresh tomatoes and watermelons, always a big part of our summer diet.

When we grew older, we'd scour the beach collecting wood for bonfire parties. The boys dragged up big logs for chairs and we'd cozy up to the fire telling stories, and roasting hot dogs and marshmallows on sticks, until the fire shrank to glowing embers.

During all those contented summers, I soaked up the basics of beachside entertaining without even realizing it. First and foremost, I learned this simple truth: from boiled shrimp to long-simmered gumbos, everything tastes better at the beach. Sun and sand make everyone hungry; whatever you serve, they'll like. Stick to what's local and fresh and keep it simple, or do it ahead.

Beach rules dictate that parties stay relaxed and informal. You're on vacation, too, so share the work of entertaining. What may seem like drudgery when you're solo in the kitchen can turn into a happy giggle-fest when everyone's working together. Invite a few trusted friends to show up early to help with the cooking, or if the party is small, make prep an integral part of the festivities. Don't be afraid to assign tasks that play to your guests' strengths. Let the cooking-averse set the table. Suggest that the amateur bartender fix drinks. Ask friends to help decorate by bringing something that's beach related—shells, small bits of driftwood—and pile everything into a large, shallow glass bowl to serve as the centerpiece. As always, when it comes to entertaining, you set the tone: if you are having a good time, you can be sure your guests will, too.

Chicken-fried Shrimp

Chicken-fried tenderloin steak was a top seller at Rebecca's Table, but I have my bartender to thank for the idea that led to this variation. One night, a couple sat down to eat dinner at the bar, and the husband ordered chicken-fried steak. His wife liked the idea, just not the red meat part of it. So the bartender says, "Why don't we do some shrimp for you?" She was thrilled.

Served with chipotle ketchup, adapted from a recipe by Texas chef and author Terry Thompson-Anderson, chicken-fried shrimp became a best-selling appetizer. It's also a natural for informal entertaining. Once guests arrive, fire up the skillet, and enlist a helper to dip the buttermilk-soaked shrimp in the seasoned flour mixture. Other guests would be well advised to stay nearby. Chicken-fried anything is best fresh from the frying pan. Set the shrimp on a communal platter accompanied with a big bowl of chipotle ketchup and let guests serve themselves. I guarantee the shrimp won't last long.

Serves 8 as an appetizer

3 large eggs, lightly beaten

2 cups buttermilk, or enough to cover the shrimp

2 teaspoons kosher salt

1/4 teaspoon cayenne pepper

1 teaspoon freshly ground black pepper

24 extra-large (16/20 count) shrimp (about 1 1/4 pounds), peeled and deveined

2 1/2 cups all-purpose flour

1 teaspoon Cajun seasoning (such as Paul Prudhomme's Seafood Magic)

1/4 cup canola oil, or more as needed, for frying

Chipotle Ketchup (page 254), for accompaniment

Combine the eggs, buttermilk, 1 teaspoon of the salt, cayenne, and 1/2 teaspoon of the black pepper in a large bowl. Add the shrimp and stir so it is completely submerged (add more buttermilk, if needed). Marinate the shrimp at room temperature for at least 15 minutes.

Combine the flour, Cajun seasoning, the remaining 1 teaspoon of salt, and the remaining 1/2 teaspoon of black pepper in a large bowl.

Have a baking pan or sheet of parchment paper ready near the stove top. Dip the shrimp, 1 at a time, in the flour mixture, coating evenly. Set the floured shrimp in the pan. Pour 1/4 cup of the oil into a large skillet set over medium-high heat.

Once all the shrimp have been coated and the oil is shimmering with heat, add as many shrimp to the pan as will fit in a single layer without crowding. Cook the shrimp until golden brown and crisp, 1 to 2 minutes per side (flip with tongs). Serve immediately with ketchup. Continue until all the shrimp is cooked, adding more oil to the skillet if necessary.

DO IT EARLY

The shrimp can sit in the buttermilk mixture, covered and refrigerated, for up to 4 hours before cooking. The seasoned flour mixture can be prepared in advance and held at room temperature. Prepare the ketchup ahead, up to 2 weeks, and store in a covered container.

Campechana

The origin of the name campechana *is a mystery, but just about every Texan I know loves this cool, tomatoey seafood cocktail stocked with plump chunks of ripe avocado and served with a pile of crisp tortilla chips. (I hear it is big in some parts of California, too.) I got stuck on campechana at a place run by legendary Houston restaurateur Jim Goode. He parlayed a small Texas barbecue joint into a homegrown restaurant dynasty that includes a Tex-Mex eatery and two Gulf Coast seafood spots.*

Campechana is incredibly versatile. As an appetizer, serve in long-stemmed glasses set on plates and surrounded with tortilla chips for dipping. Serve as a main course in a huge bowl, surrounded by chips. Offer individual bowls and let guests ladle up servings themselves. For outdoor or beachside festivities, transport in a large plastic container set in a cooler and serve in clear acrylic stemmed glasses or in disposable plastic glasses. Don't forget plenty of chips.

Serves 8 to 10 as a main course; double that as an appetizer

2 tablespoons olive oil

1 large yellow onion, coarsely chopped (about 2 cups)

1 green bell pepper, cored, seeded, and coarsely chopped

1 red bell pepper, cored, seeded, and coarsely chopped

6 medium cloves garlic, minced (about 2 tablespoons)

1 teaspoon kosher salt

$1/4$ to $1/2$ teaspoon cayenne pepper

$1^1/2$ pounds extra-large (16/20 count) shrimp, peeled and deveined

1 (28-ounce) can Rotel tomatoes (see Tip, page 138), or Muir Glen fire-roasted tomatoes with green chiles

1 (12-ounce) bottle V8 juice

$2/3$ cup tomato ketchup

1 tablespoon Worcestershire sauce

2 tablespoons freshly squeezed lime juice (about 1 medium lime)

2 tablespoons freshly squeezed lemon juice (about 1 medium lemon)

2 tablespoons prepared horseradish

1 pound lump crabmeat

4 ripe avocados

1 tablespoon chopped fresh cilantro

1 tablespoon chopped fresh Italian parsley

Lime wedges, for accompaniment

Tortilla chips, for accompaniment

Heat the olive oil in a large pot set over medium heat and sauté the onion, bell peppers, and garlic. While the vegetables cook, combine the salt and cayenne in a small bowl and rub on the shrimp; cut each shrimp into 3 bite-size pieces. Add the shrimp to the pot and sauté on medium-high for about 2 minutes. Add the tomatoes with their juice, V8 juice, ketchup, and Worcestershire sauce, and bring the mixture to a simmer, about 5 minutes. Remove the mixture from the heat and stir in lime and lemon juices, horseradish, and crab. Refrigerate until cold, preferably overnight, so the flavors meld.

Just before serving, peel and pit the avocados and cut them into bite-size chunks. Gently stir them in along with the cilantro and parsley. Serve with plenty of lime wedges and chips.

Marinated Crab Claw Cocktail

As a kid, I loved the crab claw cocktail at Don's Seafood and Steakhouse in Beaumont, Texas. My take on this childhood favorite seems so right for a Gulf Coast party: It's easy to make ahead, is light and refreshing, and highlights the glorious blue crab that inhabits the Gulf Coast.

Finding fresh crab claws can be tough if you are not at the beach during crab season, but they're available canned, and they taste almost as good as fresh. Make sure you are getting the meat with the little claw attached, so they can be plucked out of the marinade and eaten. Here in Texas they're called crabmeat fingers.

Serves 12 as an appetizer

1 medium yellow onion, halved crosswise and thinly sliced

1 red or yellow bell pepper, cored, seeded, and thinly sliced

1 green bell pepper, cored, seeded, and thinly sliced

6 medium cloves garlic, minced (about 2 tablespoons)

1/4 cup freshly squeezed lemon juice (about 2 medium lemons)

1/4 cup red wine vinegar

1/2 teaspoon dried oregano, or 2 teaspoons fresh, chopped

1 cup extra-virgin olive oil

1 teaspoon kosher salt

1 teaspoon seafood seasoning (such as Paul Prudhomme's Seafood Magic)

2 (16-ounce) cans pasteurized blue crabmeat fingers

Toasted or plain sourdough baguette slices, for serving (optional)

In a large bowl, combine the onion, bell peppers, garlic, lemon juice, vinegar, oregano, oil, salt, and seafood seasoning. Stir until thoroughly mixed. Add the crab claws and gently stir them in. Refrigerate for at least 2 hours to let the flavors meld. This is best if marinated overnight. Remove the cocktail from the refrigerator about 1 hour before serving. Just before serving, stir gently to mix all the ingredients. Serve with sliced baguettes, lightly toasted or not, as your mood strikes.

DO IT EARLY

This recipe can be made up to 1 day in advance, covered, and refrigerated.

White Balsamic-Jicama Slaw

Summer at the beach is unthinkable without coleslaw, but I sometimes I hanker for something a bit out of the ordinary. I combined napa cabbage, a more delicate cousin to regular cabbage, with crunchy jicama, dressed it with white balsamic vinegar and mayo, and sprinkled on fennel seed to create what has become my new summer fave. This sturdy salad travels with ease, whether you're taking it to the beach or to a summer party with friends. Another plus: you can make it up to 24 hours in advance.

Serves 12

SALAD

- 1 medium head napa cabbage (about 2¹/₂ pounds)
- 3 medium carrots, grated on the large holes
- 1 large jicama (about 1¹/₂ pounds), peeled and cut into large matchsticks
- 1 bunch chopped green onions, white part only
- 2 Granny Smith apples, peeled, cored, and cut into large matchsticks
- ³/₄ cup dried currants or dried cranberries

WHITE BALSAMIC DRESSING

- 3 cloves garlic, minced (about 1 tablespoon)
- 2 tablespoons freshly squeezed lime juice (about 1 medium lime)
- 3 tablespoons honey
- ¹/₄ cup canola oil
- ¹/₄ cup Dijon mustard
- ¹/₂ cup white balsamic vinegar
- 1 cup mayonnaise
- 1 tablespoon fennel seeds

TO MAKE THE SALAD: Trim off the cabbage's root end, thinly slice crosswise, then chop into pieces that can be easily picked up with a fork. Combine the cabbage, carrots, jicama, green onions, apples, and dried currants in a large bowl.

TO MAKE THE DRESSING: Vigorously whisk together the garlic, lime juice, honey, oil, mustard, balsamic vinegar, and mayonnaise in a medium bowl until the dressing is thoroughly combined. Whisk in the fennel seeds and pour the dressing over the cabbage mixture. Stir until the dressing evenly covers the slaw. The slaw will be a little soupy, which is just the way I like it. Cover and refrigerate for at least 1 hour or until ready to serve.

TIP Instead of by hand, you can mix the dressing in a food processor fitted with the metal blade, which will save you the hassle of chopping up garlic (you add it whole). You cannot, however, escape the slight hassle of peeling off the papery skin and slicing off the tips of each clove.

VARIATION

For those who plan to wear their summer shorts short, you can lighten the dressing: for the 1 cup mayonnaise, substitute ¹/₄ cup reduced-fat mayonnaise plus ³/₄ cup nonfat or low-fat yogurt.

Seafood Gumbo

Okay, gumbo takes time and patience, especially if you make the effort to prepare a nice, dark roux. On the plus side, you can make it a day ahead and heat it when your guests arrive, leaving you free to mingle, chat, and have a great time with your friends. In addition, it feeds a whole lot of hungry people, and if you are very, very lucky you'll have leftovers for lunch the next day. (Sometimes I squirrel away a little in the refrigerator for insurance.) Serve with long-grain rice and some crusty bread.

Serves 12

ROUX

- 2 cups canola oil
- 2 cups all-purpose flour

GUMBO

- 1 pound andouille sausage (a spicy, smoked pork sausage), cut into bite-size pieces
- 2 tablespoons canola oil
- 2 large onions, chopped
- 10 cloves garlic, minced
- 4 green bell peppers, cored, seeded, and cut into medium dice
- 6 stalks celery, chopped
- 1 tablespoon Cajun seasoning (such as Paul Prudhomme's Seafood Magic)
- 1 teaspoon dried thyme leaves
- $1/2$ tablespoon freshly ground black pepper
- $1/2$ teaspoon plus $1/4$ teaspoon cayenne pepper
- 1 tablespoon Tabasco sauce
- 3 bay leaves
- 4 quarts shrimp stock (see Tips, opposite)
- 2 pounds extra-large (16/20 count) shrimp, peeled and deveined (save shells to make stock)
- 1 tablespoon plus $1/2$ teaspoon kosher salt
- 2 pounds crayfish tail meat
- $1/2$ cup chopped fresh Italian parsley
- 1 (16-ounce) bag frozen sliced okra, thawed
- 1 quart fresh oysters (optional)

Filé powder, for sprinkling at the table

- 1 bunch green onions, white and green parts only, thinly sliced, for garnish
- 6 cups cooked long-grain white rice, for accompaniment

TO MAKE THE ROUX: Heat the oil in a large, heavy-bottomed skillet or pot set over medium-low heat. Whisk in the flour and cook, stirring constantly, until dark chocolate brown, about 30 minutes. Remove the pan from the heat and continue whisking for another 6 to 7 minutes. (The heat of the pan will continue to cook the roux, and it will turn an even deeper brown.) Set aside.

TO MAKE THE GUMBO: In a large skillet, brown the sausage over medium heat. Drain the sausage on paper towels. Heat the 2 tablespoons oil in a heavy-bottomed stockpot. Add the onions, garlic, peppers, and celery. Sauté over medium heat until the vegetables are soft, about 5 minutes. Stir in the Cajun seasoning, thyme, black pepper, $1/2$ teaspoon cayenne pepper, Tabasco, bay leaves, roux, and stock. Bring the gumbo to a boil over medium-high heat, then decrease the heat to medium-low and simmer for 30 minutes.

Rub the shrimp with the remaining $1/4$ teaspoon cayenne and $1/2$ teaspoon salt. Add the cooked sausage, crayfish, shrimp, parsley, okra, and remaining 1 tablespoon salt, and cook until the okra is heated through. Stir in the oysters at the last minute, if you wish, and cook just until they are heated. Set the green onions and filé on the table so guests can help themselves. Serve the gumbo hot with the rice.

TIPS Filé powder is made from ground, dried sasafrass leaves; it's a traditional thickener for gumbo.

To make shrimp stock, heat 2 tablespoons olive oil in a large stockpot set over medium-high heat. Add 1 large quartered, unpeeled onion, 1 large quartered carrot, 2 quartered stalks celery, and 2 peeled garlic cloves. Sauté 5 minutes over medium heat until the vegetables begin to soften. Add reserved shrimp shells and sauté about 5 more minutes, until they turn light brown. Stir in a 6-ounce can tomato paste, 2 cups dry white wine, 4 quarts water, and $1/2$ teaspoon kosher salt. Bring to a boil, reduce the heat to medium-low and simmer, uncovered, for 1 hour. Strain the stock and discard the solids.

Farmstand Tomato Soup with Arugula Pesto

I love coming home with friends from a steamy day at the beach knowing that I've got a batch of cold tomato soup ready. I dish it up, swirl in a tablespoon of vibrant green arugula pesto, and pass it around. We sit on the porch and savor the flavor of sun-sweetened summer tomatoes enhanced with a touch of cream and a nip of vodka. The rest of dinner will come later, but for now, we're assuaging our hunger, chatting, laughing, and reliving the events of the day.

This is a great make-ahead soup. In fact, it becomes more flavorful with age. Although I like it cold, it's equally good heated. If storm clouds gather and the temperature plunges, take the soup from refrigerator to stove, heat it up, and serve it in mugs.

Serves 8 to 10

SOUP

10 medium or 4 very large ripe tomatoes (about 4 pounds), cored

1/4 cup olive oil

2 shallots, coarsely chopped

2 cloves garlic, chopped

1 (28-ounce) can fire-roasted crushed tomatoes

1 tablespoon kosher salt

1/8 teaspoon sugar

1/4 to 1/2 cup heavy whipping cream

1/4 cup good-quality vodka (optional)

ARUGULA PESTO

1/2 cup pine nuts

5 ounces baby arugula

2 cloves garlic, coarsely chopped

1/2 teaspoon kosher salt

1 tablespoon freshly squeezed lemon juice (about 1/2 medium lemon)

3/4 cup extra-virgin olive oil

1/2 cup freshly grated Parmesan cheese

TO MAKE THE SOUP: Preheat the oven to 400°F. Set the cored tomatoes on a rimmed baking sheet. Drizzle with 2 tablespoons of the olive oil and roast them until they look wrinkly, about 30 minutes; set aside. While the tomatoes cool, heat the remaining 2 tablespoons olive oil in a small sauté pan. Add the shallots and 2 cloves chopped garlic and sauté over medium-low heat until they turn golden brown and caramelized, 15 to 20 minutes; set aside.

When the tomatoes are cool enough to handle, peel off the skins, which should slip off easily. Put the peeled tomatoes in the jar of a blender along with the sautéed shallots and garlic, crushed tomatoes (with juice), 1 tablespoon salt, and sugar. Process until the soup is smooth. Stir in the cream and vodka, if desired. Refrigerate in a covered bowl for at least 6 hours, or preferably overnight.

TO MAKE THE PESTO: Toast the pine nuts, stirring occasionally, in a skillet set on medium heat

continued

until they turn golden brown, about 4 minutes. Combine the arugula, pine nuts, 2 cloves garlic, $^1/_2$ teaspoon salt, and lemon juice in the jar of a blender or the work bowl of a food processor fitted with the metal blade, then slowly add in the olive oil through the feed tube and process. Transfer the pesto to a bowl and stir in the Parmesan.

TO SERVE: Ladle the chilled soup into individual serving bowls, and swirl 1 tablespoon of pesto into each.

DO IT EARLY

The soup can be made up to 4 days in advance and refrigerated. Ditto for the pesto. Both should be well covered. Arugula pesto does not brown when exposed to oxygen as does its more common cousin, basil pesto.

VARIATION

The more traditional-minded may prefer a basil pesto (page 31). Also, you can eliminate the cream and top the soup with a dollop of crème fraîche or Greek-style yogurt and a drizzle of pesto.

Gulf Coast Entertaining, Rockport Style

Carol Hicks Bolton and her husband, Tim, entrepreneurs and owners of Fredericksburg's Homestead antiques store, try to escape to their Gulf Coast beach home near Rockport at least twice monthly. They bought the place so they could "kick the door in, drop our shoes, and not think about the next day until we have to," says Carol. Not a surprising sentiment from a woman who, on top of designing her own line of furniture and helping with Homestead's business, also home-schools her two children, thirteen-year-old Mac and nine-year-old Augusta. No one wants to attend another fancy party at the beach, she says. But they do want to spend time with those they care about.

"Our home is so simple. Our kitchen is simple. Our parties are the same," Carol says. Entertaining chez Bolton is often a group effort, and informality is a given. "Sometimes we don't even sit at the table—we gather around that huge bar and sample appetizers. Then everyone cooks their specialty dish on that tiny little stove or our cheap little grill and it all is laid out on the table on the deck or dragged to the fishing pier. No frills, just chunky white ironstone plates, old silver that can fall through the cracks with no worries, the frying pan as serving dish, slubbed linen napkins that used to be curtains. It's beyond easy."

Gardens in the Boltons' beachside village of Fulton begin producing well before their counterparts in Fredericksburg, Carol says, setting the stage for garden parties with a delightfully local flavor. "If you are fortunate enough to be friends with a gardener, you certainly will be invited to a garden party as soon as the first good tomatoes come in and the larder is stocked. If you aren't the dirt type, you'll be asked to bring something from the city—handmade goat cheese and fresh pecans from the Hill Country, bread from Rather Sweet, mozzarella from Dallas, a homemade balsamic salad dressing. Locals bring tomatoes along with the most incredible things you have ever tasted—arugula, butter lettuce from their sandy dirt, something fresh caught from the bay, made-today pico de gallo, those big, lime-green avocados from Mexico. The host makes a huge salad with everyone's bringings—it reminds me of stone soup. There is usually a big pot of cucumber water to drink with a few strawberries thrown in. The salad bowl is huge and as the guests arrive, they cut up their contributions and throw it into the bowl."

The Boltons' favorite family party takes place on their deck overlooking the bay, and the fun is multiplied when the neighbors are around. The family shares a pier with two families who love to fish. "Oh, what trading goes on upon that pier—flounder for crabs, redfish for sea trout," Carol says.

During the past few decades, the Vietnamese population has grown in the area. "They have taught us about noodles and seafood and cilantro all in a bowl," Carol says. "We have taken a cue from that. Guests bring their catch of the day, throwing it on the grill and then into a big bowl of pasta and good olive oil. It seems like most entertaining here is very impromptu—so different from the Hamptons, or any other beach for that matter. So unpretentious! I love it here."

Cajun Catfish Tacos with Chipotle Mayonnaise

My spicy, tangy catfish tacos are a great way to feed a hungry beach crowd without the hassle of frying or grilling. Load up a rimmed baking sheet with fish fillets, pour on the marinade, refrigerate overnight, and just before serving, bake for less than 30 minutes. Heat flour or corn tortillas in a tortilla warmer along with the fish, and set it all out on the table with a bowl of chipotle mayo and a platter of thin-sliced cabbage. Now everybody chow down! The fish is just the way I like it—juicy and flavorful thanks to long marination (at least 6 hours) and oven baking.

I've allowed two tacos per person to ensure you'll have enough even for man-size, sun-fueled appetites. (What is it about playing on the beach that makes men so hungry?) If you have a smaller crowd or guests with smaller stomachs, halve the recipe.

Serves 12; 2 tacos per person

CATFISH

12 large catfish or other white fish fillets

1/4 cup Cajun seasoning (such as Paul Prudhomme's Seafood Magic)

2 (7-ounce) cans chipotle chiles in adobo sauce (reserve 2 whole chipotle chiles for the mayo, recipe follows)

1/4 cup freshly squeezed lemon juice (about 2 medium lemons)

1 cup olive oil

24 medium corn or small flour tortillas

1 head red or green cabbage, thinly sliced, for accompaniment

2 large limes, cut into wedges, for accompaniment

Cucumber-Tomato-Avocado Salad (recipe follows), for accompaniment

CHIPOTLE MAYONNAISE

2 cups mayonnaise

2 reserved chipotle chiles

3 tablespoons freshly squeezed lime juice (about 1 1/2 medium limes)

1 tablespoon Creole mustard

1 1/2 teaspoons kosher salt

TO MARINATE THE FISH: Pat the fillets dry and spread them in 1 layer on a rimmed 13 by 18-inch baking sheet. (They can be close together, even touching, but not overlapping.) Liberally sprinkle Cajun seasoning on both sides of the fillets. Puree the chipotle peppers (minus the 2 reserved chiles) and their sauce in the work bowl of a food processor fitted with the metal blade. Add the lemon juice and olive oil and pulse a few times until the mixture is combined. Pour the mixture over the seasoned catfish. Cover the fish with plastic wrap and refrigerate for at least 6 hours or overnight.

Preheat the oven to 350°F. Bake until the fish begins to flake when pulled apart with a fork, 20 to 25 minutes. Keep warm.

TO MAKE THE CHIPOTLE MAYONNAISE: Whirl the mayonnaise, reserved 2 chipotle chiles, lime juice, Creole mustard, and salt in the work bowl of a food processor fitted with the metal blade until blended. Scrape into a small bowl and refrigerate until ready to serve.

TO SERVE: Use a spatula to cut the fish into manageable portions and leave them on the baking sheet so guests can serve themselves. Set out the warm tortillas, sliced cabbage, chipotle mayo, and lime wedges, allowing guests to custom-build their own tacos. Have the salad on the table to serve with the tacos.

DO IT EARLY

As long as the chipotle mayo is prepared with commercially made mayonnaise, it will keep for up to 2 weeks in the refrigerator.

Cucumber-Tomato-Avocado Salad

Makes twelve ¹/₃-cup servings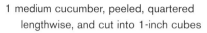

1 medium cucumber, peeled, quartered lengthwise, and cut into 1-inch cubes

1 pint cherry tomatoes, halved

2 large ripe avocados, peeled, pitted, and cut into bite-size pieces

2 tablespoons red wine vinegar

1 teaspoon Dijon mustard

¹/₄ teaspoon kosher salt

Freshly ground black pepper

¹/₄ to ¹/₂ cup extra-virgin olive oil

Place the cucumber, tomatoes, and avocados in a large bowl. In another bowl, whisk together the vinegar, mustard, salt, freshly ground pepper to taste, and olive oil. Add the dressing to the vegetables and toss to coat. Serve immediately.

Champagne-marinated Shrimp Boil

A day of lazy dipping in Gulf Coast waters calls for a cold bowl of cooked shrimp dipped in a sweet-savory sauce. That's what my mom thought, anyway, and she always had cold shrimp on hand when we stayed at the beach. I love it, too, and it's a great do-ahead that lets you set out something for your hungry guests as soon as you step inside after a day of sand and sun.

I cook the shrimp and make the dipping sauces the day before and stick 'em all in the fridge. When I pull them out, everyone thinks I'm an organized genius. (Naturally, I politely demur.) Snacking on shrimp, nobody notices if I disappear into the kitchen for a little main-course prep work. I usually figure about one-third pound per person. The shrimp usually runs out before anyone's hunger does, but that works for me. I want my friends to have room for dinner and dessert. If I don't feel much like cooking, I allow about one-half pound of shrimp per person for a hands-on main course. Of course, I always offer dessert, often as simple as cookies (like Vanilla Sand Dollars, page 83) and ice cream.

Serves 12

SHRIMP

- 1 bottle (750 ml) brut Champagne, sparkling wine, or cava
- 1/4 cup freshly squeezed lemon juice (about 2 medium lemons)
- 1 tablespoon chopped fresh oregano leaves (preferably Mexican)
- 1 teaspoon cayenne pepper
- 4 pounds large (21/30 count) shrimp, deveined, with shells
- 1/4 cup prepared shrimp boil seasoning (such as Old Bay)
- Typical Red Sauce (page 254), for dipping
- Spicy Remoulade (page 255), for dipping

TO MAKE THE SHRIMP: In a large bowl, stir together the Champagne, lemon juice, oregano, and cayenne. Add the shrimp and refrigerate for at least 1 hour but no longer than 3 hours, or the shrimp could turn mushy.

Fill a large stockpot with about 2 gallons water. Add the shrimp boil seasoning. Bring the seasoned water to a boil over high heat, add the shrimp, and return the water to a boil. Decrease the heat to medium and simmer the shrimp until they turn pink, 1 to 2 minutes. Drain the shrimp, dump them into a large bowl, and cover with ice cubes to stop the cooking. Once the shrimp are cool, drain the ice, and refrigerate for up to 24 hours.

Serve cold with dipping sauces.

DO IT EARLY

Cooked shrimp can be refrigerated for up to 1 day. The red sauce will keep, refrigerated, for up to 1 month, and the remoulade for about 2 weeks.

Crab in Shells

In my book, lump crabmeat spells luxury, and I can't think of a better way to pamper my guests than starting off with a sumptuous serving. Offering my friends a mound of crab in crab or scallop shells makes me feel as if I'm bringing the sea to the table. Scallop shells are usually easier to find than crab shells, although I've seen both at kitchen supply stores. If you can't find shells, use small ramekins.

For a speedy main course, double the recipe and bake the crab in larger ramekins. Serve with a green salad and loaves of crusty bread.

Makes about eight ¹/₂-cup servings

1 tablespoon olive oil

¹/₂ cup diced red onion (about half a medium onion)

¹/₂ green bell pepper, cored, seeded, and cut into small dice

¹/₂ red bell pepper, cored, seeded, and cut into small dice

¹/₂ cup mayonnaise

2 tablespoons Creole or Dijon mustard

2 tablespoons drained nonpareil capers

1 teaspoon Cajun seasoning

2 large eggs, lightly whisked

2 shakes Tabasco sauce

¹/₄ cup chopped fresh Italian parsley or fresh dill

1 pound jumbo lump crab

1¹/₂ cups panko (Japanese) breadcrumbs

¹/₄ teaspoon kosher salt

Pinch of freshly ground black pepper

2 tablespoons unsalted butter

Preheat the oven to 375°F. Lightly coat 8 scallop shells, crab shells, or 2¹/₂-inch-diameter heat-proof ramekins with cooking spray.

Place the oil in a large skillet set over medium heat. When the oil is hot but not smoking, add the onion and bell peppers and sauté until softened, about 3 minutes. (No need to wash the skillet yet.)

In a bowl, stir together the mayonnaise, mustard, capers, Cajun seasoning, eggs, Tabasco, and parsley. Stir in the sautéed vegetables, crab, 1 cup of the panko crumbs, salt, and pepper. Spoon about ¹/₂ cup of the crab mixture into each of the prepared shells. Set aside.

Melt the 2 tablespoons butter over medium-low heat in the skillet used to sauté the vegetables. Add the remaining ¹/₂ cup of panko and stir to coat the crumbs with butter. Top each portion of crab with about a tablespoon of the buttered crumbs. Bake until the crumb topping turns golden brown and the crab mixture is heated through, 10 to 15 minutes (a little longer if the crab mixture has been refrigerated).

Serve immediately.

DO IT EARLY

The dish can be prepared and refrigerated, covered, for up to 24 hours before baking.

TIP Don't want the hassle of preparing individual servings? Add the crab mixture to a large, shallow, ovenproof casserole coated with cooking spray. Top with buttered panko crumbs and bake until the crab casserole is warm throughout, at least 15 minutes.

VARIATION

For a passed appetizer, shape the crab mixture into bite-size cakes. Coat them in panko crumbs and sauté in a skillet heated with 1 tablespoon each of butter and olive oil. Cook over medium heat until the crab cakes are golden brown on both sides and heated all the way through, about 3 minutes per side.

Beach House Memories

The only timepiece in the McNeill family's historic, two-story summer place in Caplen, Texas, resided in the kitchen. "We took our wristwatches off at the door, woke up when the sun came up, and went down when we felt like it," Barbara Gordon McNeill recalls. "Napping was a priority, at least for the adults." Although Barbara and husband, Alan, have hosted plenty of folks at their beachfront home known as The Breakers, entertaining at their Bolivar Peninsula getaway tended to be as informal and easygoing as a one-clock abode would suggest.

Neighbors like the McNeills signaled their arrival by hoisting the flag, and "a very casual socializing began." Deck time with wine was a late afternoon ritual that rarely ended before the sun slipped into the water, and "supper" was always "whenever." If the family spotted friends strolling by on the beach, they'd wave and invite them up. Barbara might say, "I've got shrimp, let's do something tonight."

Fixing large quantities became an important beach-house custom; there was always a crowd—from Barbara and Alan's children and grandchildren to neighbors, friends, and assorted houseguests. They cooked up big pots of gumbo and seafood Creole, fixed huge cast-iron pans of cornbread and plates of fried fish, feasted on fresh shrimp from Milt's seafood or from Veronica, The Shrimp Lady, whose memorable motto was, "U Ring, We Bring." Platters of fresh tomatoes from the McNeills' garden and fruits from the nearby High Island stand appeared repeatedly. Dessert included homemade cakes and cookies brought from their Beaumont home, Blue Bell ice cream, and dewberry cobbler made from the blackberry look-alikes picked on the property. Barbara and family did most of the cooking—a far cry from the afternoon beach parties her great-uncle W. D. Gordon and his wife, Ruth, favored after buying the home in 1905: they'd arrive by train from Beaumont, servants in tow, and while they "bathed" in the warm Gulf Coast waters, the hired help prepared meals.

Barbara and Alan inherited The Breakers from Barbara's mother and painstakingly restored it. In 1998 it was placed on the National Register of Historic Places. A year later the McNeills moved the home 150 feet inland to protect it from severe beach erosion. Through it all, Barbara displayed her knack for easy, imaginative entertaining. She decorated with treasures that washed up on her beachfront property. A big old platter filled with seashells sat on the front porch table, along with the examples from her shark tooth collection. (Several of the largest teeth were mounted as a necklace.) On display around the house were numerous mementos from the Gulf—including fifty conch shells, a glass Japanese fishing float, and candlesticks fashioned from porch latticework. When she grew tired of paper napkins, Barbara substituted vintage dishtowels, and she unearthed her bib collection when barbecued crab was served. For those unfamiliar with Bolivar, she set out placemats that featured a map of the peninsula.

No one cooked lunch. Barbara stocked the refrigerator with homemade pimiento cheese, along with chicken and tuna salad for sandwiches, because, she says, guests and family alike enjoyed setting their own beach schedules for swimming, walking the beach, bird-watching, fishing, crabbing, or even napping. (There was always a pot of hot coffee going for sleepyheads in need of a caffeine pick-me-up.)

Five generations of the Gordon family enjoyed The Breakers until, tragically, the house was swept away by Hurricane Ike in September 2008. Losing the home came as a terrible shock, especially for a structure that had withstood so much. It survived the famous 1900 Galveston hurricane, still considered one the most destructive storms to hit U.S. soil. In 1915, a second devastating storm took a few nearby summer cottages but merely knocked The Breakers off its foundation blocks, leaving much of the house intact. Ike proved not so forgiving, and when the storm abated, all that remained were two iron beds tangled up in the shrubbery and a few birdhouses on poles.

"I'd like to think that it is still intact somewhere, like Dorothy's house in *The Wizard of Oz*," Barbara says. "We are still grieving." But they haven't given up on the place. Alan returned recently to broadcast wildflower seeds over the property. "We're not going to sell the land," Barbara says. "If the children want it, it will be there."

Big Easy Whole Flounder

This dish got its "Big Easy" name from the New Orleans–inspired Cajun seasoning that defines its flavor, and also because it's one of the biggest, easiest party dishes I know. The fish can be prepared and in the oven in less than 15 minutes, and it doesn't take much longer to cook. Cleanup is a snap, too, as long as you line the baking pan with foil. (Once the fish is cooked, just toss out the foil and return the pan to the cabinet.) For a simple dinner party after a day at the beach, it can't be beat. I serve whole flounder whenever I can find it because I'm smitten with the clean, light taste of this white fish, and for sentimental reasons, too. I spent many a summer on the Texas Gulf Coast, sunning, swimming, and fishing on the Bolivar Peninsula near Galveston. At night we'd step into our old tennis shoes, and armed with a flashlight and a spear, we'd wade into the Gulf up to our knees, shine the flashlight in the water, and when we spotted a bottom-dwelling flounder, we'd spear it. We tried really hard not to spear our own feet, and succeeded, though we did end up at the local ER a couple of times—never for a speared foot, though. This recipe pairs nicely with One-Pot Cajun New Potatoes, page 75.

Serves 6 to 8

1 whole (3- to 4-pound) flounder, cleaned and scaled

1 to 2 teaspoons Cajun seasoning (such as Paul Prudhomme's Seafood Magic)

1/2 to 1 cup dry white wine

2 tablespoons freshly squeezed lemon juice (about 1 medium lemon)

2 pints cherry tomatoes

1/4 cup drained nonpareil capers

1/4 cup (1/2 stick) unsalted butter, cut into 4 pats

Arrange the oven rack in the center of the oven. Preheat the oven to high broil. Cover the bottom of a large metal baking pan with heavy-duty aluminum foil and lightly grease it with cooking spray. Season the fish inside and out with Cajun seasoning. Set it in the prepared baking pan. Around the sides of the fish, pour the wine and lemon juice and scatter the cherry tomatoes and capers. Arrange the pats of butter in a line on top of the fish. Broil until the flesh of the fish is opaque throughout, about 20 minutes (cut a little slit in the thickest part of the fish to check).

For a dramatic presentation, take the whole fish to the table on a platter. Then whisk it back to the kitchen to debone for serving. Arrange equal portions of fish on individual plates along with a generous helping of tomatoes. Pour a bit of pan juice over each piece of fish.

TIP Aside from flounder, any mild white whole fish will do for this recipe, such as trout, snapper, bass, or grouper. If you can't find a big enough fish to feed everyone, buy two and broil them in the same pan.

One-Pot Cajun New Potatoes

This is the easiest, simplest recipe and it is guaranteed to draw raves from potato lovers everywhere. Okay, anything with a good dose of butter is bound to taste great. Point taken. But adding Cajun seasoning gives a plain-Jane dish a jolt of heat and energy. Finally, it all goes together in one pot, so even the post-party dishwasher (usually me) gets a break.

Serves 12

25 red potatoes (about 2^{1}/$_2$ pounds) about the size of golf balls, halved

^{3}/$_4$ cup unsalted butter (1^{1}/$_2$ sticks), at room temperature

1 tablespoon Cajun seasoning

^{1}/$_4$ teaspoon kosher salt

^{1}/$_4$ cup Italian parsley leaves, for garnish

Put the potatoes in a large pot and cover them with water. Bring the water to a simmer over high heat and decrease the heat to medium so the water doesn't boil over. Cook until the potatoes are fork-tender (literally when you stick a fork in a spud, it slides out with ease), about 20 minutes, and drain.

Return the potatoes to the pot and add the butter, Cajun seasoning, and salt. Using a metal spatula, stir in the butter and seasonings, and coarsely chop the potatoes until they are somewhat smashed, but not mashed.

Serve immediately from the pot, or if you feel the need to get fancy, pile them into a warm serving bowl and let guests serve themselves. Garnish with the parsley.

VARIATION

For a lower-fat version of this dish, you can cut back on the butter. Try adding 6 tablespoons. If the potatoes seem a little dry, add 1 or 2 tablespoons of low-fat milk.

Lemony Artichokes au Gratin

This simple, delicious side dish was inspired by a meal at one of my favorite Gulf Coast outposts, Stingaree Restaurant. This casual Bolivar Peninsula eatery (there's a bait shop on the ground floor) serves all-you-can-eat Gulf blue crab, oysters on the half shell, shrimp in many guises, and a seeming barge-load of other fresh seafood dishes. Stingaree is proof that you can't keep a good thing down—it was among the first to reopen following hurricane Ike, the ferocious September 2008 storm that leveled much of the peninsula. The building was damaged, but unlike many of the peninsula's structures, it wasn't swept away, and the owners managed to reopen just five months post-Ike.

I like to serve this with any simple fish or shellfish preparation. Try it with Big Easy Whole Flounder, page 73, or Champagne-marinated Shrimp Boil, page 67.

Serves 8

1 cup (2 sticks) unsalted butter, melted

4 (14-ounce) cans quartered artichoke hearts, drained (about 6 cups artichokes)

1 cup thinly sliced green onions, white part only (about 2 large bunches)

1 teaspoon Cajun seasoning

1/4 teaspoon red pepper flakes

1/2 teaspoon freshly ground black pepper

1/4 cup freshly squeezed lemon juice (about 2 medium lemons)

Dash of Tabasco sauce

3 cups freshly grated Parmesan cheese

1 cup shredded Monterey Jack cheese

1 1/2 cups panko (Japanese) breadcrumbs

Preheat the oven to 350°F. Using a pastry brush, lightly coat the bottom of a large gratin dish with a bit of the melted butter. Spread the artichoke hearts evenly over the bottom of the gratin dish and sprinkle with the green onions.

In a bowl, stir together the remaining melted butter, Cajun seasoning, red pepper flakes, black pepper, lemon juice, and Tabasco. Add the Parmesan, Monterey Jack, and panko crumbs and stir to combine. Spoon the mixture evenly over the artichokes.

Bake until the breadcrumb-butter mixture is golden brown and the casserole is hot throughout, 20 to 30 minutes. Serve immediately.

DO IT EARLY

The gratin can be assembled up to 1 day ahead, then covered and refrigerated. Bake just before serving.

Pineapple Bundt Cake

I know it's tough to keep things fresh in the salt air, but my favorite cousin's pineapple Bundt cake stays delectably moist for days—even at the beach. Sometimes I make it ahead and tote it to the beach; other times I make it there and keep it on hand. Who knows when we might be inspired to host a last-minute party? My cousin Vicki has been making this cake forever. She still bakes it in her grandmother Hille's cast-iron Bundt pan, which she inherited along with a boxful of prized family recipes. Vicki says, "Every time I make this cake I feel like my grandmother is watching over me."

Serves 12

CAKE

1 cup (2 sticks) unsalted butter, at room temperature

2 cups granulated sugar

5 large eggs

2 cups all-purpose flour

$1/2$ teaspoon kosher salt

1 (20-ounce) can crushed pineapple in heavy syrup, drained, with juice and 2 tablespoons pineapple reserved for glaze

1 teaspoon vanilla extract

PINEAPPLE SYRUP

1 cup granulated sugar

Reserved syrup from crushed pineapple

2 tablespoons reserved crushed pineapple

Powdered sugar, for dusting the finished cake

TO MAKE THE CAKE: Preheat the oven to 350°F. Grease a 10-cup Bundt pan.

Using an electric mixer fitted with the paddle attachment, beat the butter and the 2 cups granulated sugar on medium-high speed until light and fluffy, about 3 minutes. Add the eggs, 1 at a time, beating on medium speed after each addition until incorporated. Add the flour and salt and mix on medium-low just until incorporated. Reserve 2 tablespoons of the drained pineapple to use for the syrup; stir the remaining pineapple and the vanilla into the batter. Spoon the batter into the prepared pan. Bake until a toothpick inserted into the center of the cake comes out clean, about 50 minutes.

TO MAKE THE PINEAPPLE SYRUP: In a large saucepan set on medium-high heat, stir together the 1 cup granulated sugar and reserved pineapple syrup; bring to a boil. Decrease the heat to medium and continue cooking, stirring, until the mixture thickens, about 5 minutes. Remove from heat and stir in the 2 tablespoons reserved pineapple. Set aside.

TO FINISH THE CAKE: Cool the cake in the pan for about 10 minutes. Using thin wood or metal skewers, poke holes in the cake 1 to $1^1/2$ inches apart, reaching almost to the bottom. Pour the pineapple syrup evenly over the cake. Let it sit another 10 minutes to let the syrup penetrate; invert the cake onto a cake stand or plate. Dust with powdered sugar. Serve warm or at room temperature.

continued

Covered and kept at room temperature, this cake can be made at least 5 days in advance; or wrap it in plastic wrap and aluminum foil and freeze for up to 3 weeks. Defrost in its wrapping at room temperature.

TIP Although my cousin says the recipe doesn't work unless she uses canned pineapple in heavy syrup, I've found a way to compensate. If you can only find canned pineapple in its own juice, follow the recipe for the pineapple syrup above, but add 3 tablespoons corn syrup along with the sugar. Works like a charm.

Beachside Frozen Pops

Who can resist a frozen pop at the beach? But I am beyond tired of the artificially colored electric blue and fire-engine red pops that leave garish stains on lips and tongues. I keep a set of frozen pop molds at the ready and fill them up with my favorite fruit juices. If I want to get fancy I puree fruits such as berries or peaches, and mix with a matching fruit juice. Or I drop bite-size bits of fresh fruit into the molds along with a complementary juice. Below are a few suggestions to get you going.

JUICES

Orange

Grape

Pomegranate

Peach, mango, pear, or apricot nectar

Pineapple

Piña Colada (pineapple and coconut)

Any juice blend found in the refrigerator case at your local grocery

WHOLE FRUIT ADD-INS

Pomegranate seeds

Quartered seedless red or green grapes

Canned mandarin oranges, drained and cut in thirds

Thinly sliced banana

Blueberries

Raspberries

Peaches, peeled and cut into small dice

Mangoes, peeled and cut into small dice

Pineapple tidbits

Cocoa Cloud Icebox Pies

I've never forgotten the icebox pies I used to eat as a child at Luby's Cafeteria. Those pies, along with the jewel-colored servings of Jell-O, were too tantalizing to resist. I always selected an icebox pie and a bowl of Jell-O, agonizing over which color to choose. I always finished the pie, but never touched the Jell-O. The Jell-O was for looks, the pie for flavor.

My version of icebox pie is a stunning party animal—dramatic and devilishly rich. For parties, I prepare this recipe in stages: the crust one day, the filling the next, and the whipped cream topping the day of my party.

A word of warning: These are large and very rich pies. Only under extreme circumstances do I recommend eating a whole one in a single sitting. (For example, you're starring in a new movie and have been asked by your big-time director to gain fifty pounds pronto.) So you may wish to serve a half or quarter pie per person.

Makes 12 pies

CRUST

2 (16-ounce) packages Newman-Os or other chocolate sandwich cookies (preferably organic)

1 cup (2 sticks) unsalted butter, melted

TRUFFLE FILLING

3 cups whole milk

1 cup heavy whipping cream

2 whole vanilla beans, split

12 large egg yolks

1 cup granulated sugar

8 tablespoons all-purpose flour

1 pound bittersweet chocolate (at least 70 percent cacao), chopped in small pieces

$1/4$ cup ($1/2$ stick) unsalted butter

Pinch of salt

COCOA CLOUD CREAM

4 cups chilled heavy whipping cream

$1^{1}/4$ cups powdered sugar

$1/2$ cup high-quality unsweetened cocoa (such as Green & Black's or Scharffen Berger)

TO MAKE THE CRUST: In 1 or 2 batches, whirl the cookies in the work bowl of a food processor fitted with the metal blade until ground into coarse crumbs. Add the melted butter and pulse until the butter is thoroughly combined. Press the mixture into twelve $4^{3}/8$-inch-diameter (1-cup) foil tartlet pans, making sure the crumbs cover the pans' sides. Refrigerate until ready to fill.

TO MAKE THE FILLING: Heat the milk and 1 cup cream with the split vanilla beans in a large, heavy-bottomed saucepan over medium heat until hot but not boiling. Remove from the heat.

In a large bowl, vigorously and thoroughly whisk together the egg yolks, the granulated sugar, and the flour, about 30 seconds. Remove the vanilla beans from the milk mixture and discard. Slowly pour about $1/4$ cup of the milk mixture into the egg mixture, whisking constantly. Set the saucepan with the remainder of the milk mixture

continued

over medium-low heat. (This "tempers" the eggs, ensuring that they do not curdle.) Whisking constantly, slowly pour in the egg mixture. Continue whisking until the mixture thickens into a pudding-like consistency, 4 to 5 minutes. The mixture should be thick enough that the whisk leaves visible tracks as it passes through. Whisk in the chocolate, the ¼ cup butter, and the salt, and stir until melted.

Pour the chocolate filling into the individual pie pans to just below the top of the cookie crust. Immediately cover with plastic wrap, making sure it touches the filling at all points to prevent a skin from forming. Refrigerate for at least 4 hours (overnight is better to make sure the chocolate sets up).

TO MAKE THE COCOA CREAM: Using an electric mixer fitted with the whisk attachment, whip the 4 cups cream in a large bowl on high speed until firm peaks form. Add the powdered sugar and cocoa and whip until thoroughly combined. Cover each pie with a generous mound of whipped cream.

TO SERVE THE PIES: Gently push the bottom of the each foil pan to slip the pie onto individual dessert or serving plates.

DO IT EARLY

You can refrigerate the crust-lined tart pans up to 4 days ahead. The filled pies can chill up to 3 days in advance. You can add the cocoa cream the day they are ready to serve.

VARIATIONS

Garnish each pie with chocolate shavings: draw a vegetable peeler along the edge of an 8-ounce chocolate bar, letting the shavings fall onto waxed paper. Alternatively, use a gourmet hot chocolate mix, many of which are made with chocolate shavings, such as Williams-Sonoma Hot Chocolate.

For single servings, use standard nonstick muffin tins. To release the pies, run a sharp paring knife around the edges and they'll pop out.

Vanilla Sand Dollar Cookies

I recently happened upon a sand dollar cookie stamp at Der Kuchen Laden, Fredericksburg's top-notch kitchen store, and snapped it up, thinking what a great hit beach-themed cookies would be during Gulf Coast getaways. For kids summering on Bolivar Peninsula, a day at the beach meant a fistful of sand dollars, sugar shells, and colorful beach glass as smooth and opaque as Texas honey. Sand dollars were the hardest to find because the disk-shaped marine creatures habitually burrow into the sand. We'd swim out to the sand bars and dig for dollars by burying our feet a few inches into the sand and sliding along until our toes hit the critters' hard internal shells. We'd pluck them out of the sand and haul them home. Popular legend holds that sand dollars are really mermaid's coins. If I'd heard that as a little girl, I surely would have gathered even more.

This recipe is a variation on the common shortbread cookie, without eggs or other leavening, because, according to the cookie stamp people, the rising of the cookies obscures the pattern left by the stamp. Makes sense to me. Although it is expensive, I like to use vanilla bean paste because it has little flecks of vanilla seed in it, giving the cookie a sandy, beachy look. It is available at kitchen specialty stores and at many upscale grocers.

Makes about 5 dozen 2-inch cookies

2 cups (4 sticks) unsalted butter, at room temperature

1 cup firmly packed golden brown sugar

2 tablespoons vanilla bean paste or vanilla extract

4 cups all-purpose flour

$^1/_2$ teaspoon salt

Preheat the oven to 325°F. Line baking sheets with parchment paper or silicone liners or grease generously with butter or cooking spray. With a pastry brush, lightly coat a cookie stamp with a neutral-tasting vegetable oil, such as canola, or mist it with cooking spray.

Using an electric mixer fitted with the paddle attachment, mix the butter, sugar, and vanilla on medium-low speed until combined. Add the flour and salt and mix on low speed just until thoroughly combined. (Don't overmix here or the cookies can be tough.) Using a $1^1/_4$-inch scoop, drop the dough on the prepared baking sheets about 2 inches apart. Stamp each dough ball firmly enough to make an imprint, but don't press so hard that the cookie flattens to less than $^1/_4$ inch thick. Bake until the cookies begin to look golden brown around the edges, about 10 minutes. The cookies will keep for a few days in an airtight container.

TIP You'll find cookie stamps in many patterns at most well-stocked specialty kitchen stores, or check out www.rycraft.com. In addition to ones depicting sand dollars, they stock numerous others that are sea-related, including seahorses, sea turtles, crabs, starfish, and dolphins.

S'mores Cupcakes

When I was a teenager, summer meant the beach. If I was lucky, I'd arrive in time for one of the great big beach-bonfire fiestas staged frequently by my friends, complete with roasted weenies, just a touch of beer (I swear!), and my total favorite—bonfire s'mores. Sadly, times have changed. Only a few Texas beach communities allow bonfires, so I came up with a s'more cupcake that puts me into a beach party mood no matter where I happen to be. The only fire necessary to bring their marshmal-lowy topping to the pitch-perfect golden brown of a genuine s'more is the skinny blue flame that shoots from my portable kitchen torch.

These cupcakes are sure to bring smiles to just about any kid who shows up for a casual party, whether it takes place in the kitchen, at the shore, or on a beachfront deck. Now that my daughter is a seasoned college student, I make the cupcakes in advance, and whip up the marshmallow topping just before party time. I provide disposable plastic pastry bags fitted with open star tips so Fran and her friends can decorate the cupcakes themselves. Then it's time for me to pass the torch—the kitchen torch, that is. Now that I think of it, it's not the only torch I'm passing.

Makes 12 Texas-size or 18 standard cupcakes

GRAHAM CRACKER BASE

2 cups graham cracker crumbs
    (about 16 whole crackers)

1 cup (2 sticks) unsalted butter, melted

1/4 teaspoon kosher salt

CHOCOLATE CUPCAKES

1 cup (2 sticks) unsalted butter

1/2 cup high-quality unsweetened cocoa (such as Green & Black's or Scharffen Berger)

3/4 cup brewed coffee, or 1 tablespoon espresso powder fully dissolved in 3/4 cup hot water

2 cups sugar

2 large eggs

1 cup buttermilk

2 tablespoons vanilla extract

2 cups all-purpose flour

1 teaspoon baking soda

1/4 teaspoon kosher salt

1 (12-ounce) bag large milk chocolate chips (such as Ghirardelli)

MARSHMALLOW TOPPING

8 large egg whites, at room temperature

1 1/2 cups sugar

TO MAKE THE GRAHAM CRACKER BASE: In a bowl, stir together the crumbs, the 1 cup melted butter, and the 1/4 teaspoon salt. Set aside.

TO MAKE THE CUPCAKES: Preheat the oven to 350°F. Line Texas or standard-size cupcake tins with paper cupcake liners. For the crust, press the graham cracker base into the bottom of each well: about 3 tablespoons for a Texas-size cupcake; about 2 tablespoons for a standard-size.

Melt the 1 cup butter in a large saucepan over medium-low heat. Add the cocoa and whisk until smooth. Add the coffee and whisk until smooth. Add the 2 cups sugar, eggs, buttermilk, and vanilla to the warm cocoa mixture. Whisk

continued

until smooth. Add the flour, baking soda, and $\frac{1}{4}$ teaspoon salt and whisk until incorporated. Stir in the chocolate chips.

Evenly divide the batter to fill each cup almost to the top of the muffin papers. Bake until a toothpick inserted into the center comes out clean and the cupcakes feel firm when lightly pressed in their center, 20 to 25 minutes. Cool for 10 minutes and invert onto wire cooling racks. Cool for at least 30 minutes before decorating.

TO MAKE THE MARSHMALLOW TOPPING: Set a large, perfectly clean metal bowl over a pot filled with 2 inches of lightly simmering water. Add the egg whites and the $1\frac{1}{2}$ cups sugar and heat, whisking constantly, until the sugar melts and there are no visible sugar grains in the meringue. (Rub a little bit of meringue between your fingers to make sure all the sugar has melted.) Remove the meringue from the heat and beat it with an electric mixer fitted with the whisk attachment on high speed until the meringue is stiff and shiny, about 5 minutes.

TO ASSEMBLE TO CUPCAKES: Spoon the marshmallow topping into a pastry bag fitted with an open star tip. Pipe the topping onto each cupcake in a circular motion, starting at the outside edge of the cupcake and working toward the center. I like to pipe it on generously so that it comes to a peak in the center that is 2 to $2\frac{1}{2}$ inches high. Or pile the topping on top of the cupcakes. Style it with your fingers by plucking at it to tease it into jagged spikes, or shape it with a spoon. Using a kitchen torch, brown the marshmallow by moving the flame slowly around the topping (avoiding the cupcake papers) until it is evenly golden brown. Alternatively, you can brown the topping under a broiler: Set the cupcakes on a baking sheet on the middle rack of the oven and broil until the meringue topping turns golden brown, about 1 minute. Watch the cupcakes closely, as they can go from browned to burnt in seconds. Serve the same day you make them.

DO IT EARLY

The cupcakes can be made in advance, but not frosted, and frozen for up to 2 weeks. Defrost them completely before finishing with the marshmallow topping. With topping, they will keep for about 2 days uncovered in the refrigerator.

Watermelon Mojitos

The fading sun, an ocean breeze, a pitcher of mojitos waiting in the fridge. Open the door, fill the ice bucket, and let the party begin. Invented in Cuba and beloved by many, the rum-based mojito is an inherently festive drink.

Friend and colleague cocktail specialist David Alan has created this refreshing watermelon mojito and thoughtfully devised a shortcut to reduce the workload for even the most laid-back party-throwers. Preparing the base drink ahead makes it easy to crank out drinks quickly. Adding the club soda at the last minute ensures that all drinks retain the proper level of fizz. So before you set out for the beach, muddle the mint leaves, lime juice, sweetener, and rum in a large pitcher. Stow it in the refrigerator along with several bottles of soda water and a bowl of peeled, seeded, and chunked-up watermelon. Leave a dozen or so eight-ounce Collins glasses on the kitchen counter and when you arrive home with your friends—dazzled and thirsty from a day in the sun—chilly, refreshing mojitos are just moments away.

Makes 8 drinks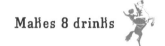

MOJITO BASE

- 1/4 cup agave nectar
- 1/4 cup freshly squeezed lime juice (about 2 medium limes)
- Handful of fresh mint leaves
- 1 cup light rum (such as locally distilled Treaty Oak)
- 1/2 cup aged rum (such as Mount Gay)

ADDITIONS

- Per drink: 3 or 4 chunks peeled, seeded ripe watermelon
- Ice cubes
- Club soda
- Watermelon slices and sprigs of mint, for garnish

TO MAKE THE BASE: Add the agave nectar, lime juice, and mint leaves to a large glass pitcher and lightly bruise the leaves with a wooden spoon or muddler. Add both rums.

FOR EACH DRINK: Add the watermelon to a tall 8-ounce glass and lightly mash with a wooden spoon or muddler. Add a generous amount of ice, and fill the glass two-thirds full with mojito base. Top off with club soda and garnish with a slice of watermelon and sprig of mint.

CHAPTER THREE

HOMECOMING

FOR MANY TEXANS, homecoming means football, friends, tailgate parties, beer, and barbecue. But when I think "homecoming," I see a modest white church in East Texas and the tree-shaded cemetery behind it dotted with family headstones reaching back seven generations. For me, homecoming means baked beans and crisp fried chicken, tender potato salad, pecan crunch, and at least one lofty layer cake all set out on picnic tables overlooking the more than 100-year-old cemetery. Every June, I make the five-hour drive to Longview for the Elderville Cemetery Association's annual homecoming picnic, which has been held there for the past 75 years.

"Generation after generation of cooks bring their family's favorite dishes," explains my cousin Vera, who lives nearby and never forgets to bring her mother's old red-and-white tablecloth to cover our table. "Many attend from other places, and sometimes we don't know if we are hugging cousins or old friends!" Similar celebrations called "dinner on the grounds" are held throughout Texas, keeping families connected to each other and their family histories.

Last year my great-uncle Jack Shoultz, a retired Methodist minister who retains the sharpness and vigor of a man much younger than his more than 80 years, delivered the homecoming sermon at Longview's Centre Presbyterian Church.

"When I come to this part of Texas, I feel I am on holy ground," Uncle Jack said. "I am surrounded by so great a cloud of witnesses," referring to generations of our East Texas relatives "who gave me my values as a Christian and my values as a man."

He named several who are buried behind the church: his great-grandfather Bill Wright, wounded at the Battle of Mansfield, and his great-grandmother, Jeannette, who nursed her Civil War veteran husband back to health. He spoke of Aunt Emma, "who told me she would die a Presbyterian and a Democrat and as far as I know she did. I didn't try to remove her from either one," he added.

He described how his father first saw his mother driving by the church in a buggy and enlisted his cousin to ask her for a date. Her response was direct and pointed: "If he wants a date with me, you tell him to ask himself," she said. "Here I am." But was she impressed enough to consider it? "Well," she said, "he has a beautiful horse." With that story I understood more clearly than ever what a long line of strong, feisty women have come before me.

Every year at our homecoming picnic I learn something new about my past, and I like to believe that wisdom will help carry me through in the future. The food on the picnic tables, often treasured family recipes made with care by relatives I see but once a year, strengthens the link to earlier generations.

This chapter includes homecoming family favorites as well as recipe ideas for potlucks, picnics, tailgate celebrations, birthday parties, and church suppers. These informal get-togethers can be the best kind of entertaining. Everyone contributes—sharing the workload and bringing tastes from varying traditions. What better way to build the connections that hold us together, as friends, neighbors, colleagues, and families?

Deviled Eggs

Here's a portable egg favorite for those who like eggs and bacon for lunch or dinner (who doesn't?) that's certain to disappear at any gathering. The recipe comes from my friend Penny Perry-Hughes, co-owner with husband, Jerry, of Der Kuchen Laden, a first-rate kitchen shop located just across Main Street from Rather Sweet. As a student at London's Le Cordon Bleu years ago, she remembers promising to bring her family's prized deviled eggs to a party thrown by a group of fellow Americans. "My mother almost died laughing that I called from London to get her deviled egg recipe," she says. Worst part was, Penny prepared the deviled eggs in advance, but got sick just before the party and couldn't go. The eggs went without her, never to be seen again.

Makes 12

6 large eggs

3 slices bacon, cooked crisp, drained, and crumbled

1/4 teaspoon sugar

1 tablespoon distilled white vinegar

1 teaspoon yellow mustard (Penny uses French's)

1 1/2 to 2 tablespoons mayonnaise

Salt and freshly ground black pepper

Finely chopped fresh Italian parsley, or paprika, for garnish (optional)

In a large saucepan, set the eggs in a single layer and add enough water to cover them by 1 inch. Bring the water to a boil over medium-high heat. Immediately remove the saucepan from the heat, cover, and let the eggs sit for 15 minutes. Drain the eggs, run cool water over them, dry, and refrigerate. To peel the eggs, hold in the palm of your hand and knock on a hard surface to crack the shells. Submerge in a bowl of cool water to remove the peel, rinsing well to ensure all of the shell bits are removed. Halve each peeled egg lengthwise.

Scoop out the egg yolks and place in a small bowl. Mash the yolks with a fork. Stir in the crumbled bacon, sugar, vinegar, mustard, and mayonnaise; season with salt and pepper. Spoon a tablespoon of the yolk mixture into each egg-white half. Sprinkle with finely chopped parsley or paprika, for garnish. Cover the eggs with plastic wrap and refrigerate until ready to serve.

DO IT EARLY

According to the American Egg Board, refrigerated, unpeeled hard-cooked eggs will keep for up to 1 week. If covered and refrigerated, the deviled eggs will keep for up to 3 days. Make sure to wrap them well; they can absorb odors easily from other foods stored in your refrigerator.

Layered Salad in a Jar

I love the simplicity of individual salads in jars. Make the salad, toss it in an ice chest, and off you go. Once you arrive at your destination, the salad is ready to eat right out of the jar. Alternatively, you can skip the jars and toss the salad ingredients together in a large bowl.

Serves 12

DRESSING

- 1/4 cup freshly squeezed lemon juice (about 2 medium lemons)
- 1/2 cup white balsamic vinegar
- 2 tablespoons mild honey
- 2/3 cup extra-virgin olive oil
- Kosher salt and freshly ground black pepper
- 1 cup feta cheese, crumbled

- 1 pound orzo pasta
- 1 (16-ounce) bag baby greens, spinach, arugula, or romaine
- 5 green onions, white and green parts, thinly sliced
- 1 cup cherry tomatoes, halved
- 1/2 cup pitted kalamata olives, coarsely chopped
- 1 cucumber, coarsely chopped (with peel)
- 1/2 cup feta cheese, crumbled
- 1 tablespoon dried oregano, or 2 tablespoons chopped fresh oregano leaves
- 1/4 cup pine nuts

TO MAKE THE DRESSING: In a bowl, whisk together the lemon juice, vinegar, honey, and olive oil; season with salt and pepper. Whisk in the feta. Cover and refrigerate until ready to use.

TO MAKE THE SALAD: In a large pot, cook the orzo in salted water according to the package instructions. Drain and run cold water over the pasta to stop the cooking. Put the orzo in a large bowl and toss with 1/2 cup of the dressing. In a small bowl, stir together the green onions, tomatoes, olives, and cucumber. In a separate small bowl, stir together the 1/2 cup feta and the oregano.

Preheat the oven to 350°F. Arrange the pine nuts on a baking sheet in a single layer and bake until golden, about 5 minutes; set aside. (Keep checking; they burn easily.)

TO ASSEMBLE THE LAYERS: Have 12 (1-pint) wide-mouth canning jars with lids ready. Spoon 1/3 cup of the orzo into the bottom of each jar, and follow with 1 layer each of the following: 1/4 cup green onion-tomato-olive-cucumber mix, 2 teaspoons feta-oregano mix, and 1/2 cup packed greens. Spoon about 1 tablespoon of the dressing on top of each salad and sprinkle each with about 1 teaspoon of the pine nuts. (You will have some dressing left over for another use.) Top with lids and refrigerate until needed. To serve, shake the jar to distribute the dressing.

DO IT EARLY

The dressing and orzo can be prepared up to 1 day in advance and refrigerated. Assemble the salad in jars up to 6 hours before it is to be served. Keep it cold until serving time.

You *Can* Go Home Again
Potato Salad

Someone always complains if there's no potato salad at our annual homecoming reunion in Longview. And while I never tire of getting together with my extended family, I do grow weary of eating the same old spud salad over and over. I decided a new version was in order and combined potatoes, buttermilk, sour cream, and blue cheese into a fresh-tasting, mayonnaise-free salad flavored with fresh tarragon.

Serves about 8

3 pounds medium red potatoes, quartered or
    cut into bite-size pieces if large

$^1/_2$ cup crumbled blue cheese

1 cup sour cream

$^1/_2$ cup buttermilk

2 tablespoons Dijon mustard

$^1/_2$ teaspoon kosher salt

A few grinds of black pepper

1 tablespoon chopped fresh tarragon leaves

1 cup chopped celery

4 green onions, green parts only, sliced

Fill a large stockpot half full with water and bring to a boil over high heat. Add the potatoes to the boiling water. Decrease the heat to medium and simmer, uncovered, until they are fork-tender, about 12 minutes. While the potatoes are cooking, combine the blue cheese, sour cream, buttermilk, mustard, salt, pepper, and tarragon in a bowl. When the potatoes are done, drain them and let cool in a large, shallow bowl for about 15 minutes. Add the celery, onions, and blue cheese mixture and gently stir the ingredients together. Cover and refrigerate until cold.

DO IT EARLY

The salad can be made 24 hours in advance and stored, covered, in the refrigerator. In fact, a night in the fridge improves the flavor.

VARIATIONS

To add a Texas-style chile kick, stir in 2 small stemmed, seeded, and diced jalapeños along with the celery and onions.

Reduce the fat quotient by substituting low-fat or nonfat sour cream for the regular stuff.

96

Curried Jasmine Rice Salad

When I've got a crowd to feed and a tight budget, I turn to rice salad. I love its versatility: Simply add meat or shellfish for a heartier dish, but omit them for vegetarians. Sometimes I divide the rice mixture into two serving bowls before adding meat or shellfish, reserving one for my non-meat eating friends. It's hard to beat homemade mayonnaise, which tastes fresher and richer than the commercial stuff. I've included a recipe for the mayonnaise we use at Rather Sweet Bakery & Café.

Serves at 10 to 12

4 cups water

1/2 teaspoon kosher salt

2 1/2 cups jasmine rice

2 1/2 cups mayonnaise (preferably homemade, page 255)

2 tablespoons freshly squeezed lemon juice (about 1 medium lemon)

3 tablespoons Major Grey's chutney or Fischer & Wieser Whole Lemon Fig Marmalade (available online)

1/4 cup curry powder

1/2 teaspoon ground white pepper

2 1/2 cups diced celery (about 7 large stalks)

1 cup thinly sliced green onions, green and white parts

1 1/4 cups dried cherries or dried cranberries

1 cup chopped, cooked ham, shrimp, turkey, or chicken (optional)

1 cup slivered almonds

Bring the 4 cups water and salt to a boil in a large saucepan over medium-high heat; add the rice, decrease the heat to medium-low, and simmer, covered, until the water is absorbed, 15 to 20 minutes. Spoon the rice into a large bowl, fluff it with a fork, and cool for about 15 minutes.

In a bowl, stir together the mayonnaise, lemon juice, chutney, curry powder, and white pepper. Stir the mayonnaise mixture into the rice along with the celery, green onions, dried cherries, and cooked meat or seafood, if you're using it. Refrigerate the salad for at least 4 hours, or preferably overnight, which allows the flavors to meld and develop.

Preheat the oven to 350°F. Arrange the almonds on a baking sheet in single layer and bake until golden, about 5 minutes; set aside. Stir in the almonds at the last minute.

DO IT EARLY

The rice salad can be made up to 2 days in advance, covered, and refrigerated. Stir in the almonds just before serving to keep them from getting soggy.

VARIATION

For nutrition bonus points, use brown jasmine rice in this recipe. Make sure to follow cooking instructions on the package: it takes about twice as long to cook, but in return, contributes firm texture and a subtle nutty flavor.

TIP For a lighter dressing, use 1 1/4 cups each of mayonnaise and low-fat yogurt or reduced-fat sour cream. (I am not a big fan of nonfat yogurt or sour cream. No-fat translates—to my taste—to no flavor.)

Double-dipped
Buttermilk Fried Chicken

My uncle Roger Glenn is known for his terrific fried chicken, which we look forward to eating all year. We count on him to bring a loaded basket of his impossibly crisp specialty to our homecoming reunion held annually on the shaded grounds next to the Elderville cemetery, where many of our relatives are buried. But Roger Glenn didn't show up last year, and we were just a touch put out.

"We tell 'em we don't care if he comes, we just want his chicken," says Cousin Vera. But Roger got the dates mixed up and scheduled some sorry old hunting trip instead, so we all had to suffer.

Roger's chicken is so good that Vera and her sisters Barbara and Gloria always toss one of his chicken legs over the fence and onto the grave of their dear deceased brother Vance Mitchell, who died eight years ago. Before his death, Vance made it known that even after he was gone, he just might crave another bite of chicken. Every year his sisters make sure that he gets one. Always one to think ahead, Cousin Vance also carefully selected his future gravesite.

"Vance said, 'I want mine right here, near the barbecue pit, where all the food is going to be,'" recalls Vera.

I missed Roger's chicken so much last year that as soon as I got home from our reunion, I set about figuring out how to replicate it. I already had a few things to go on: He once told me he marinates his chicken in buttermilk. I'd also heard he's a devoted double-dipper—dredging the chicken in flour twice with a dip in the buttermilk marinade in between. It makes the chicken super-crispy. I'm pleased with how my version turned out. If Uncle Roger doesn't show up next year, at least we won't be grumbling about missing his chicken.

Serves 10 to 12

4 cups buttermilk

$1/2$ tablespoon dried thyme

2 tablespoons Tabasco sauce

2 tablespoons Worcestershire sauce

2 tablespoons kosher salt

$2^1/2$ teaspoons freshly ground black pepper

2 frying chickens (about 3 pounds each), cut up

3 cups all-purpose flour

1 tablespoon Cajun seasoning

Olive oil or vegetable oil, for frying

Combine the buttermilk, thyme, Tabasco, Worcestershire, 1 tablespoon of the salt, and $1^1/2$ teaspoons of the pepper in a nonreactive bowl large enough to contain all of the chicken pieces with at least 1 inch to spare. Add the chicken and turn to coat fully in the marinade. Cover with plastic wrap and marinate in the refrigerator for at least 6 hours or overnight. Remove the chicken from the refrigerator about 45 minutes before frying.

Line a large baking sheet with aluminum foil. In a large, shallow bowl, combine the flour,

continued

remaining 1 tablespoon salt, Cajun seasoning, and 1 teaspoon pepper. Remove the chicken from the buttermilk marinade and roll it around in the seasoned flour until completely covered. Set it on the prepared baking sheet; repeat with the remaining chicken. Dip the coated chicken pieces once more in the marinade, then again in flour. Return the pieces to the baking sheet (a few minutes' rest makes for a sturdier, crisper coating).

Have a wire cooling rack set over paper towels ready. In a large, heavy Dutch oven, heat 1½ inches of oil over medium heat until it reaches 350°F on a deep-fat thermometer. Using kitchen tongs, add a few chicken pieces at a time to the hot oil (crowding will lower the temperature, making for greasy chicken). Fry the chicken until the internal temperature reaches 180°F, about 10 minutes per side (watch carefully, it can easily burn). Transfer the cooked chicken to the wire rack. Serve immediately or at room temperature (don't let the chicken sit more than 2 hours).

DO IT EARLY

The chicken can be fried up to 2 days in advance, covered, and refrigerated. Serve it cold—a classic Texas picnic food—or reheat on wire racks set on baking sheets in a 375°F oven for 15 to 20 minutes.

TIP If the chicken looks pretty dark before it is cooked through, transfer to wire racks set on baking sheets and bake in a 375°F oven until the meat reaches an internal temperature of 180°F on an instant-read thermometer. Keep fried chicken warm in a 200°F oven. Using a digital thermometer eliminates the need to stand over the chicken. When the alarm sounds, the meat is done.

Slow-baked Brisket with Bourbon Mustard Barbecue Sauce

In these parts, everyone knows that "low and slow is the only way to go" when it comes to making barbecued brisket. Whether prepared in the oven, on the grill, or in an old-fashioned barbecue pit, it takes hours and a gentle heat to transform this tough cut into the tender, flavorful dish that shows up at shindigs throughout Texas—from UT tailgate parties, where on game days folks set up steel-drum barbecues in parking lots during the wee morning hours, to family get-togethers, ranch weddings, and backyard cookouts. My mom, who adored brisket, took it often to parties and family events, and I've recently resurrected the tradition. James DeWolf helped develop this recipe. I carted our brisket halfway across Texas—from Fredericksburg five hours' drive east to Longview—to share it with my family at our annual homecoming potluck.

Serves 10 to 12, quite possibly with leftovers

RUB

- ¹/₂ cup firmly packed golden brown sugar
- ¹/₄ cup Spice Mix (page 102)
- 2 tablespoons kosher salt

BRISKET

- 1 (8-pound) beef brisket, preferably with fat cap intact
- ¹/₂ cup Dijon mustard
- ¹/₂ cup Creole mustard
- ¹/₄ cup bourbon
- 2 tablespoons cider vinegar

BOURBON MUSTARD BARBECUE SAUCE

- 1 tablespoon olive oil
- 1 large yellow onion, diced
- 1 tablespoon minced garlic (about 3 medium cloves)
- ¹/₄ cup Dijon mustard
- ¹/₂ cup firmly packed golden brown sugar
- 1 cup beef stock or brisket drippings (fat skimmed off)
- ¹/₂ cup bourbon
- ¹/₂ cup ketchup
- 3 tablespoons tomato paste
- 2 tablespoons Worcestershire sauce
- 2 tablespoons freshly squeezed lemon juice (about 1 medium lemon)
- 1 tablespoon soy sauce

TO MAKE THE DRY RUB: Combine the ¹/₂ cup brown sugar, spice mixture, and salt in a small bowl.

TO MAKE THE BRISKET: Preheat the oven to 275°F. Using your fingers, evenly coat the brisket with dry rub. Combine the mustards, ¹/₄ cup bourbon, and cider in a small bowl. Spread the mustard paste evenly over the brisket. Set the brisket in a large roasting pan, fat side up. Tightly cover

continued

the pan with aluminum foil and bake until the meat is tender, at least 6 hours.

TO MAKE THE BARBECUE SAUCE: In a large skillet, heat the olive oil over medium heat and cook the onion until wilted, about 3 minutes; stir in the garlic and cook 1 minute more. Stir in the $^1/_4$ cup mustard, the $^1/_2$ cup brown sugar, beef stock, the $^1/_2$ cup bourbon, ketchup, tomato paste, Worcestershire sauce, lemon juice, and soy sauce and bring the mixture to a boil. Decrease the heat to medium-low and simmer until the sauce is slightly thickened, about 15 minutes.

To serve, slice the brisket thinly across the grain and serve hot or at room temperature with barbecue sauce.

DO IT EARLY

The brisket can be baked up to 2 days in advance, covered, and refrigerated until ready to serve. Reheat in a 275°F oven for 1 hour. The spice mixture will keep in an airtight container at room temperature for about 2 months.

TIPS Leftovers make great hot sandwiches. In a medium saucepan, heat thin slices of brisket over low heat with enough barbecue sauce to coat them generously. Serve on soft rolls, such as Honey Grain Rolls, page 104.

Creole mustard, a Louisiana favorite, is made with crushed mustard seeds and often a touch of horseradish. If you can't find it, substitute any whole grain Dijon-style mustard

Spice Mix

Makes about $^3/_4$ cup

2 tablespoons chili powder

1 tablespoon ground cumin

1 tablespoon freshly ground black pepper

1 tablespoon onion powder

1 tablespoon garlic powder

1 tablespoon dry mustard powder

1 tablespoon ground coriander

1 tablespoon paprika

$^1/_4$ teaspoon cayenne pepper

$^1/_2$ teaspoon dried thyme leaves

In a small bowl, combine the chili powder, cumin, black pepper, onion powder, garlic powder, dry mustard, coriander, paprika, cayenne, and thyme leaves. Measure out $^1/_4$ cup and reserve the rest in an airtight container for future use.

Ralph's Six Rivers Tuna with Honey Grain Rolls

I first tasted Ralph Watterson's Six Rivers Tuna last year when he and his group of bicycling buddies passed through Fredericksburg on a four-day cycling trip. His tuna provides hearty lunches for the group as they cover 300 miles and cross six rivers on their annual spring cycling trip. I asked for the recipe, which he described as his mother's version, plus a few embellishments of his own. I made it, tried it out at the bakery, and our tuna sandwich sales skyrocketed. Ralph's Six Rivers Tuna is now a part of our regular menu.

Given its proven track record as a recipe that travels, I figured it would be great for an outdoor picnic or a potluck. On bike trips, Ralph says he often serves it with crackers. I wanted something more substantial and created a soft, honey-kissed roll that when split and filled with tuna makes a memorable and satisfying sandwich that travels with ease.

Makes about 5 cups

TUNA

- 2 (12-ounce) cans tuna packed in water, drained
- 3 hard-boiled eggs, coarsely chopped (see page 93)
- 1 Granny Smith apple, cored but not peeled, chopped
- 1 large dill pickle, coarsely chopped
- 1/4 cup chopped red onion
- 1/2 to 3/4 cup mayonnaise
- 1/4 cup Creole or Dijon mustard
- 2 tablespoons freshly squeezed lemon juice (about 1 large lemon)
- 1/2 teaspoon cracked black pepper
- 3/4 cup dried cranberries
- 1/4 cup roasted sunflower seeds
- Honey Grain Rolls (recipe follows)

In a large bowl, break up the tuna with a fork. Stir in the eggs, apple, pickle, onion, mayonnaise, mustard, lemon juice, pepper, cranberries, and sunflower seeds. Cover and refrigerate until ready to serve.

To serve, spoon into a bowl and let guests help themselves.

Honey Grain Rolls

Makes about 2 dozen 3½-inch rolls

SPONGE STARTER

- 2 tablespoons active dry yeast
- 2 cups lukewarm water (105° to 115°F)
- 2/3 cup honey
- 1 cup whole wheat flour
- 1 cup all-purpose flour

ROLLS

3 large eggs, lightly beaten

1 cup old-fashioned oats, plus more
    for sprinkling

$^1/_3$ cup wheat germ, plus more for sprinkling

$^1/_3$ cup unsalted butter, melted

$^1/_3$ cup whole-grain cracked wheat

2 teaspoons kosher salt

2 cups whole wheat flour

3 cups all-purpose flour, plus 2 tablespoons
    for kneading

2 large eggs

2 tablespoons water

TO MAKE THE SPONGE: In a large bowl, whisk together the yeast, water, honey, 1 cup whole wheat flour, and 1 cup all-purpose flour. Set aside in a warm draft-free spot until it foams and increases in volume, about 30 minutes.

TO MAKE THE ROLLS: Grease 2 half-sheet (13 by 18-inch) pans with butter or cooking spray. Stir the 3 beaten eggs, oats, wheat germ, melted butter, cracked wheat, and salt into the sponge. Add the flour, $^1/_2$ cup at a time, and work the dough with your hands until it becomes less sticky. Sprinkle a work surface with a few tablespoons of flour. Transfer the dough to the work surface and knead until it becomes smooth and elastic, about 5 minutes. (Or knead in a heavy-duty electric mixer fitted with a dough hook on medium speed, 2 to 3 minutes.)

Lightly grease a large bowl with butter or cooking spray and place the dough in the prepared bowl. Cover it with a tea towel and let it rise in a warm, draft-free spot until it doubles in bulk, about $1^1/_2$ hours. Punch down to deflate. Shape into 3-ounce rounds, about the size of golf balls, and place on the prepared pans. Set in a warm, draft-free spot until they rise and resemble marshmallows in texture, 30 to 40 minutes.

Preheat the oven to 375°F. In a small bowl, lightly beat the 2 remaining eggs and 2 tablespoons water. Just before baking, with a pastry brush, lightly coat the tops of the rolls with the egg wash. Sprinkle with a pinch of oatmeal or wheat germ. Bake until the rolls are golden brown on the top and bottom, 40 to 50 minutes. Serve warm or at room temperature.

DO IT EARLY

The tuna can be made in advance and refrigerated for up to 3 days. The dough for the rolls can be made through the first rising, covered, and refrigerated for up to 3 days. On baking day, remove the dough from the fridge, divide it into 3-ounce balls, let it rise a final time, and bake according to recipe directions.

The Six Rivers Ride

The annual Six Rivers Ride brings a collection of avid Texas cyclists together for a four-day, 300-mile trip through the Texas Hill Country fueled by, among other things, Ralph Watterson's protein-dense rendition of tuna salad (page 104).

Every spring, Ralph and up to six of his friends load up his extended Dodge van for a party on wheels through some of the most scenic country Texas has to offer. This year marks the sixth time Watterson, owner and founder of Old Home Supply House in Fort Worth, joins Austin-based National Public Radio correspondent John Burnett and a revolving group of riders that has included a federal judge, a retired military man, a bike shop owner, an Episcopal priest, and a lobbyist.

The group makes it a point to cross six rivers, starting at the Colorado and eventually passing over the Blanco, Pedernales, Guadalupe, Frio, and Nueces. Not that the guys, aged forty-something and up, are completely roughing it. They cover an average of seventy-five miles a day on two wheels topped with a harder, narrower saddle than any used by a Texas cowboy, but their nights are spent in cozy beds at nice hotels, and they plan their route to ensure they'll enjoy evening meals at one of the many restaurants dotting the Hill Country landscape. During the day, they sustain themselves with provisions that Ralph stows in his van, including his signature tuna recipe, plenty of fruit such as watermelons and cantaloupes, chocolate, and an ample stock of liquid libations, including high-quality beer, which, Ralph reports, is really big on long-distance rides. In fact, he adds, beer is considered a carbohydrate in the cycling world, and his group always hits a few local breweries during their Hill Country ride. Ralph also brings along the ingredients for his "Traveling Margarita," another important Six Rivers tradition. Strong, simple, and easy to make and remember, Ralph and company subscribe to the 1-1-1 method for margaritas: 1 part inexpensive tequila blanco (Ralph advises to save the expensive stuff for sipping), 1 part Triple Sec, 1 part freshly squeezed lime juice. Stir them together and serve over ice.

With all of his talk about beer and tequila one might get the impression that the group is more serious about drinking than cycling, but moderation is key, except, of course, when it comes to cycling. Shortly after their Six Rivers Ride, Ralph and pal John Burnett head to New Mexico for The Santa Fe Century, a 100-mile single-day ride described by organizers as having no easy turnarounds, putting the pressure on participants to complete the circuit. Thanks to Six Rivers, Ralph and John should be in fine shape to finish the job.

Gangy's Spoon Bread

Spoon bread is an old Southern favorite, and it's beloved in many parts of Texas, too. I've heard numerous stories about the origin of its name—some say it is derived from a similar-sounding Indian precursor, others suggest it's named for the utensil customarily used to eat this softer, smoother version of cornbread. I often bring spoon bread to potlucks, where it can be counted on to stir up old memories. (A version reportedly was served at Thomas Jefferson's Monticello.) This recipe came from Gangy—the favorite grandmother of one of my oldest and dearest friends, Kristen Ohmstede. Kristen's grandmother served it often with butter and blackberry jam and to this day, that's the only way Kristen will eat it.

Makes 12

3 cups whole milk

2 tablespoons unsalted butter

1¼ cups yellow cornmeal

1¾ teaspoons baking powder

1 teaspoon kosher salt

3 large eggs

Butter and jam, for accompaniments

Preheat the oven to 350°F. Grease an 8 by 8-inch square pan with butter or cooking spray. Heat the milk and butter in a large saucepan over medium-high heat until the mixture begins to boil. Decrease the heat to medium-low and slowly sprinkle in the cornmeal, whisking constantly, until the mixture thickens slightly, about 5 minutes. Remove the pan from the heat; whisk in the baking powder, salt, and eggs, beating until the batter is smooth and the eggs are thoroughly incorporated. Pour the batter into the prepared baking pan and bake for about 30 minutes, until golden and puffy. (The bread will deflate somewhat as soon as it comes out of the oven.) Cut into squares, and serve warm or at room temperature with butter and jam.

DO IT EARLY

Spoon bread is best eaten the day it is prepared, but it can be baked early in the day and eaten later.

Butternut Squash Bread

Everyone makes zucchini bread, but somehow it feels so blah to bring another loaf of this admittedly delicious stuff to a potluck. Here's a new take on the old theme, using butternut squash, which lends a golden hue and a delicate flavor to the bread. Large loaves, which can be sliced on-site, work beautifully as potluck fare. Wrapped mini loaves tied with ribbons and adorned with handwritten tags make memorable party favors. For family reunions, spell out the family name, the date, and the reunion site, such as "Wright Family Reunion, May 2009, Elderville Churchyard." Just about any event, from wedding showers and baptisms to graduations and birthday parties, can be commemorated this way, leaving guests with a nonperishable memento that can be saved in scrapbooks long after the last scrap of bread disappears.

Makes 2 standard-size loaves or 8 mini loaves

1 cup canola oil

$^1/_2$ cup pure maple syrup

3 cups butternut squash, peeled, seeded, and grated (about 1$^3/_4$-pound squash)

1 Granny Smith apple, peeled and grated

4 large eggs

1 cup granulated sugar

1 cup firmly packed golden brown sugar

3 cups all-purpose flour

1 teaspoon baking powder

$^1/_2$ teaspoon baking soda

1 teaspoon kosher salt

2 teaspoons ground cinnamon

1 teaspoon grated nutmeg

1 cup chopped toasted pecans (see page 168)

Preheat the oven to 350°F. Grease 2 standard-size (9 by 5-inch) loaf pans or 8 mini (5$^1/_2$ by 3-inch) loaf pans with butter or cooking spray.

In a large bowl, whisk together the oil, maple syrup, butternut squash, apple, eggs, and sugars. Stir in the flour, baking powder, baking soda, salt, cinnamon, nutmeg, and $^1/_2$ cup of the pecans until the dry ingredients are incorporated. Divide the batter evenly between the loaf pans. Sprinkle both loaves with the remaining $^1/_2$ cup pecans.

Bake the loaves until they are firm to the touch and a toothpick inserted in their center comes out clean: 1 hour for the large loaves, about 40 minutes for the mini loaves. Cool the breads for 30 minutes in their pans. Remove from the pans and cool on wire racks before serving or wrapping for storage.

DO IT EARLY

The bread can be made in advance, wrapped, and frozen for up to 1 month, or refrigerated for up to 1 week.

VARIATION

Add 1 cup raisins or dried cranberries to the batter. Or to add a little sparkle, combine $^1/_2$ cup diced candied ginger with the chopped pecans used to top the loaves; sprinkle the mixture over the loaves before baking.

TIP Grating any squash, but especially tough butternut squash, can be grating on the nerves and the knuckles. I avoid the pain by using my food processor's grating disk. Push hunks of peeled squash through the feed tube and the grating is done in minutes. While I'm at it, I grate the apple—peeled, seeded, and quartered—right along with the squash. If you end up with too much grated squash, spoon it into a plastic bag, squeeze out the air, and freeze for future batches of bread.

Walnut Baked Beans

Last year, my cousin Gloria showed up at our homecoming reunion with a huge pan of baked beans topped with a layer of walnuts. Walnuts? Walnuts are my least favorite nut, and I've never seen them paired with baked beans. But Gloria is a fine home cook, so I asked her where she got the idea. "I dreamed it last night," she said. I tried her beans, and those crispy, toasted walnuts added a lovely crunch to an old standby. By adding walnuts to beans, Gloria has given a delicious new meaning that old maxim: "Live your dreams." I can't wait to see what she "dreams up" for next year's homecoming.

Serves 12

6 slices applewood-smoked bacon

1 medium red onion, coarsely chopped

2 tablespoons minced garlic (about 6 medium cloves)

2 teaspoons chili powder

2 (28-ounce) cans baked beans (preferably Bush's)

1 cup Bourbon Mustard Barbecue Sauce (page 101) or your favorite bottled barbecue sauce

3/4 pound chopped walnuts

DO IT EARLY

Assemble and cook the beans without baking up to 2 days ahead and refrigerate. Sprinkle on the walnuts and bake the day you plan to serve.

TIP When I don't feel like making my own barbecue sauce, I turn to Stubbs Original Bar-B-Q Sauce, a tried-and-true Texas brand available across the country.

In a large skillet or a large Dutch oven, cook the bacon until crisp; drain on paper towels. Pour off all but 2 tablespoons of the bacon grease. Sauté the onion in the bacon drippings over medium heat until it softens, about 3 minutes. Add the minced garlic and chili powder and sauté for another minute. Crumble the bacon, and stir it into the onion-garlic mixture along with the baked beans and barbecue sauce. Cook over medium heat until the mixture simmers. If using a Dutch oven, top the beans with an even layer of walnuts. Otherwise, pour the beans from the skillet into a greased 17 by 12-inch ovenproof casserole and top with nuts. Bake, uncovered, until the beans are hot and bubbling, about 30 minutes. Serve the beans hot or at room temperature.

Butterscotch Brownies with Brown Sugar Butter Icing

My friend Stirling Greenlee's sense of humor is as well developed as her cooking skills. She admits to being a fervent potluck lover, and I suspect it may be because she says that for years her idea of formal dining was eating from a tablecloth without cat hair. One of her most amusing potluck stories involves a less than successful event where guests were asked to bring something that "reminds you of your childhood." Much to her horror, everyone brought white food—bland grits, milk toast, angel food cake. "As soon as everyone got out of there I imagine they bolted and went straight to Burger King," she recalls. Too bad no one thought of butterscotch brownies, a childhood favorite of mine. This version features a sugary, lightly caramelized butter icing that ensures the brownies stay moist and travel well. On top of that, the king-size recipe makes it a top-tier candidate for large potlucks, as well as picnics and family gatherings.

Makes about 2¹⁄₂ dozen 2 by 3-inch bars

BROWNIES

- 1 cup (2 sticks) unsalted butter, at room temperature
- 3 cups firmly packed golden brown sugar
- 4 large eggs
- 1 tablespoon vanilla extract
- 3 cups all-purpose flour
- 1 tablespoon baking powder
- 1 teaspoon kosher salt
- 2 cups chopped pecans, toasted

ICING

- 1 cup (2 sticks) unsalted butter
- 2 cups firmly packed golden brown sugar
- 4 cups powdered sugar
- ¹⁄₃ cup half-and-half
- 1 tablespoon vanilla extract

TO MAKE THE BROWNIES: Preheat the oven to 350°F. Line a half-sheet (13 by 18-inch) pan with aluminum foil and grease with butter or cooking spray. Using an electric mixer fitted with the paddle attachment, beat the 1 cup butter and the 3 cups brown sugar on medium-high speed until fluffy, about 2 minutes. Add the eggs and 1 tablespoon vanilla and continue beating for another minute. In a bowl, stir together the flour, baking powder, and salt. Beat the flour mixture into the butter mixture on low speed until incorporated. Stir in the pecans. Pour into the prepared pan, smoothing the top. Bake until the bars are set and slightly puffed, 25 to 30 minutes. Cool completely before icing.

TO MAKE THE ICING: In a saucepan set over medium heat, melt the 1 cup butter and 2 cups brown sugar. Once the mixture is lightly bubbling, decrease the heat to medium-low and cook, stirring occasionally, for 2 more minutes; set aside. Using an electric mixer fitted with the paddle attachment, beat the powdered sugar, half-and-half, and vanilla on medium speed until creamy, about 1 minute. Add the melted butter mixture

continued

and beat until combined. Pour over the cooled brownies and spread evenly. Let the brownies sit for about 30 minutes to allow the icing to firm up before cutting into squares.

DO IT EARLY

Left uncut in the pan, the bars will keep at room temperature, covered, for up to 3 days. Cut them the day you'll serve them. Once cut, they can be wrapped and frozen for up to 3 weeks.

TIP For an old-fashioned look that doubles as brownie holder and sticky finger protector, wrap each brownie in parchment paper halfway up. For an attractive presentation, stack them overlapping and at an angle on a serving tray.

Peach-Almond Bars

Here's an all-around bar that goes anywhere with ease. I've taken it to school dinners, church suppers, and outdoor picnics. The almond paste adds a distinctive dimension that gives the bars a touch of exotic appeal. Canned almond paste can be purchased at most grocery stores. Make sure you buy almond paste, not its similar cousin, marzipan. Food authorities do not always agree on the exact difference between the two, but generally speaking almond paste contains a higher ratio of ground almonds to sugar than marzipan.

Makes about 20 bars

CRUST

²/₃ cup (about 11 tablespoons) chilled unsalted butter

¹/₂ cup sugar

2 cups all-purpose flour

Pinch of salt

FILLING

1 (13-ounce) jar high-quality peach preserves (such as Bon Maman)

4 cups thinly sliced peaches, thawed and drained, if frozen

TOPPING

¹/₂ cup all-purpose flour

¹/₄ cup sugar

¹/₄ cup (¹/₂ stick) chilled unsalted butter

1 (8-ounce) can almond paste

1 cup sliced almonds

TO MAKE THE CRUST AND FILLING: Preheat the oven to 350°F. Grease a 9 by 13-inch baking pan with butter or cooking spray. In the work bowl of a food processor fitted with the metal blade, pulse the ²/₃ cup butter, ¹/₂ cup sugar, 2 cups flour, and salt until crumbly. Press into the bottom of the prepared baking pan. Bake for 10 minutes (the crust may not look browned;

remove it from the oven anyway). Spread peach jam evenly over the warm crust. Arrange the peaches evenly on top.

TO MAKE THE TOPPING: In a bowl, stir together the ¹/₂ cup flour and ¹/₄ cup sugar until evenly combined. Using your hands, work the ¹/₄ cup butter and almond paste into the flour-sugar mixture until it is crumbly. (Or pulse the flour, sugar, butter, and almond paste until crumbly in the food processor—no need to wash it—used to make the crust.) Spread the topping evenly over the peaches and sprinkle with almonds.

Bake until the topping is lightly browned, 35 to 40 minutes. Let the bars cool completely before cutting into squares.

VARIATIONS

For a lightning-fast alternative, spread the jam over the crust, omit the fruit layer entirely, and sprinkle on the topping and the almonds. Bake for 20 to 25 minutes.

For Raspberry-Almond Bars, substitute raspberry jam for the peach and top with 2 cups of fresh or frozen (thawed and drained) raspberries.

Hostess-with-the-Mostest Cupcakes

I felt like a modern-day Pied Piper as I carried a tray of these cupcakes to the dessert table at a picnic last fall. A throng of kids sprang up behind me, each one clamoring for a cupcake decorated with the familiar white curlicue and enriched with a hidden cream filling. Soon, all that was left was an empty tray and the hilarious chocolate smears that decorated the faces and fingers of the youngest children.

These are simpler to make than you'd imagine and, given the excitement they always inspire, they certainly are worth the effort. You'll need a pastry bag with a number 10 tip to inject the cream filling into the center of the cupcakes.

Makes 2 dozen standard cupcakes

COCOA CUPCAKES

1 ¹/₂ cups all-purpose flour

³/₄ cup granulated sugar

³/₄ cup firmly packed golden brown sugar

1 cup high-quality unsweetened cocoa (such as Green & Black's or Scharffen Berger)

2 teaspoons baking powder

1 teaspoon baking soda

¹/₂ teaspoon kosher salt

1 cup buttermilk

¹/₄ cup (¹/₂ stick) unsalted butter, melted

2 large eggs

2 teaspoons vanilla extract

³/₄ cup boiling water

FILLING

1 cup (2 sticks) unsalted butter, at room temperature

³/₄ cup powdered sugar

¹/₄ cup heavy whipping cream

ICING

6 ounces bittersweet chocolate, coarsely chopped

¹/₂ cup heavy whipping cream

¹/₄ cup Lyle's Golden Syrup or corn syrup

1 teaspoon vanilla extract

Pinch of kosher salt

TO MAKE THE CUPCAKES: Preheat the oven to 350°F. Grease standard-size (3-inch-diameter) muffin cups with butter or cooking spray, sprinkle with flour, and knock out the excess.

In a large bowl, stir together the flour, granulated sugar, brown sugar, cocoa, baking powder, baking soda, and ¹/₂ teaspoon salt. In a bowl, whisk together the buttermilk, melted butter, eggs, and 2 teaspoons vanilla. Pour the egg mixture into the flour mixture and whisk until combined. Add the boiling water and whisk until the batter is smooth. Evenly spoon about ¹/₄ cup of batter into each of the prepared muffin cups, filling

continued

about ³/₄ full. Bake until a toothpick inserted into the middle of a cupcake comes out clean, about 15 minutes. Remove the cupcakes from the pan and cool on wire racks about 20 minutes before filling and icing.

TO MAKE THE CREAM FILLING: Using an electric mixer fitted with the paddle attachment, beat the 1 cup butter and powdered sugar on medium-high speed until the mixture is light and fluffy, about 5 minutes. Add the ¹/₄ cup whipping cream and beat for 1 minute more. Set aside.

TO MAKE THE ICING: Set the chocolate in a bowl. In a saucepan set over medium heat, bring the ¹/₂ cup whipping cream to a gentle boil. Pour the hot cream over the chocolate, stirring constantly until it melts completely. Stir in the syrup, 1 teaspoon vanilla, and pinch of salt. Let the icing cool for about 20 minutes before spreading over the cupcakes.

TO ASSEMBLE THE CUPCAKES: Using a spoon, fill a pastry bag fitted with a round number 10 tip three-quarters full with the cream filling. Set the cupcakes upside down on a work surface. For each cupcake, push the metal pastry tip into the center of the bottom of the cupcake three-quarters of the way in, squeezing filling out as you go. Refill the pastry bag as needed and repeat with each cupcake. (There will be extra filling; you'll use it to decorate the tops of the cupcakes.) Turn the cupcakes right side up and use a spatula to ice their tops. Let the icing harden for about 15 minutes.

TO FINISH: Embellish the top with curlicues of the leftover filling piped with the same number 10 tip; 2 or 3 plumpish curls will fit on top of each cake. For a more authentic look, spoon the leftover filling into a plastic sandwich bag, snip off a tiny corner, and squeeze out the filling to make 5 or 6 thin curls on each cupcake.

DO IT EARLY

The cupcakes can be made, filled, and stored on a tray or platter and covered in plastic wrap up to 1 day in advance without refrigeration. Covered and refrigerated, they'll keep 2 days. Ice before serving.

TIP No buttermilk? Here's a substitute: put 1 tablespoon lemon juice or distilled white vinegar in a liquid measuring cup. Add enough milk to measure 1 cup and stir. Let the mixture sit for about 15 minutes; stir again.

Tailgating

Barbecue pits so big they're towed in on trailers. Generator-powered air-conditioned tents. Flat-screen TVs with satellite hookups. Converted school buses outfitted with bars, grills, and awnings. Vehicles plumbed to tap beer. Tailgating in Texas has grown big enough to be considered a sport all its own. Tailgate parties spring up wherever there's a football stadium and a game to be played, but college and pro games draw the biggest crowds. When the University of Texas Longhorns play at Memorial Stadium, the tailgaters spread out for blocks in every direction and the school's burnt orange color blossoms on everything from T-shirts to tattoos. The UT Web site displays four pages of Longhorn paraphernalia custom-made for tailgaters, including Texas Longhorn brushed metal wine stoppers, collapsible rolling coolers, cutlery sets, mom-and-dad car decals, "glo mugs," and team streamers emblazoned with the team motto: Hook'em Horns.

Stephanie Moore, a Texas A&M graduate, regularly tailgates with her family outside the Houston Texans' Reliant Stadium. The Moores' menus are inspired by the indigenous cuisine of the home team's opponents. When the Texans faced Florida, the menu featured mahimahi; for the game against the Saints, they served gumbo. In her family, it's the guys on the grill, the girls on the sides. Grilled pineapple basted with rum and brown sugar is one of Stephanie's favorite tailgate desserts, along with a "sopaipilla cheesecake" made with two layers of rolled-out crescent rolls filled with a cream cheese, sugar, and vanilla mixture and topped with cinnamon sugar and butter.

Stephanie is a self-avowed Bloody Mary person, especially for afternoon games, when tailgating festivities can start in the early morning. But she's also partial to a drink called the Pain Killer made with rum, coconut milk, and nutmeg, an especially useful concoction given the kind of season the Texans just endured.

Despite all this tailgate fun, Texans take their football very seriously, and team rivalries can endure for generations. That's the way it is with fans of rivals Texas A&M and UT, she says. In the fall, her dad, an A&M graduate, tells her only half in jest, "You don't talk to your friends at UT until football season is over."

Stephanie's friend Natalie Cunningham, who graduated from UT a few years ago, says all is well on the tailgating front as long as you are wearing the team colors. "If you are a Longhorn and they are a Longhorn, they will take you in," she says. "You will probably start a conversation and you will become best friends."

All in all, tailgating isn't all that different from hosting a backyard barbecue, says Kelli Lemke, another veteran tailgater and recent UT graduate. But it's happening on game day and in a parking lot. Of course, there is one big difference, and that's what makes tailgating so much more exciting than your average backyard bash: you can hear the roar of the crowd and even if you never set foot inside of the stadium, it's almost as though you were there.

White Chocolate Cake with Spiky Meringue Frosting

In my family, it wouldn't be homecoming without at least one old-fashioned layer cake, so I developed one inspired by a recipe from my Grandma Nez, the cake champion of her generation. As a child I wasn't sure which I loved better, her cakes or her ample lap. I'd nestle into her smooshy interior and feel so comfy and protected there underneath her big bosoms.

I admit this cake is a lot of work, but bring it to any event and no one will forget it. It makes a great cake for birthdays, wedding or baby showers, and anniversaries.

Serves 12 to 14

CAKE

1 cup (2 sticks) unsalted butter, at room temperature

1 1/2 cups granulated sugar

3 cups cake flour

3 teaspoons baking powder

1 teaspoon kosher salt

1 teaspoon vanilla extract

1 cup heavy whipping cream

1 1/2 cups coarsely chopped macadamia nuts

5 large egg whites

FILLING

1 (10-ounce) bag white chocolate chips (about 2 cups)

2 cups (4 sticks) unsalted butter, at room temperature

2 cups powdered sugar

1/4 cup heavy whipping cream

MERINGUE FROSTING

10 large egg whites

3 cups granulated sugar

1 cup (about 6 ounces) white chocolate chips, melted and cooled for about 15 minutes

1/4 cup chopped macadamia nuts, for sprinkling

TO MAKE THE CAKE: Place 1 oven rack in the top third of the oven and the second in the bottom third. Preheat the oven to 350°F. Line three 9-inch cake pans with parchment paper rounds, grease with butter or cooking spray, dust the pans with flour, and knock out the excess.

Using an electric mixer fitted with the paddle attachment, cream the 1 cup butter and 1 1/2 cups granulated sugar on medium-high speed until light and fluffy, about 3 minutes. Use a rubber spatula to scrape down the sides of the bowl. In a bowl, stir together the flour, baking powder, and salt. Stir the vanilla into the 1 cup whipping cream. Add the flour mixture and cream in alternating batches, beginning and ending with flour. After each addition, mix on low speed just to combine the ingredients. Stir in the 1¹/₂ cups nuts.

In a separate bowl, using an electric mixer fitted with the whisk attachment, whip the 5 egg whites on high speed until stiff, but not dry, peaks form. Gently fold the egg whites into the batter.

Spoon the batter evenly into the prepared cake pans. Set 2 layers on 1 rack and the third on the other. Stagger the cake layers on the oven racks so that no layer is directly over another. Bake until the cake is firm to the touch, and a toothpick inserted into the middle comes out clean, 25 to 30 minutes. Monitor the layers carefully for doneness; each may be done at a different time. Cool the layers in their pans about 10 minutes; unmold onto wire racks to cool completely.

TO MAKE THE FILLING: Melt the 2 cups white chocolate chips in a metal bowl set over a saucepan with 2 inches of lightly simmering water. Stir constantly until the chocolate is melted completely. Or melt the chocolate in a glass bowl in the microwave at 50 percent power— 30 seconds at first, then in 15-second increments, stirring the chocolate between each heating until melted. Let the chocolate cool for about 15 minutes.

Using an electric mixer fitted with the paddle attachment, cream the 2 cups butter on medium-high speed, about 1 minute. Add the powdered sugar and ¹/₄ cup whipping cream and beat on medium-high speed for about 2 minutes. Beat in the cooled white chocolate until it is completely incorporated.

TO MAKE THE MERINGUE FROSTING: Set a large, perfectly clean metal bowl over a pot filled with 2 inches of lightly simmering water. Pour in the 10 egg whites and the 3 cups granulated

sugar. Heat the egg whites and sugar, whisking constantly, until the sugar melts and there are no visible grains in the meringue. (Rub a little bit of meringue between your fingers to make sure all sugar grains have melted.) Remove the meringue from the heat and beat it in a mixer fitted with a whisk attachment on high speed until the meringue is stiff and shiny, about 5 minutes. Fold in the 1 cup cooled melted chocolate.

TO ASSEMBLE THE CAKE: Place 1 cake layer on a serving plate and spread the top with half of the filling. Repeat with a second layer. Stack the final cake layer on top of the first 2 and generously cover the top and sides with meringue frosting. Sprinkle with chopped macadamia nuts.

DO IT EARLY

You can make and assemble the cake layers and filling up to 1 day in advance. Wrap and refrigerate. Make the icing within a few hours of serving.

TIPS   For a spectacular presentation, use a kitchen torch to toast the meringue frosting until it is a light golden brown. Hold it 2 to 3 inches away from the meringue and move the flame slowly around the frosted cake until it is golden all over. I love the way it makes the cake look like a giant meringue.

White chocolate is made with just cocoa butter, the fat component of the cacao bean, plus milk solids, sugar, and, depending on the brand, other flavorings and ingredients. But some manufacturers replace all or most of the cocoa butter with vegetable oils—even partially hydrogenated vegetable oils. For best results, I recommend Sunspire white chocolate chips, Bernard Callebaut white chocolate drops, or Guittard white chocolate wafers.

Peanut Butter and Jam Cake

This cake is a riff on my great-aunt Lorena's 1-2-3-4 cake, a classic confection dating back to at least the mid-1800s, made with one cup butter, two cups sugar, three cups flour, and four eggs. It's a simple cake, perfect for the likes of Aunt Lorena, who was better known for her prowess as a drama teacher than for her ability in the kitchen. (The auditorium in the Grapeland, Texas, high school where she taught for many years is named after her.)

My favorite story about Aunt Lorena comes from Uncle Jack, Lorena's middle son, who says he was in high school history class before he discovered the South did not win the Civil War. As he tells it, his mom was so proud of her grandfather, William Burroughs Wright, who fought in the war alongside his brother and his brother-in-law, that she managed to brush over the fact that the North won.

Serves 12 to 14

CAKE

1 cup (2 sticks) unsalted butter, at room temperature

2 cups granulated sugar

4 large eggs

3 cups all-purpose flour

1 tablespoon baking powder

1/2 teaspoon kosher salt

2 teaspoons vanilla extract

1 cup whole milk

1 (10-ounce) bag peanut butter chips

1 cup high-quality strawberry jam, for filling

FROSTING

1 cup (2 sticks) unsalted butter, at room temperature

1 1/2 cups smooth peanut butter

1 cup powdered sugar

1/4 cup heavy whipping cream

2 teaspoons vanilla extract

1 cup chopped salted peanuts, for decorating

TO MAKE THE CAKE: Place 1 oven rack in the top third of the oven and the second in the bottom third. Preheat the oven to 350°F. Line three 9-inch cake pans with parchment paper rounds, grease with butter or cooking spray, dust the pans with flour, and knock out the excess.

Using an electric mixer fitted with the paddle attachment, cream the 1 cup butter and granulated sugar on medium-high speed until light and fluffy, about 3 minutes. Use a rubber spatula to scrape down the sides of the bowl. Add the eggs all at once and beat on medium speed until combined. In a bowl, stir together the flour, baking powder, and salt. Stir the 2 teaspoons vanilla into the milk. Add the flour mixture and milk in alternating batches, beginning and ending with flour. After each addition, mix on low speed just to combine the ingredients. Stir in the peanut butter chips.

Divide the cake batter evenly among the prepared cake pans. Set 2 layers on the top rack and the third on the lower rack. Stagger the cake layers on the oven racks so that no layer is directly over another. Bake until the cake is golden, firm to the touch, and a toothpick inserted into the middle comes out clean, 25 to 30 minutes. Monitor the layers carefully for doneness; each one may be done at a different time. Cool the layers in their pans about 10 minutes; unmold onto wire racks to cool completely.

TO MAKE THE FROSTING: Using an electric mixer fitted with the paddle attachment, beat the 1 cup butter and peanut butter on medium speed until fluffy, about 3 minutes. Add the powdered sugar, cream, and the 2 teaspoons vanilla and beat on medium speed until light and fluffy, about 2 more minutes.

TO ASSEMBLE THE CAKE: Place 1 cake layer on a serving plate and spread the top with half of the jam. Repeat with a second layer. Stack the final cake layer on top of the first 2 and cover the cake's top and sides with frosting. Press the chopped peanuts around the sides of the frosted cake.

Syrup Cake

I first ate syrup cake in the deep, piney woods of East Texas with a boy I once dated. We were visiting his grandma. She served squirrel stew with biscuits and syrup cake. I don't eat squirrel now and I didn't then, but I got that recipe for syrup cake. I later found out the simple cake is a Cajun country favorite, typically made with cane syrup. It seems that almost everyone in Louisiana swears by Steen's brand. If you can't find cane syrup, substitute molasses, maple syrup, or Lyle's Golden Syrup.

Serves 10 to 12

³/₄ cup vegetable oil

1 cup sugar

³/₄ cup cane syrup, plus more (optional)
　for drizzling

³/₄ cup buttermilk

2 large eggs

2 cups all-purpose flour

¹/₂ teaspoon grated nutmeg

¹/₂ teaspoon ground ginger

2 teaspoons baking soda

¹/₄ teaspoon kosher salt

Powdered sugar, for garnish

DO IT EARLY

The cake can be made up to 24 hours in advance and kept at room temperature or it can be wrapped and frozen for up to 3 weeks.

Preheat the oven to 350°F. Grease an 8 by 8-inch pan with butter or cooking spray. In a large bowl, whisk together the oil, sugar, ³/₄ cup syrup, buttermilk, and eggs. In another bowl, mix the flour, nutmeg, ginger, baking soda, and salt in another bowl. Stir the dry ingredients into the oil and sugar mixture. Bake until a toothpick inserted into the middle comes out clean, about 30 minutes. Sprinkle with powdered sugar and serve it straight out of the pan you baked it in. Provide extra syrup for guests to drizzle over the cake, if desired.

Graham Cracker-Pecan Crunch

My cousin Vera sent me this recipe from Ann (Mrs. Dan) K. Lucy, a regular at the Elderville Cemetery Association's annual homecoming picnic held on the grounds of the modest East Texas church where my great-great-grandparents met. It did not look promising. How could a layer of common graham crackers with butter, sugar, nuts, and toffee tossed on top amount to much? Then I made them—and repented. (My sincerest apologies to Mrs. Lucy.) I have taken this confection to several potlucks and have yet to escape without someone (or two or even three fellow guests) begging me for the recipe. I have made them a day in advance and been unable to resist snacking on them—just a few at a time, mind you—so that by the time they arrived at their intended destination their numbers were severely diminished. These crisp little squares are divine, seriously addictive, and making them is almost as easy as dropping dollar bills into the church-offering basket.

Makes about 4$\frac{1}{2}$ dozen 2-inch-square confections

15 double graham crackers

1$\frac{1}{2}$ cups chopped toasted pecans

1 (8-ounce) package toffee bits

1$\frac{1}{2}$ cups (3 sticks) unsalted butter

$\frac{3}{4}$ cup sugar

Preheat the oven to 350°F. Line a half-sheet (13 by 18-inch) pan with aluminum foil. Arrange graham crackers side by side and end to end to cover the pan in a single layer. Sprinkle pecans evenly over the crackers and cover with toffee bits. In a heavy skillet or saucepan set over medium-high heat, bring the butter and sugar to a boil; continue boiling for 2$\frac{1}{2}$ minutes. Immediately pour over the cracker-pecan-toffee layers. Bake for about 12 minutes. While still hot, use a pizza cutter to cut the bars into squares or diagonally into diamonds. Cool in the pan, then lift the foil lining out and stack the squares on a serving platter.

DO IT EARLY

These can be made up to 3 days in advance and kept in an airtight container at room temperature. Well wrapped, they can be frozen for up to 3 weeks. Do not leave them out for too long in humid weather, or they lose their crunch and become sticky. If the weather is terribly humid, keep them in the refrigerator until serving.

TIP I've substituted crushed chocolate-covered toffee bars for the toffee bits with great results. I used six 1.4-ounce bars—as close as I could come to matching the recipe's 8-ounce package of toffee bits. Whatever size toffee bars you use, just do the math—most candy bars list weight in ounces on the package—to determine how many you'll need. To crush, smack them, fully wrapped, with a pestle, heavy mallet, or rolling pin.

Grandma Olfers's Malted Mocha Bars

Discovering something new to bake is half the fun of attending potlucks. I'm always on the lookout for new recipes that others might enjoy. One of my servers gave me this recipe, which her grandmother has been making for as long as she can remember. I took these bars to a recent potluck supper, where they drew raves and more than a few requests for copies of the recipe.

Makes about 20 bars

CRUST

1³/₄ cups all-purpose flour

³/₄ cup (1¹/₂ sticks) unsalted butter, at room temperature

²/₃ cup firmly packed golden brown sugar

¹/₂ teaspoon kosher salt

TOPPING

¹/₂ cup granulated sugar

3 large eggs

³/₄ cup chocolate malted milk powder

¹/₄ cup all-purpose flour

1 teaspoon baking powder

¹/₄ teaspoon kosher salt

2 teaspoons vanilla extract

1 cup chopped pecans

1 cup sweetened shredded coconut (optional)

ICING

3 tablespoons chocolate malted milk powder

1 tablespoon instant espresso coffee powder

2 tablespoons hot water

2 tablespoons unsalted butter, at room temperature

1 teaspoon vanilla extract

1¹/₂ cups powdered sugar

Pinch of kosher salt

TO MAKE THE CRUST: Preheat the oven to 350°F. Using an electric mixer fitted with the paddle attachment, combine the 1³/₄ cups flour, ³/₄ cup butter, brown sugar, and ¹/₂ teaspoon salt and beat on medium speed until the mixture is crumbly. Press evenly into an ungreased 13 by 9-inch pan. Bake for 10 minutes. Maintain the oven temperature.

TO MAKE THE TOPPING: In the same (unwashed) mixing bowl used for the crust, beat together the granulated sugar, eggs, the ³/₄ cup malted milk powder, ¹/₄ cup flour, baking powder, the ¹/₄ teaspoon salt, and the 2 teaspoons vanilla on medium speed until combined. Stir in the pecans and coconut, if desired. Spread the mixture over the baked crust. Bake until the topping is set, 25 to 35 minutes more. Cool.

TO MAKE THE ICING: In a large bowl, whisk together the 3 tablespoons malted milk powder, instant coffee, and hot water. Whisk in the 2 tablespoons butter, the 1 teaspoon vanilla, the powdered sugar, and the pinch of salt until smooth. Spread evenly over the bars. (Thin it with a few drops of water if it is too thick to spread easily.) Let the icing set for about 15 minutes, cut the bars, and serve. (The bars can be made up to 3 days in advance.)

Homecoming Iced Tea

Those of us who grew up within spittin' distance of Louisiana know that unsweetened iced tea is practically un-American. Furthermore, a family get-together in Texas just isn't right without a big, fat, sweating pitcher of sweet iced tea. So here's my latest, most favorite iced tea recipe, inspired (ironically) by a vendor at New York City's biggest farmers' market—the Union Square Greenmarket. I discovered it on a broiling August afternoon after buying a paper-cupful for one dollar. It was beyond refreshing, with a hint of mint, a kiss of citrus, and just the right touch of New England maple syrup. Naturally, I substitute Texas honey for my version.

My mother always made iced tea the old-fashioned way, by boiling water, steeping the tea, and cooling it off with loads of ice. But my coauthor's mother, Patricia Oresman, gave me a better idea. She used to make sun tea by leaving a pitcher full of water and tea bags in the sun for several hours. One day she put the tea bags in a pitcher full of water but never did get around to setting it out on her sunny backyard porch. She returned to the kitchen a few hours later to find perfectly brewed no-sun sun tea. Now she makes kitchen-counter iced tea year-round, no solar energy needed. How long does she let the tea bags steep? "I let it sit until it gets the color I think it should be," she says.

Makes 8 cups

8 cups cool tap water

8 (black-tea) tea bags of your choice (English breakfast is good)

2 tablespoons freshly squeezed lime juice (about 1 medium lime)

2 tablespoons freshly squeezed lemon juice (about 1 medium lemon)

$^1/_3$ to $^1/_2$ cup local honey, heated for 30 seconds in the microwave

6 sprigs fresh mint

TIP Hate watery iced tea, a casualty caused by melting ice cubes that dilute the tea? Make an extra half batch of sweetened tea and freeze it in ice cube trays. Once cubes are completely frozen, punch them out, stow them in plastic bags, and store them in the freezer. They'll be ready to keep your iced tea cold and strong whenever you need them.

Fill a large pitcher with the 8 cups water. Submerge 8 tea bags in the water. Twist the tea bag strings several times to hold them together and let the paper ends dangle over the outside edge of the pitcher for easy retrieval later. Let the tea bags steep until the tea tastes sufficiently strong, 1 to 1$^1/_2$ hours. Stir in the citrus juices, honey, and mint. Refrigerate until cold. Serve in glasses of your choice with plenty of ice.

CHAPTER FOUR

SAN ANTONIO TEX-MEX FIESTA

I COULD LIVE ON Tex-Mex fare for the rest of my life and die happy. Creamy guacamole sparkling with the tang of citrus, irresistible chile con queso, chile gravy enriched with smoky anchos, and juicy fajitas fresh off the grill. It's the ultimate party food—casual, the opposite of fussy, and supremely delicious.

When planning a Tex-Mex party I often gather ideas and inspiration from nearby San Antonio, considered by many to be the capital of Tex-Mex, and a city with a rich Spanish and Mexican cultural heritage. Decorating is easy: I often turn to Fiesta on Main, located just north of downtown and a treasure trove of whimsical piñatas, multicolored paper flags, bright woven table runners, and papier-mâché animals. I buy paper flowers in every color imaginable, handmade in San Antonio in honor of the Battle of Flowers Parade, one of four major Fiesta parades. The flowers come in several styles and colors and make adorable, inexpensive arrangements that can be plunked in vases and spread all over the house. *Cascarones*—dried eggshells stuffed with confetti and designed to be broken over someone's head—are another Fiesta tradition guaranteed to liven up any party. Just be sure to keep them outside, or figure to spend some serious time behind your vacuum cleaner when the party ends.

For drinks, I stick to Mexican beers and colorful Mexican sodas in ice-filled buckets, and I almost always offer margaritas, because a Tex-Mex party doesn't seem complete without them.

One of my students at a San Antonio cooking class suggested a "Margarita Pour-Off" that she and her husband hosted for a group of friends. Steve and Sandy White provide 100 percent Agave Hornitos Brand Silver tequila, and possibly a reposado tequila, which makes a great splash on the top, Sandy says. They also stock fruit for fresh-squeezed juice, including limes, lemons, oranges, and blood oranges, as well as agave nectar, Triple Sec, and margarita salt.

Guests are asked to bring whatever they wish to create a margarita with a "unique twist" such as a specialty tequila, Controy (orange liqueur from Mexico), Grand Marnier, or any fruit the Whites aren't supplying. "The fun part is to try everyone's concoctions. You could go as far as crowning a Margarita King and Queen," Sandy says. It's a great idea. I'm hoping to stage my own Margarita Pour-Off real soon.

Pork and Tomatillo Quesadillas with Ancho Dipping Salsa

A fresh-off-the-griddle appetizer offered just after guests arrive makes for an especially warm welcome. Pork quesadillas were standard fare during my catering days, when we passed them on trays as appetizers. Most of the components for this dish are made in advance, but assembling and grilling them is a last-minute thing. Frances, my college-age daughter, is a quesadilla pro, and at a recent party she stepped right in, saying, "I know how to do this, Mom." She kept on turning out quesadillas until the tortillas were gone and guests had moved on to filling their plates from the buffet. It reminded me how handy it is to have a young adult around to help out, freeing me to greet and mingle. My daughter is away at college for most of the year, but teenagers—yours, a friend's, or even a neighbor's—can be valuable helpers at parties. Money is a strong motivator, so I always pay my teen helpers, and I always train them beforehand, letting them know exactly what I expect. Oh, and I always feed them, too.

Makes 6 quesadillas for about 12 appetizer portions

PORK

- 2 tablespoons chili powder
- 2 tablespoons ground cumin
- 1 tablespoon coriander seed, lightly crushed
- 1 tablespoon kosher salt
- 1 1/2 teaspoons freshly ground black pepper
- 4 pounds pork butt (also sold as shoulder)

TOMATILLO SAUCE

- 2 pounds fresh tomatillos, papery covering removed, and washed
- 1 medium yellow onion, peeled and quartered
- 1 1/2 jalapeño chiles, seeded
- 3 cloves garlic
- 2 tablespoons freshly squeezed lime juice (about 1 medium lime)
- Coarsely chopped fresh cilantro
- 2 teaspoons kosher salt
- 1 ripe medium avocado

QUESADILLAS

- 2 tablespoons olive oil
- 2 medium yellow onions, sliced
- 4 poblano chiles, stemmed, seeded, and sliced in long strips
- 2 Anaheim chiles, stemmed, seeded, and sliced in long strips
- 12 large (8-inch) flour tortillas
- 3 cups shredded Monterey Jack cheese (about 12 ounces)
- Ancho Dipping Salsa (recipe follows), for accompaniment

TO MAKE THE PORK: Preheat the oven to 325°F. Combine the chili powder, cumin, coriander seed, the 1 tablespoon salt, and black pepper in a small bowl. Place the pork in a roasting pan and evenly rub the spice mixture all over the meat. Add enough water to the pan to cover the first inch of the meat, which will ensure the pork stays moist as it cooks. Cover the pan

continued

135

tightly with aluminum foil. Roast until the meat reaches an internal temperature of 190°F on an instant-read thermometer, 5 to 6 hours. (When it's done, stand back when first removing the foil to avoid a blast of heat and steam in your face.) The meat will be fork-tender and almost falling off the bone. Let the meat stand until it is cool enough to handle. Remove the bone and pull the meat apart into bite-size chunks. The meat can be stored in a covered bowl and refrigerated until ready to use.

TO MAKE THE TOMATILLO SAUCE: Place the tomatillos, quartered onion, jalapeños, and garlic in a large saucepan, cover with water, and bring to a boil over medium-high heat; decrease the heat to medium-low, bring the vegetables to a low boil, and cook until the tomatillos are soft and their bright green color turns a dull yellow-green, about 7 minutes. When any of the tomatillos bursts and falls apart, the vegetables are done; remove from the heat immediately. Pour the tomatillo mixture into a colander set over a bowl or the sink to strain out the liquid. In the work bowl of a food processor fitted with the metal blade, puree the tomatillo mixture, lime juice, cilantro, and 2 teaspoons salt. Just before serving, peel, pit, and cut the avocado into coarse chunks, and puree with the tomatillo mixture until smooth in a food processor.

TO ASSEMBLE AND SERVE THE QUESADILLAS: Pour the olive oil into a large skillet set over medium heat. Once the oil begins to shimmer, add the sliced onions and the poblano and Anaheim chiles and sauté, shaking the vegetables occasionally, until they are soft and lightly caramelized, 10 to 15 minutes.

Preheat an ungreased griddle or large skillet over medium heat. Have the shredded pork, tomatillo-avocado sauce, tortillas, caramelized vegetables, and shredded cheese within easy reach. Put as many tortillas on the griddle as will fit without touching. Spread about $1/4$ cup shredded cheese on each tortilla, then cover half of them with about $3/4$ cup of the shredded pork, a heaping spoonful of the caramelized vegetables, and 2 tablespoons tomatillo sauce each. Reserve the remaining sauce for dipping. Flip the cheese-only tortillas on top of the pork tortillas and cook, flipping if necessary, until the tortillas are crispy and browned on the bottom. Once grilled, using a long sharp knife or a pizza cutter, slice the quesadillas into quarters. Serve immediately on warmed platters with Ancho Dipping Salsa and remaining tomatillo sauce.

DO IT EARLY

The pork can be roasted up to 2 days in advance, covered and refrigerated until ready to use. If you really want to get a jump on things, the pork can be frozen for up to 3 weeks. Make sure it is double-wrapped in plastic wrap, then foil, to keep it from drying out. The tomatillo sauce can be made up to 4 days in advance, covered, and refrigerated, with the exception of the avocado, which should be added the day you plan to serve the dish. The caramelized onions and chiles can be made up to 1 day in advance, covered and refrigerated. The refrigerated ancho salsa will keep for up to 5 days.

Ancho Dipping Salsa

Makes about 3 cups

8 Roma tomatoes, cored

3 cloves garlic

1 medium yellow onion, quartered

2 jalapeño chiles, stemmed and seeded

1 tablespoon olive oil

4 ancho chiles, stemmed and seeded

2 chipotle chiles, stemmed and seeded

1 1/2 teaspoons kosher salt

Pinch of sugar

2 tablespoons freshly squeezed lime juice
    (about 1 medium lime)

Preheat the oven to 425°F.

Roast the tomatoes in the oven in a large baking pan for about 30 minutes. Remove from the oven; add the garlic, onion, and jalapeños, and drizzle with olive oil. Return the pan to the oven and roast for another 20 minutes.

Meanwhile, place the ancho and chipotle chiles in a bowl and cover with boiling water. Use a plate or small bowl to weigh down the chiles, keeping them submerged. Soak them until softened, about 15 minutes. Drain the chiles. Set aside.

When the roasted vegetables are done, remove the skins from the tomatoes and discard. In the work bowl of a food processor fitted with the metal blade, pulse the roasted vegetables in 2 separate batches. Don't over-pulse or you'll end up with a pureed salsa, not a chunky one. Pour the processed salsa into a large bowl. Puree 2 of the reconstituted ancho chiles in the (unwashed) food processor. Stir the pureed chiles into the salsa mixture. Pulse the remaining anchos and the chipotles until finely chopped, but not pureed. Stir the chopped chiles, salt, sugar, and lime juice into the salsa. Cover and refrigerate until ready to use.

Queso

We Texans love our queso, and although I've seen many a fierce debate over the use of one of its signature ingredients—Velveeta—most of us grew up eating it. For us, queso spells comfort. I don't use Velveeta for anything else, but there's something about its ability to melt into a creamy smoothness that makes queso, queso. The dip shows up at so many Texas tables because, for many of us, queso means warmth, ease, and familiarity—just the recipe for an easy, congenial get-together with friends. (Pictured opposite, left side)

Makes about 8 cups

2 tablespoons vegetable oil

1 medium yellow onion, diced

1/2 cup stemmed, seeded, and chopped
    jalapeño chiles (about 3 medium)

1 tablespoon minced garlic (about 3 medium
    cloves)

3 cups whole milk

1 teaspoon ground cumin

1 teaspoon paprika

1 teaspoon cayenne pepper

1 (14.5-ounce) can tomatoes with green
    chiles

1/2 pound Monterey Jack cheese, shredded

2 1/2 pounds Velveeta, cut in 1-inch slices

6 ounces baby spinach, coarsely chopped

Tortilla chips, for dipping

In a large heavy stockpot, heat the oil over medium heat; sauté the onion, jalapeños, and garlic until soft, about 3 minutes. Decrease the heat to low; stir in the milk, cumin, paprika, and cayenne. Once the milk is warm, add the tomatoes, Monterey Jack, and Velveeta and stir until the mixture is smooth and creamy. Stir in the spinach and cook a few minutes more. Serve in a bowl set on top of a warming tray or in a slow cooker set on low, with plenty of chips.

VARIATION

For a heartier queso, remove the casing from 1/2 pound of Mexican chorizo (seasoned pork sausage), sauté until browned, drain off the fat, and stir into the cheese mixture. For a hotter queso, sauté 4 seeded and minced serrano chiles along with the onion and jalapeños and continue as directed above.

DO IT EARLY

The queso, minus the spinach, can be made a day in advance and refrigerated. Reheat slowly over low heat, stirring constantly until it is smooth. Do not overcook; the mixture will separate if overheated. Stir in the spinach and serve.

TIP Rotel diced tomatoes with green chiles are the traditional choice for queso; I've also used Muir Glen's fire-roasted diced tomatoes with green chiles.

Rosa's Red Posole

Posole is a pork-based soup that's really a cross between a soup and a stew. Apart from the pork, the main ingredient is hominy—white corn kernels that have been soaked in lye. Many Texans profess to love posole, but I've always found it impossibly bland. That is, until I tried Rosa's version, which she transformed from blah to bueno with the addition of a flavor-packed red chile sauce. Rosa, a native of Mexico City, has worked at Rather Sweet since it opened almost ten years ago. A traditional Mexican concoction, posole comes in many styles, and is often prepared on feast days or to celebrate the new year, says Rosa. Sounds like a natural party food to me.

I like to serve Red Posole as a main course for an informal dinner party on a cool night. Make a big batch of guacamole (page 255) and set out bowls with all of the traditional posole accompaniments—lime wedges, thinly sliced radishes, lettuce, and green onions. Serve the posole in the Dutch oven you made it in, or seize the chance to use that old-fashioned soup tureen you inherited from Great-Aunt Belle. Decorate your serving table with a Mexican-style tablecloth or a colorful runner. Bundle cloth napkins with the necessary silverware and set out a stack of deep soup bowls and small plates. Let guests serve themselves buffet style. Complete your stress-free, do-ahead dinner with a large pitcher of White Sangria (page 175) and a combination plate of Chile Crinkle Cookies (page 206) and Chubby's White Pralines (page 168).

Serves 8 to 10

SOUP

1 tablespoon olive oil

1 teaspoon kosher salt, plus more salt for seasoning

Freshly ground black pepper

2$\frac{1}{2}$ to 3$\frac{1}{2}$ pounds boneless pork butt (also sold as shoulder)

$\frac{1}{2}$ medium yellow onion

4 cloves garlic

10 cups water

2 (29-ounce) cans white hominy, drained

2 tablespoons freshly squeezed lime juice (about 1 medium lime)

RED CHILE SAUCE

6 guajillo chiles, stemmed and seeded

2 ancho chiles, stemmed and seeded

1 cup chile soaking water, strained

$\frac{1}{2}$ medium yellow onion, quartered

5 cloves garlic

1 tablespoon olive oil

1 teaspoon dried oregano, or 1 tablespoon minced fresh oregano leaves

1 teaspoon ground cumin

1 shake Tabasco sauce

1 teaspoon kosher salt

TOPPINGS

3 medium limes, cut in wedges

1 bunch fresh radishes, stemmed and thinly sliced

1 head romaine or iceberg lettuce, cored and thinly sliced

1 bunch green onions, white and green parts, thinly sliced

Coarsely chopped fresh cilantro (optional)

Chunks of fresh avocado (optional)

Guacamole, page 255 (optional)

TO MAKE THE SOUP: Heat the 1 tablespoon oil for about 30 seconds in a large Dutch oven or 12-quart stockpot set over medium heat. Salt and pepper the pork butt; sear it until browned, about 2 minutes per side. Remove the pot from the heat; slice the meat into 2- to 3-inch hunks and return it to the pot. Add the 1/2 onion, 4 cloves garlic, the 1 teaspoon salt, and the 10 cups water. Set the pot over high heat until the mixture boils; decrease the heat slightly to bring it down to a simmer. Simmer for about 1 hour, skimming off any scum that rises to the surface. Cover and simmer until the meat is falling-apart tender, about 1 hour more. Strain the meat from the broth, and return the broth to the pot. Skim off as much fat as possible. When the meat is cool enough to handle, shred it into bite-size pieces, removing and discarding as much fat as possible, and return it to the pot.

TO MAKE THE CHILE SAUCE: While the meat simmers, place the guajillo and chipotle chiles in a large bowl and cover with boiling water. Use a plate or slightly smaller bowl to weigh down the chiles, keeping them completely submerged. Once the chiles have softened, about 30 minutes for the unusually tough guajillos, remove from the soaking water. Strain the soaking water, reserving 1 cup. Puree the chiles in a blender with 1/2 cup of the reserved soaking water, the quartered onion, and 5 cloves garlic. Push the pureed chile-onion mixture through a strainer to catch any seeds or large, tough bits of chile. Drizzle the 1 tablespoon olive oil into a skillet set over medium heat. Add the strained chile mixture, the remaining 1/2 cup of chile soaking water, oregano, cumin, Tabasco, and 1 teaspoon salt. Cook for 2 to 3 minutes, stirring occasionally.

Stir the chile mixture into the soup; add the hominy and simmer over medium heat for about 30 minutes. Stir in the lime juice. Taste and correct the seasonings, adding salt and pepper if necessary.

When ready to serve, set out bowls of lime wedges, sliced radishes, lettuce, green onions, cilantro, avocado, and guacamole, allowing guests to choose their own toppings.

DO IT EARLY

The soup can be made 2 days ahead, covered, and refrigerated until ready to serve. It can be frozen for up to 3 weeks before serving.

TIP Pork butt can be fatty, which makes it flavorful, but it also can lead to greasy soup. One of the easiest ways to remove the fat is to refrigerate the soup overnight. The fat will rise to the top and harden, making it easy to spoon off without sacrificing any of the flavorful broth. If you don't have time to refrigerate the soup, there's another way: After the straining the cooked meat from the broth, let the broth settle for about 5 minutes without stirring. The fat will rise to the top. Set a single sheet of paper towel lightly on top and let it soak up the fat. Discard the towel and if the broth harbors more fat, repeat.

Lime Soup

I fell for this soup on a trip to the Yucatan Peninsula, where it is a mainstay. It's light and refreshing—a tasty first course that whets the appetite without ruining it for the main event. It's a smart way to go if you're serving heavier fare, such as Cheese Enchiladas with Chile Gravy (page 152) or Fiesta Chiles Rellenos (page 145) for a main course.

Serves 8 to 10

1 (4- to 5-pound) stewing chicken (preferably organic)

2 medium yellow onions

2 large carrots, halved

2 stalks celery

3 cloves garlic

2 bay leaves

1 teaspoon whole peppercorns

2 tablespoons olive oil

2 teaspoons minced garlic (about 2 cloves)

1 poblano chile, stemmed, seeded, and cut into $1/4$-inch dice

4 ears fresh corn, husked and kernels cut from the cob

1 tablespoon kosher salt

1 teaspoon dried Mexican oregano

$1^{1}/2$ cups freshly squeezed lime juice (about 6 medium limes)

TOPPINGS

Chunks of fresh avocado

Diced fresh tomatoes

Chopped fresh cilantro

Lime wedges

Fried tortilla strips

Set the chicken in a large, heavy stockpot and fill it with cool water to cover by at least 1 inch. Halve 1 of the onions. Add the carrots, the onion halves, celery, garlic cloves, bay leaves, and peppercorns and bring to a boil over medium-high heat. Decrease the heat to medium and simmer gently for 2 hours, skimming off any scum that rises to the top. Remove the chicken from the broth and let rest in a large dish until it is cool enough to handle. Strain the chicken broth and return it to the stockpot. You'll have 10 to 12 cups of broth. Remove the skin from the cooled chicken and discard; shred the meat and return it to the broth in the stockpot.

Heat the oil in a large skillet set over medium heat. Cut the remaining onion into $1/4$-inch dice. Sauté the diced onion, minced garlic, poblano, and corn for about 3 minutes until the vegetables are soft. Stir the sautéed vegetables into the chicken stock, stir in the salt, oregano, and lime juice and bring the mixture to a simmer. Taste and add more salt and lime juice if needed. Serve hot with the toppings of your choice.

DO IT EARLY

The soup can be made up to 2 days in advance, covered, and refrigerated.

Fiesta Chiles Rellenos

I'm always trying to get Rosa to make chiles rellenos for the bakery's lunch special. Customers love them and they always sell out. But they are messy and a lot of work. Even after you've roasted and peeled the chiles and finished making the meat filling, you're only halfway there: they still need dipping in egg-white batter, individual deep-frying, and an immediate mouth to feed, because nobody likes cold chiles rellenos.

I complained about this to Yvonne Bowden, a favorite party-throwing partner. She told me about a relleno casserole that bypassed the deep fryer. It's still a lot of work, but the casserole configuration is more party friendly. We worked on the dish together and Fiesta Chiles Rellenos were born. Serve with small bowls of Beans a la Charra (page 150).

Makes 12 rellenos

RANCHERO SAUCE

1 tablespoon olive oil

1/2 cup diced red onion

1 tablespoon minced garlic (about 3 cloves)

1 green bell pepper, cored, seeded, and coarsely chopped

3 serrano chiles, stemmed, seeded, and cut in small dice

4 stalks celery, coarsely chopped

1 teaspoon kosher salt

1 teaspoon dried Mexican oregano

1 cup dry white wine

1 cup beef broth

1 (28-ounce) can diced tomatoes

FILLING

1 cup pine nuts

2 pounds ground beef

1/2 cup diced red onion

1 tablespoon minced garlic (about 3 medium cloves)

1 large baking potato, peeled and diced

1/2 teaspoon ground cinnamon

1 1/2 teaspoons kosher salt

1 1/2 cups beef broth

2 (15-ounce) cans tomato sauce

6 ounces high-quality dark chocolate, coarsely chopped

1 3/4 cups golden raisins (about 10 ounces)

CHILES

12 large poblano chiles

1 cup shredded Monterey Jack cheese (about 4 ounces), for topping

BATTER

12 large egg whites

1/2 cup all-purpose flour

1 teaspoon baking powder

1/2 teaspoon kosher salt

1 tablespoon chili powder

1/2 teaspoon onion powder

1/2 teaspoon garlic powder

TO MAKE THE RANCHERO SAUCE: Heat the oil in a large skillet set over medium heat. Sauté the 1/2 cup onion, 1 teaspoon garlic, bell pepper, chiles, and celery until the onion is soft, about 3 minutes. Stir in the 1 teaspoon salt, oregano,

continued

wine, broth, and tomatoes with juice. Simmer over medium heat until the flavors meld but the celery retains a slight crunch, about 15 minutes.

TO MAKE THE FILLING: Toast the pine nuts, stirring occasionally, in a large, heavy skillet set on medium heat, until they turn golden brown, about 4 minutes. Set aside in a small bowl. In the same skillet, brown the beef along with the $1/2$ cup onion, 1 tablespoon garlic, and potato, breaking up the meat with a spatula. Pour off the fat and discard. Stir in the cinnamon, the $1^1/2$ teaspoons salt, beef broth, tomato sauce, dark chocolate, and raisins. Simmer until the potatoes are tender, about 30 minutes. Stir in the pine nuts.

TO ROAST AND STUFF THE POBLANOS: Preheat the oven to 450°F. Grease a large baking sheet with cooking spray.

Arrange the poblanos in a single layer on the baking sheet and roast, turning once halfway through, for about 30 minutes. The peppers should be blistered and slightly blackened. Using an oven mitt, place the peppers in large plastic or paper bags. For plastic bags, leave enough room to twist the bag shut. For paper bags, leave enough room to fold the top over twice to seal. Let the peppers steam in the bags for at least 10 minutes, remove them, and peel off the skin, which should slide off easily. Meanwhile, grease a large ovenproof dish with butter or cooking spray. (If the stuffed chiles will not fit in a single layer, use a second baking dish for the overflow.)

Starting just below the pepper's stem, make a lengthwise slit three-quarters of the way down, leaving an opening large enough to scrape the seeds out with a spoon. Be careful not to tear the chile's flesh. Stuff each pepper with the ground beef mixture, filling it only enough so that the seams still fit together. Set the filled peppers seam side up in the prepared casserole dish. Reduce the oven temperature to 375°F.

TO MAKE THE BATTER: Using an electric mixer fitted with the whip attachment, beat the egg whites on high speed until they form soft peaks. Add the flour, baking powder, the $1/2$ teaspoon salt, chili powder, onion powder, and garlic powder and beat until combined. Spoon the batter over the stuffed poblanos. Bake until the batter is golden brown, about 30 minutes. Remove from the oven and spoon on an even layer of ranchero sauce. Top with shredded cheese and bake until the cheese and the rellenos are heated through, about 5 minutes. Serve warm.

DO IT EARLY

The chiles can be roasted, stuffed, and set in prepared casserole dishes 1 day in advance. Just before serving, spread the batter on the stuffed chiles and bake as directed, adding about 10 minutes to the baking time to compensate for the chill of the refrigerated chiles.

TIP If serrano peppers are too hot for your taste, substitute an equal number of jalapeños.

Fiesta

Every April, San Antonio throws Fiesta, one of the Lone Star State's oldest and grandest parties—an eleven-day extravaganza packed with parades, pageantry, military observances, food and music festivals, carnivals, sports, and more than a touch of royalty, Texas style.

It's a celebration of Texas history and the rich multiethnic heritage of one of the state's oldest cities, and just about everyone who lives in San Antonio takes part, according to my friend Sam Bell Steves. He ought to know, he is a former Fiesta king and a recent Lord High Chamberlain, the official who presides over the coronation of the Queen of the Order of the Alamo, one of Fiesta's oldest events. The Fiesta Queen and her court—twelve duchesses from San Antonio proper and twelve from other Texas cities—don spectacular dresses for a night of pageantry and music at San Antonio's Municipal Auditorium.

Fiesta began more than 100 years ago with the Battle of the Flowers parade to honor heroes of the Alamo and the Battle of San Jacinto—the decisive fight that won Texas its independence from Mexico. The parade started as a procession of horse-drawn carriages, bicycles, and floats festooned with fresh flowers, which participants tossed at each other. The parade has grown to become the second largest in the country, and the only U.S. parade run exclusively by women. Today's Fiesta consists of 107 events that organizers say draw about 3.5 million participants annually.

Sam recalls his first Fiesta memory, being let loose as a ten-year-old at Night in Old San Antonio, a four-night festival celebrating historic San Antonio. Filled with music and food, the event is held at La Villita on the banks of the San Antonio River, site of the city's earliest neighborhood. Like many of Fiesta's events, NIOSA, as it is known by locals, was conceived to raise money for the community, in this case the San Antonio Conservation Society, a driving force behind San Antonio's vibrant preservation movement.

For young Sam, NIOSA offered a first, very exciting taste of freedom. His mother, one of the event's organizers, allowed Sam and his siblings to wander the festival on their own, with strict orders to meet her at the "hitching post" at 8:30 P.M.

As senior vice president of Fiesta's executive committee, Sam's connection to the event has continued through his adulthood. In 2004 he followed in his father's footsteps to become a second-generation King Antonio, the oldest of Fiesta's kings. King Antonio is elected from the ranks of the Texas Cavaliers, a civic group that sponsors the annual evening River Parade down the San Antonio River, which cuts through the city. More than 250,000 spectators fill the restaurants and storefronts that line the river to watch the evening event, one of the few parades where, as residents joke, floats really float. In 1980, the Paseo del Rey Feo, the Ugly King Parade sponsored by League of United Latin American Citizens, joined the Fiesta lineup. Both King Antonio and El Rey Feo (the Ugly King) crisscross the city, attending numerous Fiesta events, as well as conducting whirlwind tours of local schools, hospitals, and nursing homes, spreading Fiesta coins and medals and, hopefully, a few laughs along the way. At night they make appearances at the numerous balls, dinners, and parties that have become woven into the fabric of Fiesta.

Chicken with Banana-Basil Mole

My old friend David Garrido, a supremely talented chef, came up with a fresh take on mole that combines guajillo chiles with fresh basil, bananas, and dates to create a lively, fruit-sweetened sauce that marries beautifully with chicken. I love this dish for a relaxed but elegant dinner party at home. Skinny bi***es take note: the dish contains little fat, lots of flavor.

Serves 8

1 large ripe banana, halved (with peel)

10 fresh basil leaves

2 tablespoons freshly squeezed lemon juice (about 1 medium lemon)

8 boneless, skinless chicken breasts (about 5 ounces each)

Kosher salt

3 tablespoons olive oil

1 clove garlic, chopped

1/2 medium yellow onion, sliced

2 guajillo chiles, stemmed and seeded

3 large pitted dates

1 cup chicken stock

TO MAKE THE BANANA-BASIL GARNISH: Peel 1 banana half and cut the fresh into small dice. Mince 4 of the basil leaves; combine the minced basil and diced banana with 1 tablespoon of fresh lemon juice. Set aside.

TO COOK THE CHICKEN: Preheat the oven to 350°F. Season the chicken breasts with salt. In a large skillet, heat 2 tablespoons of the olive oil over high heat. In batches, cooking only as many as will fit in the skillet at once without crowding, sear the chicken until light brown, 1 to 2 minutes on each side. Transfer the breasts to a large baking dish in a single layer. Bake, uncovered, until cooked through, 6 to 8 minutes.

TO MAKE THE MOLE: Meanwhile, in the same skillet set on medium heat, heat the remaining 1 tablespoon olive oil and cook the garlic and onion until the onion is translucent, about 3 minutes. Peel and coarsely chop the remaining banana half and mince the remaining 6 basil leaves; add to the onion mixture along with the guajillos, dates, the remaining tablespoon of lemon juice, and the chicken stock. Cook for 4 to 6 minutes. Use tongs to remove the softened guajillos (see Tip). Pour the remainder of the mixture into the jar of a blender and puree until smooth. Season with salt.

To serve, place a generous amount of banana mole on each plate and place 1 chicken breast on the sauce. To garnish, top each chicken breast with a spoonful of banana-basil garnish.

TIP Guajillos are slim dried chiles with a red-brown cast and a famously tough skin. They can be quite hot. Unless you are a heat-loving fiend, remove them from the mole sauce before pureeing it as directed above. Just by simmering in the sauce they lend enough heat to satisfy most American palates. If, after tasting the sauce, you crave additional heat, puree the guajillos separately in the blender, adding a couple of tablespoons of chicken stock, and pass the mixture though a sieve before combining with the mole sauce. Don't skip the straining, as the tough skin of these chiles won't process to a fully smooth puree.

Beans a la Charra

You may not think of beans as a party dish, but there's something deeply comforting and welcoming about a big pot of beans simmering on the stove top. First, it fills the house with a wonderful earthy aroma. Second, it gives friends the feeling that they're worth fussing over—almost everyone knows homemade beans take a little extra time and some advance planning. Finally, I enjoy serving beans for a party because I have several gorgeous terra-cotta bean pots and I can't resist showing them off.

Serves 8 to 12

1 pound dried pinto beans (about 2 cups)

12 cups water

1 poblano chile

2 dried ancho chiles, stemmed and seeded

12 slices applewood-smoked bacon

3 cups chopped yellow onions

2 jalapeño chiles, stemmed, seeded, and diced

3 tablespoons minced garlic (about 9 cloves)

1 (10-ounce) can tomatoes with green chiles, with juice

1 tablespoon kosher salt

1 (12-ounce) bottle Corona (or other Mexican) beer

1/2 cup chopped fresh cilantro, for garnish

Sort through the beans and rinse them in cold water. In a large stockpot set over high heat, boil the beans in the 12 cups water for 2 minutes. Remove the pot from the heat, cover, and let the beans soak for 1 hour. Roast the poblano chile with a kitchen torch, over a gas burner, or under an oven broiler until evenly charred. Rinse it in cold water to remove the charred skin, then stem, seed, and chop it into small dice; set aside.

Place the ancho chiles in a medium bowl and cover with hot water. Use a plate or small bowl to weigh down the chiles, keeping them submerged. Soak them until softened, about 15 minutes. Drain the chiles, reserving 1/4 cup of the soaking water. Puree the softened chiles and the reserved chile soaking water in the jar of a blender or the work bowl of a food processor fitted with the metal blade. Use a wooden spoon to push the pureed chiles through a strainer and into a bowl; set aside.

In a large skillet, brown the bacon over medium heat until crisp; drain on paper towels. In the same skillet, sauté the onions, jalapeños, garlic, and poblano in the bacon fat over medium heat. Add the onion mixture to the beans and their soaking water in the stockpot.

Add the tomatoes, pureed ancho chiles, salt, and beer. Bring the beans to a gentle simmer over medium heat and cook, uncovered, until the beans are tender, about 1 1/2 hours. Crumble the cooked bacon and stir into the beans. Serve warm in small bowls, sprinkled with cilantro.

DO IT EARLY

The beans can be made up to 5 days in advance and refrigerated.

Cheese Enchiladas with Chile Gravy

For those who don't speak Tex-Mex, chile gravy is a smooth sauce made with reconstituted dried chiles, broth, flour or some other thickener, and fat. The canned version—enchilada sauce—is stacked in grocery aisles all over the country. It's worth the effort to make homemade, though, because fresh chile gravy is about as far from the canned stuff as Texas is from Toronto. I serve my cheese enchiladas topped with gravy, diced yellow or sweet onions, and sides of refried beans (page 161) and Rosa's Mexican Rice (page 161).

Serves 12, two enchiladas per person

CHILE GRAVY

8 ancho chiles, stemmed and seeded

1 pasilla chile, stemmed and seeded

5 cloves garlic

1/4 cup vegetable oil (or lard, for real Tex-Mex authenticity)

1/4 cup all-purpose flour

2 teaspoons ground cumin

1 1/2 teaspoons chili powder

1 teaspoon dried Mexican oregano

2 teaspoons kosher salt

1 teaspoon freshly ground black pepper

Pinch of sugar

2 cups chicken stock

2 (15-ounce) cans plain tomato sauce

CHEESE ENCHILADAS

24 corn tortillas

1 cup vegetable oil

2 cups shredded sharp Cheddar cheese (about 3/4 pound)

3 cups shredded Monterey Jack cheese (about 3/4 pound)

3 large yellow onions, diced, for garnish

TO MAKE THE CHILE GRAVY: Place the ancho and pasilla chiles in a large bowl and cover with hot water. Use a plate or small bowl to weigh down the chiles, keeping them submerged. Soak them until softened, about 15 minutes. Drain the chiles, reserving 1 1/2 cups of the soaking water.

In a large skillet set on low heat, brown the garlic cloves, shaking occasionally, about 10 minutes. Puree the garlic, softened chiles, and the 1 1/2 cups reserved chile soaking water in the jar of a blender or the work bowl of a food processor fitted with the metal blade. Use a wooden spoon to push the pureed chiles through a strainer and into a bowl.

In the skillet used to brown the garlic, stir together the 1/4 cup vegetable oil and flour until smooth and cook over medium heat, stirring constantly until the mixture turns a light brown, 5 to 6 minutes. Stir in the cumin, chili powder, oregano, salt, black pepper, sugar, pureed chiles, chicken stock, and tomato sauce and simmer until the sauce thickens and the flavors meld, about 15 minutes.

TO MAKE THE CHEESE ENCHILADAS: Preheat the oven to 400°F. Grease a 9 by 13-inch baking dish with butter or vegetable oil. Warm the 1 cup vegetable oil in a large skillet set over low heat. Using tongs, dip the tortillas, 1 at a time, into the vegetable oil to soften; drain on paper towels. In a large bowl, stir together the shredded cheeses. Fill the center of each tortilla with about 3 tablespoons cheese, roll it up, and place it, seam side down, on the prepared baking dish. Repeat with the remaining tortillas, arranging them close together in 1 layer. Cover the enchiladas with the chile gravy. Sprinkle with $1/4$ cup of the leftover shredded cheese. Bake until hot and bubbling, about 15 minutes. Serve with diced onion scattered over the top.

DO IT EARLY

The chile gravy can be made up to 3 days ahead and refrigerated, or frozen for up to 3 weeks. The enchilada casserole can be made, but not baked, up to 1 day ahead and refrigerated. Add 5 minutes to the baking time if taking the casserole straight from refrigerator to oven.

VARIATIONS

Enchiladas can be filled with shredded, seasoned meat or beans, with or without the cheese. Other possible additions include chopped black olives, chopped green onions, or just about anything that sounds good to you.

For a lighter, thinner sauce substitute 30 ounces tomato juice for the tomato sauce.

153

Rib-eye Fajitas on the Grill

My idea of party perfection is a backyard fajita fest. I have the guys roast the peppers until blistery and browned, then I send them into the kitchen to seed and slice them. Next they grill up the steaks and cut them into nice, thin strips. Meanwhile I've already set out bowls of guacamole, sour cream, salsa, and chips. We all gather around my outdoor table, each of us making our dream fajita with just the right balance of steak and peppers, sour cream and guacamole.

Serves 8 to 12

3 tablespoons soy sauce

3 tablespoons freshly squeezed lime juice
(about 1 1/2 medium limes)

3 tablespoons Worcestershire sauce

6 cloves garlic, crushed

1 1/2 cups red wine

1/4 cup vegetable oil

5 pounds boneless rib-eye steaks

1 poblano chile

4 Anaheim chiles

8 bell peppers (2 green plus 6 in any
assortment of red, yellow, or orange)

2 tablespoons freshly squeezed lemon juice
(about 1 medium lemon)

Pinch of kosher salt

12 tortillas (flour or corn)

2 large yellow onions, cut in 2-inch-thick
slices

Sour cream, for accompaniment

Guacamole (page 255), for accompaniment

Beans a la Charra (page 150), for
accompaniment

TO MARINATE THE MEAT: In a large (4-cup) measuring cup, combine the soy sauce, lime juice, Worcestershire sauce, garlic, wine, and vegetable oil to make the marinade. Put the steaks in a large, heavy-duty, self-sealing plastic bag, pour in the marinade, seal, and refrigerate for at least 4 hours or overnight.

Preheat an outdoor grill; preheat the oven to 250°F. Grill the chiles and bell peppers whole until they blister and brown, turning with tongs every few minutes to ensure they roast on all sides; remove from the heat. Core and seed them, slice them lengthwise into 1/2-inch strips, and sprinkle them with lemon juice and a pinch of salt. Wrap them in aluminum foil and keep them warm in the oven until ready to serve. Wrap the tortillas in foil and put in the oven to warm with the peppers. Remove the steaks from the marinade, drain, and grill according to your preference. Grill the onion slices along with the steak, about 5 minutes per side.

To serve, slice the steaks thinly; arrange on a large platter with the grilled sliced onion and the chiles and peppers. Alongside the platter, set out the warm tortillas and bowls of sour cream and guacamole. Beans à la Charra, served in small bowls, is another classic fajita accompaniment.

VARIATION

Substitute boneless, skinless chicken breasts or shrimp for the beef. Marinate the chicken according to the directions above. For the shrimp, skip the marinade and just rub them with a little kosher salt and pepper before grilling.

El Rancho de la Reina Casserole

My mom was a veteran entertainer, and the Mexican décor of her home often influenced the menu. She insisted on doing things ahead and served a favorite casserole she called "sopa" at informal dinner parties. I never understood why she used the Spanish word for soup as the name of her casserole, but after browsing through several Texas community cookbooks, I discovered that a commonly used ingredient in a similar chicken tortilla casserole was condensed soup—cream of chicken, celery, or mushroom. Frankly, my inner chef's code of conduct means I'd sooner come face to face with an ornery Texas longhorn than serve a casserole with a condensed soup base to my guests. But I remember loving my mom's party sopa, and since she didn't leave me her recipe, I created this meal-in-a-dish in her honor. I've nixed the soup shortcut, but I'm all for picking up a rotisserie chicken from the local market to ease the workload. Best of all, the casserole can be made ahead and refrigerated or frozen— on party day, just slide it in the oven.

Serves 8 to 10

2 tablespoons olive oil

3 cups diced yellow onions

4 Anaheim chiles, stemmed, seeded, and chopped

2 teaspoons minced garlic (about 2 cloves)

2^1/$_2$ pounds fresh tomatillos

2 Roma tomatoes, cored and chopped

3 teaspoons kosher salt

1 cup sour cream

1 large rotisserie chicken (3 to 4 pounds)

1 (28-ounce) can fire-roasted, diced tomatoes (such as Muir Glen)

1 teaspoon chili powder

1 teaspoon ancho chile powder

2 shakes Tabasco sauce

18 corn tortillas

5 cups shredded Monterey Jack or Mexican-style cheese (about 1^1/$_4$ pounds)

Grease a 9 by 13-inch baking pan with cooking spray. Preheat the oven to 375°F.

Heat the olive oil in large skillet set on medium heat. Sauté the onions, Anaheim chiles, and garlic until soft, about 5 minutes. Remove the papery husks from the tomatillos; wash and quarter them. Stir the tomatillos, Roma tomatoes, and 2 teaspoons of salt into the onion mixture; cook, stirring occasionally, until all of the tomatillos are soft, about 30 minutes. Puree the mixture in the work bowl of a food processor fitted with the metal blade. Add the sour cream and pulse until the ingredients are combined. Set aside.

Remove the meat from the rotisserie chicken, skin it, and cut or shred it into bite-size pieces. In a large bowl, stir together the chicken, canned tomatoes, chili and chile powders, the remaining teaspoon of salt, and Tabasco.

Arrange 6 tortillas evenly to cover the bottom of the prepared pan. (They will overlap on the edges.) Layer half the tomatillo sauce, half the chicken-tomato mixture, and 3 cups of the shredded cheese. Repeat another layer, but don't add more cheese. Layer the final 6 tortillas on top of the casserole, and evenly spread the remaining

2 cups cheese on top. Bake uncovered until the casserole is bubbling, 30 to 40 minutes. Serve immediately.

DO IT EARLY

This casserole can be made 1 day ahead, covered, and refrigerated before baking. Or it can be frozen for up to 3 weeks. Defrost overnight in the refrigerator before baking. The refrigerated casserole will need up to 10 minutes more baking time.

VARIATION

For an extra blast of flavor, try a white Cheddar spiked with chiles—habanero, chipotle, or any that you prefer. I've also combined equal amounts of chile-flavored Cheddar and pepper Jack cheese with great results.

Puffy Tacos with Bison Chili

Puffy tacos have become modern-day icons of the San Antonio food scene. You can find the meat-filled, deep-fried corn tortillas throughout the Alamo City and—believe it or not—on the baseball field, too, where Henry, the Puffy Taco, serves as a mascot for the San Antonio Mission, a minor league team.

I propose a build-your-own puffy taco party, where guests crowd into the kitchen to feast on hot-from-the-skillet tacos stuffed with bison chili, a dab of guacamole, and whatever other fixings you set out. Ask friends to act as revolving fry cooks, so nobody gets stuck by the stove for too long, and in the meantime, assign others to shake up batches of Silver Bullet Margaritas (page 175).

Diana Barrios Trevino, friend and the restaurateur behind San Antonio's La Hacienda de los Barrios, gave me permission to use her famous puffy taco recipe. It was the recipe that beat TV chef Bobby Flay in a puffy taco "throwdown" staged for Flay's popular Food Network show. If you can find fresh masa dough, use it to make the tortillas. Otherwise, dried masa mix will work just fine.

Serves about 8 (about 2 tacos per person)

BISON CHILI

2 tablespoons olive oil

1 large yellow onion, diced

6 cloves garlic

2 pounds ground bison

1 poblano chile, stemmed, seeded, and chopped

3 jalapeño chiles, stemmed, seeded and chopped

1 teaspoon ground cumin

1 teaspoon ground coriander

1 tablespoon ancho chile powder

2 teaspoons chipotle chile powder

1 teaspoon chili powder

1 teaspoon kosher salt

2 teaspoons freshly ground black pepper

1 (14-ounce) can crushed tomatoes, with juice

1 (12-ounce) bottle Mexican beer

1 jigger (1 ounce) Tarantula tequila (optional)

3 tablespoons plain fish fry seasoning, or corn flour

3 tablespoons unsalted butter

PUFFY TACOS

3 cups corn masa mix

$1^1/_2$ teaspoons kosher salt

$2^1/_4$ cups warm water

Vegetable oil, for frying

Shredded lettuce, for garnish

Diced tomatoes, for garnish

Guacamole (page 255), for garnish

Sour cream, for garnish (optional)

Shredded cheese, for garnish (optional)

TO MAKE THE BISON CHILI: Heat the oil in a large skillet or Dutch oven set over medium heat. Sauté the onion until soft and translucent, about 3 minutes. Stir in the garlic and cook for about 1 minute more. Add the bison, along with the poblano and jalapeño chiles, cumin, coriander, ground chiles, chili powder, the 1 teaspoon salt, and black pepper and cook until the meat is lightly browned, 10 to 15 minutes. Add the crushed tomatoes, beer, and tequila, bring to a simmer still over medium heat, and simmer uncovered for 25 to 30 minutes. Meanwhile, in a small heavy-bottomed skillet set over medium heat, stir together the fish fry seasoning or corn flour and butter and cook, stirring constantly, for about 5 minutes. Stir the butter mixture into the chili and cook for about 5 minutes, until it thickens slightly. Keep warm until ready to serve.

TO MAKE THE PUFFY TACOS: Combine the masa mix, the $1^{1}/_{2}$ teaspoons salt, and the $2^{1}/_{4}$ cups warm water in a large bowl; mix with your hands until a smooth dough forms. Roll hunks of dough into balls about the size of ping-pong balls. If using a tortilla press, first line it with plastic—slit both sides (but not the bottom) of a quart-size plastic sandwich bag to create a large rectangle. Cover the bottom of the tortilla press with half of the plastic rectangle (seam toward the hinge of the press) and set a dough ball on top. Fold the other half of the rectangle over the dough and close the press with firm pressure. (The tortilla should be about $1/_{8}$ inch thick.) If you don't have a tortilla press, cut a plastic bag as above, lay a dough ball on one side of the cut plastic bag, cover it with the other, and use a heavy skillet to press out tortillas.

Heat 2 inches of oil in a large, deep skillet or saucepan until it reaches 350°F on a deep-fat thermometer. Using kitchen tongs, set tortillas, 1 at a time, in the hot oil. Use a long-handled spatula to ladle hot oil over the top of the tortilla as it puffs up. (It should take about 10 seconds.) Once the tortilla has puffed, flip it over. With tongs, push it to the side of the pan and wedge it gently in place. At the same time, using the edge of a spatula to press lightly in the tortilla's center, make an indentation that will allow you to fold it into a taco shape. With tongs, remove the fried tortilla and set it on paper towels to drain and cool slightly. Repeat with the remaining tortillas. (If shaping the tortillas into tacos seems like too much hullabaloo, just leave them flat, cover them with toppings, and eat them that way.)

TO ASSEMBLE AND SERVE THE PUFFY TACOS: As soon as the folded tacos are cool enough to handle, fill with a spoonful of bison chili and top with shredded lettuce, chopped tomatoes, guacamole, sour cream, and shredded cheese. Eat immediately with both hands. Forks and knives work, too, but it's not nearly as much fun or as messy. No matter what, make sure you've got plenty of napkins on hand.

DO IT EARLY

The chili can be made up to 2 days in advance and refrigerated, or frozen for up to 3 weeks. The masa dough can be made 24 hours in advance, rolled into balls, wrapped, and refrigerated. Shaping and frying the tortillas is best done at the last minute: when puffy tacos are stone cold and old, you probably won't want to eat them.

TIP Keep an eye on the oil's temperature as you fry the tortillas. If it gets too hot they'll burn and likely splatter enough to burn you, too. If the oil gets too cool, it produces soggy, greasy tacos. Periodically check the temperature with a deep-fat thermometer and adjust the heat as needed.

VARIATION

Puffy tacos are not just for meat eaters. Cook up a batch of refried black beans, without the bacon, of course (page 161), for vegetarians and fill the tacos with the bean mixture, topping with desired garnishes. Others can eat the beans as a side. Other side dish possibilities include Rosa's Mexican Rice (page 161).

Rosa's Mexican Rice and San Antonio Refried Beans

Beans and rice create an unassuming but essential backdrop for the quintessential Tex-Mex meal—leave them out and you'll probably hear about it. Rosa Albiter Espinoza, who has worked for more than seven years in the Rather Sweet kitchen, makes her Mexican rice regularly for our lunch specials. She prefers Adolphus rice, a long-grain variety native to Texas. When I'm preparing a Tex-Mex spread for a party, I make sure to serve a pot of rice and plenty of refried black beans.

Rosa's Mexican Rice

Serves 8 to 10

$^1/_2$ cup vegetable oil

1 medium yellow onion, cut in medium dice

2 tablespoons minced garlic (about 6 cloves)

4 cups long-grain rice

3 medium carrots, diced

1 (14-ounce) can plain tomato sauce

7 cups chicken stock

2 cups frozen green peas

$^1/_2$ teaspoon freshly ground black pepper

$^1/_2$ teaspoon ground cumin

Kosher salt

In a large stockpot set over medium heat, heat the oil and sauté the onion and garlic for about 2 minutes; add the rice and cook, stirring frequently, until it is light brown, about 5 minutes. Add the carrots, tomato sauce, and chicken stock. Bring to a boil, decrease the heat to medium-low, and add the frozen peas. Cover and cook until the liquid is absorbed, about 15 minutes. Remove the rice from the heat and let sit for another 10 minutes. Fluff and serve.

DO IT EARLY

The rice can be made up to 1 day in advance, cooled, covered, and refrigerated. To reheat, stir in $^1/_2$ cup water and cook in a saucepan over medium heat, stirring frequently, until the rice is thoroughly heated.

San Antonio Refried Beans

Serves 8 to 10

1 pound dried black beans

8 slices applewood-smoked bacon, chopped

1 large yellow onion, chopped

1 stalk celery, chopped

2 jalapeño chiles, stemmed, seeded, and chopped

2 tablespoons minced garlic (about 6 cloves)

6 cups chicken stock or water

1 tablespoon kosher salt

3 tablespoons vegetable oil

continued

Sort the beans to get rid of any foreign matter; rinse well in a colander; and set aside. In a large stockpot set over medium-high heat, cook the bacon about 10 minutes. Decrease the heat to medium; add the onion, celery, jalapeños, and garlic. Cook until the onion gets soft, about 3 minutes. Add the beans, chicken stock, and salt; bring to a boil. Decrease the heat and simmer, uncovered, until the stock has been mostly absorbed and the beans are tender, about 2½ hours. Spoon the mixture, including the bacon and vegetables, into the jar of a blender (in batches, if necessary) or the work bowl of a food processor fitted with the metal blade and puree until smooth. Pour the vegetable oil into the unwashed stockpot set over medium-high heat. Add the pureed bean mixture to the stockpot and cook, stirring, until the beans are hot and bubbling, about 3 minutes. Serve warm.

TIPS   I'm always busy and I'm often behind. When I discover a shortcut, I take it. All of the books advise soaking black beans before cooking, but I have found that this recipe turns out just fine without a soak. While the beans take a little longer to cook, I'm spared the extra steps of soaking, rinsing, and draining. I always take the time to sort and rinse the beans; processing does not always rid them of dirt or tiny stones.

To make this dish even faster to prepare, substitute 3 (15-ounce) cans black beans for the dried beans and skip the long cooking time. Add the drained and rinsed beans to the sautéed bacon and vegetables, heat thoroughly and puree, then follow the directions as above.

Loncito's Food Salon

FIRST SOUTH TEXAS FOOD SALON
August 1, 2, and 3 at Twin Oaks Ranch

Please join chefs and retrovores spanning the distance from the Davis Mountains to the Gulf of Mexico in a celebration of Texas lamb. In the traditional South Texas house party atmosphere of wine, women, and song we will strive to raise the collective consciousness of our fellow Texas retrovores.

Swimming, skeet, evening cruises, and croquet along with great food, wine, and music.

As soon as the e-mail invitation popped into my in-box, I knew I couldn't refuse. House parties are a long-standing tradition here. It's hard to imagine a better way to see friends for those who live on Texas's far-flung ranches than to offer a couple of night's accommodations and a party that includes breakfast, lunch, and dinner.

Nobody knows house parties like my friend Loncito Cartwright, author of the aforementioned electronic invitation, who raises grass-fed lamb at the family ranch, Twin Oaks, in Dinero, 100 miles south of San Antonio. A sixth-generation Texan, he was raised at Twin Oaks Ranch, where there always was a collection of people—especially during hunting season. The ranch (along with a sizable debt) was a wedding gift to his great-uncle Holman Cartwright and wife Claire Lucas, who frequently entertained friends and business associates there. When Loncito's parents took over, his mother encouraged him to invite friends over for house parties. He's been throwing them ever since on the family's 5,000-acre spread.

"The friendships that are forged over a couple of nights, you never forget," he says. "You can't duplicate it on the golf course or at a restaurant." Being out in the country is an essential ingredient. Loncito makes certain guests take advantage of their surroundings with dove and quail hunting expeditions, skeet shoots, arm wrestling contests, and marathon croquet matches that leave friends howling one minute and arguing about the rules the next.

Loncito says that as he's grown older and as his circle of friends has extended to include "fabulous cooks," everyone pitches in with the food. Loncito's meals reflect his steadfast belief in "retrovore" eating, defined as consuming the kinds of foods that his grandparents ate: greens, grass-fed meat, beans, rice, and locally grown vegetables. There's always plenty of Loncito's lamb, the grass-fed meat he produces at Twin Oaks and markets all over the state.

The perfect dinner at Twin Oaks is three tables of eight, Loncito says, with plenty of people from varying backgrounds. Candlelight is a must because "for young folks it's cool and for old folks it makes them look prettier." Grace always precedes the meal. Not necessarily a Christian grace, Loncito says, but some sort of thanks for the food as guests join hands. "Governor Hogg of Texas said that not saying grace at the table is like being a blind pig eating acorns under an oak tree, not knowing where the acorns came from."

Loncito was pleased with his first annual house party salon, and plans to repeat the event next year. I'm waiting for my invitation.

Cinnamon Crescents

These little crescents are gone in a couple of bites and can be surprisingly addictive. Their cinnamon sugar coating reminds me of churros, the deep-fried, cinnamon-sugar-coated lengths of sweet dough so popular in Mexico and in my own home state. For a dramatic buffet presentation set them on a tiered dessert tray along with Pequeño Chocolate-Pecan Tartlets (page 166) and Chubby's White Pralines (page 168).

Makes about 32

1 cup (2 sticks) unsalted butter

1 package active dry yeast
   (about 2¹/₄ teaspoons)

Pinch of sugar

¹/₄ cup lukewarm water (105° to 115°F)

2¹/₂ cups bleached all-purpose flour

2 large eggs, lightly beaten

Grated zest of 1 medium orange (preferably
   organic)

¹/₄ teaspoon salt

1 cup golden raisins

¹/₄ cup Grand Marnier

1 cup sugar

2 tablespoons ground cinnamon

Melt the butter and let it cool for about 15 minutes. Dissolve the yeast and sugar in the ¹/₄ cup warm water; let the mixture stand for about 10 minutes. (If it does not bubble or increase in volume, the yeast is dead.)

Place 2 cups of the flour in a large bowl and make a well in the middle. Pour into the well the beaten eggs, yeast mixture, and melted butter and mix together with a large wooden spoon or—if, like me, you love the feel of dough—with your hands. Add the remaining ¹/₂ cup flour, orange zest, and salt and mix thoroughly. The dough will be somewhat soft. Gently pat it into a ball, cover with plastic wrap, and refrigerate

overnight. In a small bowl, toss the raisins with the Grand Marnier. Cover overnight.

Preheat the oven to 350°F. Grease a baking pan with cooking spray or butter, or line it with parchment paper or a silicone liner. Combine the sugar and cinnamon in a bowl. Remove the dough from the refrigerator, and divide it into 4 equal parts. Dust a work surface with a liberal amount of cinnamon sugar. Using a rolling pin, roll out each portion of dough ¹/₄ inch thick on the sugar-coated work surface. After each stroke with the rolling pin, flip the dough, adding more cinnamon sugar to the work surface as needed. Cut the dough into 2-inch triangles. (Dough scraps can reformed into a ball and rolled out at least once.) Sprinkle a thin layer of cinnamon sugar on each dough triangle. Scoop 1 teaspoon of the macerated raisins onto the wide end of the triangle; roll up the dough beginning at the wide end. Place the crescents on the prepared baking sheet and bake until they are lightly golden brown, about 20 minutes.

DO IT EARLY

The crescents can be made up to 1 day in advance and kept in an airtight container. Wrap securely and freeze for up to 3 weeks. Unwrap and defrost the day you plan to serve them.

Pequeño Chocolate-Pecan Tartlets

I make batches of these in mini muffin pans, wrap them well, freeze them, and keep them on hand for last-minute parties. What a relief it is to have a dessert ready and waiting for an impromptu dinner. The only problem: I know where they are, and sometimes, especially late at night, I can't resist unwrapping a few and eating them. (Yup, they're pretty good frozen.) Before long, my party stash has dissipated, and I have to make some more. (Pictured on page 164, center tray.)

Makes twenty-four 2-inch tartlets

CRUST

3/4 cup (1 1/2 sticks) unsalted butter, chilled and cut into 1/2-inch cubes

1 (3-ounce) package cream cheese, chilled and cut into 1/2-inch cubes

1 1/2 cups bleached all-purpose flour

2 tablespoons cold water

FILLING

1 cup chopped pecans

1/2 cup (1 stick) unsalted butter, at room temperature

1 cup firmly packed golden brown sugar

3 large eggs

1/2 cup Lyle's Golden Syrup or light corn syrup

1 teaspoon vanilla extract

1/2 teaspoon grated orange zest (preferably organic, optional)

1/2 cup chocolate chips

KAHLÚA WHIPPED CREAM

1 cup heavy whipping cream, chilled

1/4 cup powdered sugar

2 tablespoons Kahlúa

TO MAKE THE CRUST: Using a pastry blender or two knives, cut the butter and cream cheese into the flour until the mixture resembles cornmeal. Add the 2 tablespoons cold water, and combine until the dough holds together. Use your hands to gently form the dough into a log about 1 1/2 inches in diameter. Cover with plastic wrap and refrigerate at least 2 hours.

TO MAKE THE FILLING: Preheat the oven to 350°F. Spread the pecans in a single layer on a baking sheet and toast until darker in color and fragrant, 7 to 9 minutes; set aside. Using an electric mixer fitted with the paddle attachment, cream the 1/2 cup butter and the brown sugar on medium-high speed until light and fluffy, about 2 minutes. Add the eggs, 1 at a time, beating on medium speed after each addition. Add the syrup, vanilla, and zest and beat on medium speed until incorporated. Fold in the pecans and chocolate chips. Set aside.

TO MAKE THE WHIPPED CREAM: Using an electric mixer fitted with the whisk attachment, beat the cream on high speed until soft peaks form. Beat in the powdered sugar and Kahlúa. Refrigerate for up to 2 hours.

TO ASSEMBLE THE TARTLETS: Reheat the oven to 350°F. Unwrap the refrigerated dough and cut into 1/8-inch slices. Press dough slices into the bottoms and all the way up the sides of 2-inch-diameter mini muffin cups. Spoon about 1 tablespoon of filling into each cup. Bake until the crust is golden and the filling is set, 20 to 25 minutes. Let cool for 15 minutes. Turn the tartlets out of the pan. Serve warm or at room temperature with teaspoon-size dollops of Kahlúa whipped cream.

DO IT EARLY

The dough can be made 2 days ahead, covered, and refrigerated. The tartlets can be wrapped and refrigerated for up to 3 days, or frozen for up to 3 weeks.

Chubby's White Pralines

A lifelong praline devotee, I'd never seen a white version until longtime customers and friends Diane and John B. Connally III introduced me to Ginny Marye Sharman. I lamented that I'd been searching in vain for a great, new, party-worthy praline, when Ginny said, "I have the one for you. It's my daddy's."

She sent me the recipe with the following note, "Chubby Marye, my daddy, was from Alexandria, Louisiana, and loved to cook! He always made his white pralines on cold winter evenings. I learned to make them watching him. It's a family tradition that he learned from his mother, Mama Dee."

I tried it immediately. Not only was it the easiest praline recipe I've ever encountered, it was also one of the tastiest. My mother's recipe, for example, demands intensive beating with a wooden spoon. Ginny's recipe takes a beating, but for only half the time. Chubby's pralines make a fine finale for any party; or wrap them up in waxed paper, seal with an embossed sticker, pile them in a decorative bowl, and hand them out at the end of the evening as favors. (Pictured on page 164, top tray.)

Makes about 24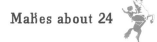

1 cup chopped pecans

2 cups sugar

1 cup whole milk

¹⁄₄ cup (4 tablespoons) unsalted butter

Pinch of kosher salt

2 teaspoons vanilla extract (preferably Mexican vanilla)

Preheat the oven to 350°F. Arrange the pecans on a baking sheet in a single layer and toast until golden brown and aromatic, 7 to 9 minutes; set aside. In a heavy-bottomed saucepan set over medium-high heat, bring the sugar and milk to a boil; decrease the heat to medium and cook until the mixture reaches the soft ball stage (234° to 240°F on a candy thermometer). Remove the saucepan from the heat and stir in the butter, salt, pecans, and vanilla. Beat the mixture for about 5 minutes with a wooden spoon, or until the mixture begins to stiffen. Quickly drop by tablespoonfuls onto waxed paper. (If you aren't fast enough, the mixture will become too hard to scoop.) Wrap individually in waxed paper, or store in an airtight container.

DO IT EARLY

Individually wrapped or stored in an airtight container, the pralines will keep for about 3 days.

VARIATION

To make even whiter pralines, omit the vanilla extract and drop in a halved vanilla bean with the sugar and milk. Remove the vanilla bean as soon as the mixture comes to a boil. Use the pointed tip of a knife to dig out the vanilla seeds and add them back to the praline mixture.

Key Lime-Coconut Cream Cake

When I brought this cake to a last-minute dinner, my hosts, Mary and Marshall Cunningham, loved it so much they begged me to take the remainder home. "Don't leave it here," they pleaded. "We'll eat it. We'll probably eat it for breakfast." A simple vanilla cake with a layer of tart Key lime curd and a blanket of lightly sweetened whipped cream, Mary dubbed it "the perfect cake for spring or summer."

Serves 8

CAKE

1 cup (2 sticks) unsalted butter, at room temperature

2 cups granulated sugar

4 large eggs

2^1/$_2$ cups all-purpose flour

2^1/$_2$ teaspoons baking powder

^{1}/$_2$ teaspoon kosher salt

1 teaspoon vanilla extract

1 cup whole milk

FILLING

1 cup granulated sugar

3 tablespoons all-purpose flour

^{1}/$_2$ teaspoon kosher salt

^{1}/$_4$ cup water

^{1}/$_4$ cup freshly squeezed orange juice (about 1 medium orange)

^{1}/$_2$ cup freshly squeezed Key lime juice (about 8 Key limes)

3 large egg yolks

2 tablespoons grated Key lime zest (preferably organic)

FROSTING

4 cups heavy whipping cream, chilled

1 cup sifted powdered sugar

3 to 4 cups flaked unsweetened coconut, for decorating

1 lime, sliced, for decorating

TO MAKE THE CAKE: Preheat the oven to 350°F. Line a 9 by 13-inch baking pan with parchment paper, grease with butter or cooking spray, dust the pan with flour, and knock out the excess.

Using an electric mixer fitted with the paddle attachment, cream the butter and the 2 cups granulated sugar on medium-high speed until light and fluffy, about 3 minutes. Scrape down the sides of the bowl with a rubber spatula. Add the eggs, 1 at a time, beating after each addition. Beat until the batter is fluffy, an additional 2 minutes. In a bowl, stir together the 2^1/$_2$ cups flour, baking powder, and salt. Stir the vanilla into the milk. Add the flour and milk mixtures in alternating batches, beginning and ending with flour. After each addition, mix on low speed just until the batter is smooth. Pour the batter into the prepared pan and bake until a toothpick inserted in the center comes out clean, 25 to 30 minutes. Remove from the oven and let cool for 10 minutes, then unmold on a wire rack to cool completely.

TO MAKE THE FILLING: Stir together the 1 cup granulated sugar, 3 tablespoons flour, and ^{1}/$_2$ teaspoon salt in a saucepan. Gradually stir in the ^{1}/$_4$ cup water and the orange and lime juices. Cook over medium heat until the mixture boils. Remove from the heat and pour ^{1}/$_4$ cup of the hot

continued

mixture into a heatproof glass measuring cup. In a bowl, whisk together the egg yolks. Slowly pour the ¼ cup hot juice mixture into the egg yolks, whisking constantly. (This tempers the egg yolks, preventing them from curdling.) In a slow, steady stream, pour the egg-juice mixture back into the saucepan with the remaining juice mixture, whisking constantly. Set the saucepan over medium heat and bring the mixture to a simmer, whisking constantly until it thickens, about 2 minutes. Pour the filling into a bowl, stir in the lime zest, and cover with plastic wrap, making sure the wrap directly touches the curd at all points, sealing out any air. Refrigerate until cool.

TO MAKE THE FROSTING: Using an electric mixer fitted with the whisk attachment, beat the cream on high speed until soft peaks form. Whip in the powdered sugar.

TO ASSEMBLE THE CAKE: Gently fold 1 cup of the whipped cream frosting into the cooled lime filling. Halve the cooled cake crosswise to make 2 layers. Place the bottom layer on a serving plate. Spread the filling over almost to the outer edge; top with the second layer and frost all over with the remaining whipped cream. Decorate with coconut and lime slices.

DO IT EARLY

Bake the cake layer in advance, wrap in plastic wrap and aluminum foil, and refrigerate or freeze for up to 3 weeks. The filling can be made up to 3 days in advance and refrigerated. Make the frosting and assemble the cake the day you plan to serve it. If it will be more than 2 hours before serving, refrigerate until ready to serve.

TIPS To make decorative lime twists, slice a lime in 8 thin crosswise rounds; for each slice, cut through the skin, stopping in the middle of each round. Use your thumb and forefinger to grasp the lime on opposing sides of the cut and twist in opposite directions. "Stand" the lime circles, cut side down, on top of the cake.

To toast the coconut: Preheat the oven to 350°F. Place the coconut in a single layer on a rimmed baking sheet and bake until lightly golden around the edges, about 6 minutes.

Corona Sorbet

Years ago, during my catering days, we served a Tsingtao beer sorbet in hollowed-out lemon halves for a Chinese New Year celebration. I remembered the idea recently as I brainstormed potential desserts for a Tex-Mex dinner. If it's good with Chinese beer, it ought to be better with a Tex-Mex beer, I reasoned. I grabbed a couple of Coronas and a handful of limes and went to work. Corona Sorbet starred at my next party and it was everything I'd hoped—lively and refreshing, sweet and tangy, just the sort of dessert I crave after a Tex-Mex feast.

Serves 12

1 1/2 cups sugar

1 1/2 cups water

1 1/2 cups freshly squeezed lime juice
    (about 12 medium limes)

2 (12-ounce) bottles Corona (or other
    Mexican) beer

Grated zest of 2 limes

In a large saucepan, bring the 1 1/2 cups water and sugar to a boil over medium-high heat; decrease the heat to medium-low and simmer until thickened, about 10 minutes. Cool for 5 minutes and stir in the lime juice, beer, and zest. Pour the mixture into an ice cream maker and follow the manufacturer's directions. For a more grainy, granita-style texture, pour the mixture into a 9 by 13-inch pan and freeze, stirring every 15 minutes for the first hour to break up the ice crystals. Let the mixture freeze for at least 2 hours or overnight and serve.

DO IT EARLY

The sorbet can be made up to 1 day ahead, but its texture will deteriorate after that.

TIP To make lime serving bowls, wash the limes before cutting them in half to juice. Once the juice has been squeezed out, freeze the skins in a plastic bag until hard, about 1 hour. When the sorbet is ready, fill each lime half with a scoop of sorbet and freeze for 1 hour more before serving.

Silver Bullet Margaritas

Just a few of us hung around the kitchen following a wonderful late-afternoon party at Sarah and Sam Bell Steves's San Antonio home. Sam's son, Tres, stopped by and we started talking margaritas. Tres broke out the family's personalized sterling silver margarita shakers, a pretty good sign that we'd stumbled into in the hands of a margarita-making marvel. We politely asked for seconds—just to make sure. Then we asked for the recipe.

Makes 1 drink

1¹/₂ ounces (3 tablespoons) tequila (the Bells suggest Tres Generaciones silver)

1¹/₂ ounces (3 tablespoons) Cointreau

1¹/₂ ounces (3 tablespoons) freshly squeezed lime juice

¹/₂ ounce (1 tablespoon) Grand Marnier

Ice cubes

Coarse salt

Combine the tequila, Cointreau, lime juice, and Grand Marnier in a cocktail shaker along with a small handful of ice cubes. Shake, shake, shake, until the mixture is "skating" with little chips of ice floating on top. Pour over ice in a salt-rimmed glass.

White Sangria

Lightly sweet and refreshingly tart, white sangria marries beautifully with just about everything Tex-Mex. It goes together easily in advance, making it one of my top picks for parties of any size.

Serves about 12

1 (1.5 liter) bottle dry white table wine

1 (6-ounce) can frozen lemonade concentrate, defrosted

¹/₄ cup freshly squeezed lime juice (about 4 medium limes)

¹/₂ cup brandy

Fruit for floating in the pitcher, such as citrus fruit slices, fresh, pitted cherries, or fresh pineapple chunks

1 (12-ounce) can soda water, or to taste

In a large pitcher, stir together the wine, lemonade concentrate, lime juice, and brandy. Cover with plastic wrap and refrigerate for at least 1 hour and up to 24 hours. When ready to serve, stir in the fruit or fruits of your choice and soda water. Add plenty of ice and serve immediately.

CHAPTER FIVE

BIG-CITY COCKTAIL PARTY

COCKTAILS ARE BACK and I couldn't be happier. My parents and their friends hosted frequent cocktail parties, and to my young eyes it all looked so glamorous and sophisticated. I know I am not the only Texan who remembers her parents' parties with excitement and nostalgia. Perhaps that's one reason cocktail parties have roared back into fashion.

"This is the second golden age of the cocktail," says bar expert David Alan, who created many of the cocktails in this book. His Tipsy Texan blog chronicles his adventures as a cocktail enthusiast, including recipes for classic drinks as well as his own creations. When planning a cocktail party, David advises taking the same care with cocktails as you do with the food: Toss the dusty bottles of prepared drink mix crouching in the corner of your liquor closet. Use only premium spirits and fresh ingredients to prepare drinks. "Treat it like the culinary art form it is," he says.

Cocktail newbies might start by learning how to mix one or two of their favorite drinks. When planning a cocktail party, unless you've hired a professional bartender, you're likely to find yourself in cocktail overload with more than two mixed-drink options. As you ponder

drink possibilities, think about varying base liquors, tastes, and colors. For example, if your first selection is a rum drink that's on the sweet and fruity side, for the second go for something more herbal and astringent made with gin.

Make sure you have plenty of ice on hand, a couple of cocktail shakers, and if fresh-squeezed fruit is involved, think about investing in one of those colorful, handheld juice presses. Not only do they squeeze out a lot of juice, but they keep the seeds at bay. Other basic tools to have on hand are a long-handled bar spoon and wooden muddler that allow you to bruise ingredients in the bottom of a glass.

Although I always see that there's plenty of comfortable seating, the best cocktail parties are stand-up affairs, allowing guests to mix, mingle, and get to know each other. The recipes in this chapter are meant to be passed on trays or scattered about on tabletops for guests to sample as they please. Many of the recipes have stood the test of time—I've been making them since my days as a caterer in Houston. Many can be made in advance. Pick a few that appeal to you, and start making your guest list. Welcome back to the new age of the cocktail party!

Savory Double Cheese Slice-and-Bake Cookies

I keep a batch of these buttery, cheese-laden cookies on hand for drop-in guests year round as they're better than a bowl of mixed nuts and just about as easy to make. Versatile, attractive, and positively addictive, they're great for a before-dinner nibble, a cocktail party hors d'oeuvre, or a pre-theater or movie snack with a glass of wine.

Makes about eighty 2-inch cookies

$^1/_2$ cup (1 stick) unsalted butter, at room temperature

2 cups grated sharp Cheddar cheese (about 8 ounces)

1 cup grated aged Asiago or Manchego cheese (about 4 ounces)

1 cup all-purpose flour

$^1/_4$ teaspoon kosher salt

$^1/_4$ teaspoon cayenne pepper

$^1/_2$ cup coarsely chopped toasted pecans (see page 168)

Using an electric mixer fitted with the paddle attachment, beat the butter and cheeses on medium speed until combined, about 1 minute. Add the flour, salt, and cayenne pepper and beat on low speed until combined. Stir in the pecans. Divide the dough in half; shape each half into a roll about 2 inches in diameter and 8 to 10 inches long. Wrap in waxed paper and chill for at least 4 hours or overnight.

Preheat the oven to 350°F. Grease baking sheets with butter or cooking spray or line with silicone liners. Unwrap the dough and slice into $^1/_8$-inch rounds. Place the rounds on the prepared baking sheets about $^1/_2$ inch apart. Bake until the cookies are lightly browned around the edges and crisp, about 10 minutes.

DO IT EARLY

Make the dough up to 2 weeks in advance, wrap in waxed paper and then a layer of plastic wrap, and refrigerate until ready to use. Or keep baked cookies in an airtight container up to 3 days, or wrap and freeze for up to 3 weeks. Bring to room temperature before serving.

TIP Asiago is an Italian cow's milk cheese that comes two ways: aged Asiago, which is a hard cheese (sometimes called the "poor man's Parmesan") that grates easily; and fresh Asiago, which is softer and lighter in color. Only aged Asiago will work in this recipe.

Polenta Rounds with Cheese, Chive Pesto, and Red Pepper

Chef Quincy Adams Erickson and I worked together in Austin during my stint as executive chef for a national chain. A graduate of the famed cooking school Le Cordon Bleu in Paris, Quincy now owns Austin's Fête Accompli, a catering company specializing in fresh, handmade appetizers. I asked Quincy to give me a cocktail party recipe for this book and, as usual, she came up with a winner. Make sure you have a small cookie cutter that will make bite-size shapes that your guests can easily pop in their mouths. Use whatever shape you'd like: circles, hearts, stars, triangles, or squares.

Makes 30 to 40 appetizers

4 cups water

Kosher salt

1 cup yellow polenta

2 tablespoons unsalted butter

1 large egg

1 cup grated Parmesan cheese

Pinch of cayenne pepper

Olive oil, for brushing

2 cups goat cheese

1/3 cup half-and-half

Freshly ground black pepper

CHIVE PESTO

1/4 cup toasted pine nuts

2 cups chopped fresh chives, chopped

1/2 cup grated Romano cheese

2 cloves garlic

1/2 cup extra-virgin olive oil

Kosher salt and freshly ground black pepper

1 red bell pepper

Grease a rimmed half-sheet (13 by 18-inch) pan with oil or cooking spray. In a large saucepan, bring the 4 cups water and 2 teaspoons of salt to a boil over medium-high heat. Stir in the polenta, decrease the heat to medium-low, and cook until thick and cooked through, about 8 minutes. Remove from the heat and immediately stir in the butter, egg, Parmesan, and cayenne. Spread evenly in the prepared baking sheet, cool for about 30 minutes, cover with plastic wrap, and refrigerate overnight.

Brush a large baking sheet with olive oil to coat. Using a small cookie cutter, cut out rounds from the cold polenta and set them on the prepared baking sheet. Brush the polenta rounds with olive oil. Set aside.

In the work bowl of a food processor fitted with the metal blade, process the goat cheese with the half-and-half until smooth. Season with salt and black pepper. Spoon the goat cheese mixture into a pastry bag fitted with a large star tip (if you don't have a pastry bag, you can use a small spoon to assemble the rounds).

TO MAKE THE PESTO: In the work bowl of a food processor fitted with the metal blade, pulse the pine nuts, chives, Romano, and garlic. Scrape down the sides and pulse again. With the food

continued

processor running, gradually add the olive oil. Season with salt and black pepper.

Using a metal fork, spear the pepper through the stem end; roast it over the flame of a gas burner, rotating it so that it is black and blistered all over. (Or blacken the pepper under the broiler or with a kitchen torch.) Place the pepper in a paper bag and fold over the top to close. Once the pepper is cool, use your hands to completely remove the blistered skin. Halve the roasted pepper and remove the seeds and membrane, then cut the pepper into $1/4$-inch strips.

TO ASSEMBLE THE ROUNDS: Preheat the oven to 400°F. Pipe goat cheese on top of each polenta round. Bake for 8 to 10 minutes. Top with a teaspoon of pesto and sprinkle with diced pepper. Serve warm or at room temperature.

DO IT EARLY

Make the polenta rounds and top with goat cheese up to 1 day in advance. Set them on the baking pan, cover, and refrigerate until ready to bake. Both the pesto and the roasted red peppers can be prepared up to 1 day in advance, covered, and refrigerated. Bake before guests arrive and top with pesto and red pepper.

Soignée Soirees

As owner and founder of Wilson Associates, one of the country's top interior architectural design firms, Tricia Wilson does a lot of entertaining—and naturally her parties demand a high level of elegance and chic. Admittedly not a cook, Tricia says she works closely with her caterer and florist to fulfill her vision for the evening. Her love of color is often expressed with a vibrant flower arrangement or boldly hued linens.

"First impressions are so important, and when I am hosting a party I always try to incorporate a special touch that will create a wonderful and memorable first impression. It may be something that relates to the party theme, such as a specialty drink offered to each guest as they arrive, or something unexpected, like having each guest choose a hat to wear for the evening, or something whimsical, such as using different place settings or china at each person's seat."

Tricia knows a thoughtfully constructed guest list ensures a successful event. She takes care to limit the party's size so that guests can easily mingle and chat. She invites a "fun, colorful mix of people" and she promotes fresh and interesting conversation by including a handful of guests who've never met. "You'll know your group is having fun if the wine is flowing and the voices are twice as loud as they were at the beginning of the party!"

She ends her soirees with a gift for her guests, something simple like a CD mix of her favorite music, or a recipe for one of the evening's dishes.

Although she's hosted many a successful evening, Tricia says that she was the honored guest, not the hostess, at one of her recent favorites.

It was a birthday celebration thrown by her dear friend Jan, who shares a similar approach to party giving. "The special touches were all there—fabulous food and drinks, gorgeous flowers, a beautifully set table, and all my closest friends.

Her special surprise touch came when we cut the birthday cake outside on the patio . . . and I was serenaded by "Bono"! He was so good I thought he was the real deal! Now that's my idea of a great party!"

Tuna Spoons

The best cocktail conversations are light, easy, and entertaining—and cocktail party food ought to follow suit. Inspired by an appetizer I enjoyed at New York City's BLT Steak, I tossed cubes of raw tuna with avocado, citrus juice, wasabi paste, and a touch of sesame oil and served the mix in ceramic spoons instead of on a plate. As simple to prepare as it is to eat, each Tuna Spoon contains just a mouthful—custom-made to enjoy with cocktails.

Makes about 16 tablespoon-size portions

1/4 cup reduced-sodium soy sauce

2 tablespoons freshly squeezed lemon juice
   (about 1 medium lemon)

2 tablespoons freshly squeezed lime juice
   (about 1 medium lime)

2 teaspoons wasabi paste

1/4 teaspoon sesame oil

3/4 pound sushi-grade ahi tuna, cut into
   1/8-inch dice

1 ripe medium avocado, peeled, pitted, and
   cut into small dice

In a ceramic or glass bowl, whisk together the soy sauce, lemon and lime juices, wasabi paste, and sesame oil. Gently stir in the tuna and avocado, being sure to coat them evenly with the soy-citrus mixture. Cover with plastic wrap and marinate for at least 30 minutes, but not more than 6 hours. Use a tablespoon to measure out portions, placing 1 tablespoon of the mixture in each of 16 ceramic spoons. Serve immediately.

DO IT EARLY

The dish can be prepared and refrigerated for up to 2 hours before serving. Make the individual portions just before serving.

TIPS
To serve this appetizer, it's easiest to use Japanese-style ceramic soup spoons, but any spoon with a flat bottom and a generous rim will do. I've also used small, shallow pitchers. Feel free to experiment with just about any small container that allows guests to easily tip the mixture into their mouths.

Wasabi paste, also known as Japanese horseradish, is available at most large supermarkets or Asian specialty markets. It's got a spicy kick that can clear your sinuses, so a little goes a long way.

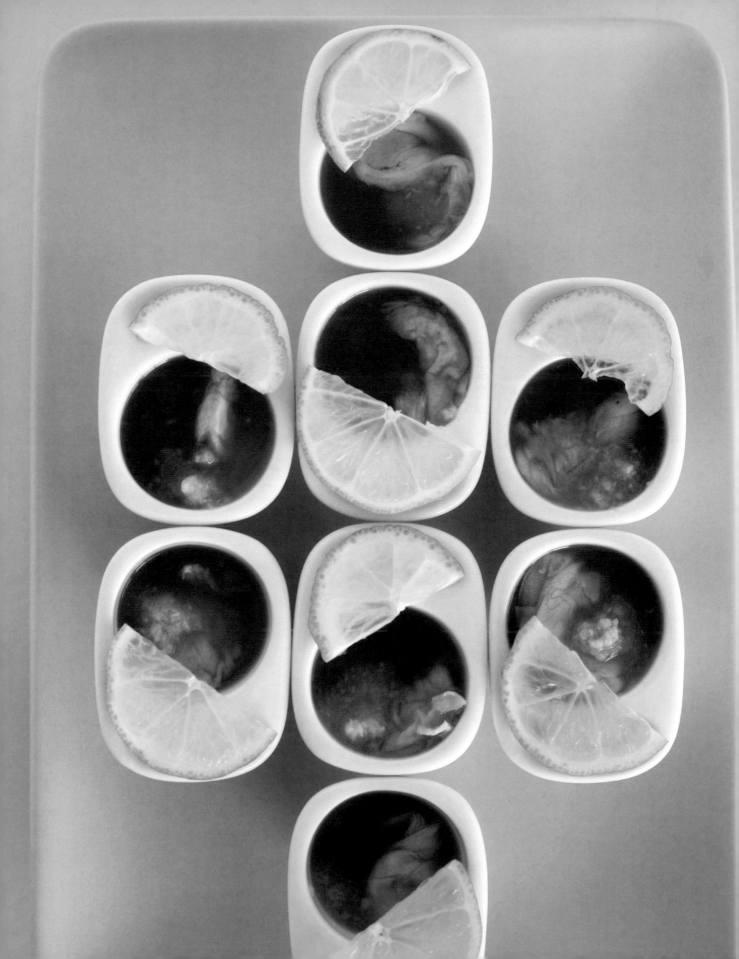

Party-in-a-Shot-Glass Oyster Shooters

My friend Yvonne and I tested my Bloody Mary oyster shooters and got lightly "toasted" at the same time. We kept draining our shot glasses and after each one we figured we needed one more, just to make sure the seasoning was right. And besides, each shot glass contained dinner (an oyster and a vegetable) and a drink (a spot of vodka), so why stop before our appetites waned? Before we knew it we'd moved from testing to party mode. We laughingly dubbed our oyster concoction a "party in a shot glass," and the name stuck. One thing is sure: start slurping these and you've got a party whether it's for just the two of you or for a crowd of your best buddies.

Makes 24 shooters

2 (12-ounce) cans V8, tomato juice, or
 Clamato juice, chilled

2 tablespoons prepared horseradish

2 tablespoons freshly squeezed lemon juice
 (about 1 medium lemon)

1 tablespoon Worcestershire sauce

3 to 4 shakes Tabasco sauce

1/2 teaspoon Cajun seasoning

1/2 teaspoon celery salt

1/2 teaspoon freshly ground black pepper

2 dozen fresh oysters (about 2 pounds)

Vodka

Halved lime slices, for garnish

In a large (at least 2-cup capacity) pitcher, stir together the V8, horseradish, lemon juice, Worcestershire sauce, Tabasco, Cajun seasoning, celery salt, and pepper. Refrigerate until ready to assemble the oyster shooters. Set 12 (1½-ounce capacity or more) shot glasses on a decorative tray. Spoon 1 oyster into each, top with 2 tablespoons tomato mix, and refrigerate until ready to serve, up to 2 hours ahead. Just before serving, float 1 teaspoon vodka on top. Garnish with lime slices.

DO IT EARLY

The Bloody Mary mix can be made up to 2 days in advance and refrigerated. Assemble the shooters, including the oysters, up to 2 hours before you plan to serve them. Float the vodka on top just before serving.

TIP Make it effortless: buy your favorite Bloody Mary mix and use it for instant oyster shooters. If you wish, spice it up with a few of your own additions, such as celery salt, prepared horseradish, or Cajun seasoning.

Wild Mushroom Turnovers

I've been making these for parties ever since I joined forces with my old friend Marianna Green. We both had little babies, and together we catered weddings, birthday parties, and more parties. I froze these two-bite nibbles by the dozen—I always had a batch on standby for last-minute events. They're still one of my favorite party hors d'oeuvres. No fuss, no muss, no sauce needed.

Makes about 35 bite-size turnovers

PASTRY

- 1/2 cup (1 stick) unsalted butter, at room temperature
- 1 (3-ounce) package cream cheese, at room temperature
- 2 tablespoons minced fresh chives
- 1 1/4 cups all-purpose flour
- 1 teaspoon kosher salt

FILLING

- 3 tablespoons unsalted butter
- 1/2 pound mixed wild mushrooms, finely chopped
- 1 small yellow onion, minced
- 1 tablespoon all-purpose flour
- 4 1/2 teaspoons sherry
- Kosher salt and freshly ground black pepper
- 1 tablespoon chopped fresh parsley
- 1/4 cup sour cream or crème fraîche

- 1 large egg yolk
- 2 teaspoons water

TO MAKE THE PASTRY: Using an electric mixer fitted with the paddle attachment, beat the 1/2 cup butter and cream cheese on medium speed until smooth. Beat in the chives; add the 1 1/4 cups flour and 1 teaspoon salt and beat on low speed to form a stiff dough. Form the dough into 2 equal disks, wrap in plastic wrap, and refrigerate for at least 30 minutes or overnight.

TO MAKE THE FILLING: In a large skillet set over medium heat, melt the 3 tablespoons butter and sauté the mushrooms and onion until the juices have evaporated. Sprinkle with 1 tablespoon flour, stirring until the mixture is combined; cook for 2 more minutes. Stir in the sherry, salt, pepper, and parsley. Cook for 2 more minutes; stir in the sour cream. Remove the skillet from the heat and let cool before assembling the turnovers.

Preheat the oven to 425°F. Grease baking sheets with butter or cooking spray or line with parchment paper or silicone liners.

Sprinkle a work surface with flour, and using a rolling pin sprinkled with flour, roll out each chilled dough disk to about 1/8 inch thick. Cut out dough rounds using a 4-inch biscuit cutter. Gather the scraps and reroll the dough to make more rounds. Add more flour to the work surface, if necessary. Place a teaspoon of the filling on each dough round, moisten the outer edges

continued

with water, and fold in half. Crimp the edges with a fork to seal. In a small bowl make an egg wash by mixing the egg yolk and the 2 teaspoons water with a fork until combined. Brush the egg wash on top of each turnover. Bake on the prepared sheets until golden brown, 13 to 15 minutes. Cool on wire racks. Serve warm or at room temperature.

DO IT EARLY

Seal the unbaked turnovers in freezer-weight plastic bags and freeze for up to 3 weeks. To serve, brush the frozen turnovers with egg wash and bake, until golden, about 16 minutes.

Better All the Time

Many know native Texan Liz Carpenter for her sharp wit, her years as press secretary to Lady Bird Johnson during the Johnsons' White House years, and the fifty-eight words she scribbled en route from Dallas to Washington, D.C., on Air Force One–Lyndon Johnson's first plane flight as president following John F. Kennedy's tragic assassination.

But among her friends, Liz is also known for her parties. From vacation house parties in Martha's Vineyard to her legendary Bay at the Moon shindigs held in her Austin backyard, Liz readily admits she loves a party. In her endearing and funny memoir, *Getting Better All the Time*, Liz writes about moving back to Texas after the untimely death of her husband, Les, and her years as a Washington, D.C., insider.

"You could have the brain of Margaret Thatcher, the wit of Joan Rivers, and still be forgotten by hostesses who think that parties, like Noah's Ark, are meant for pairs. So I do the entertaining. This keeps me popular and broke."

I visited Liz at her Austin home, Grass Roots, more than twenty years after she wrote those words, and her enthusiasm for entertaining–despite her eighty-seven years–remained unshaken. She talked with relish of the GBATTS (Getting Better All the Time Singers) and their festivities. On warm summer nights they'd move the piano outside, belt out show tunes, and howl at the moon as it rose over the city.

Liz's latter-day parties were informed in part by her association with Lady Bird Johnson, a life-long friend. When LBJ was alive, Liz recounted, he dominated the conversation. Once he was gone, "suddenly everyone had a chance to say some-thing." Lady Bird instituted new rules at the dinner table. First, only one person was to talk at a time. And second, she and Liz would come up with a question to stimulate conversation, such as "What is your oldest memory?" or "When were you most embarrassed?" Guests' answers were limited to five minutes.

Boring conversations have no place at a Liz Carpenter event, and she avoids them by devising clever themes, creative props, and by including "an interesting mix of guests." As described in her book, she invites "flaming liberals and tosses in an occasional wide-eyed conservative. . . . It does give guests something to talk about." She once presided over a storytelling party where guests were asked to bring a "tall tale of Texas" and recount it over beans and barbecue served on tin plates. At another fiesta, Liz came up with the first line of a story and her guests continued the tale from there. A traditional Labor Day party often includes a watermelon-seed-spitting contest. A party for a psychiatrist friend featured chicken à la Thorazine, crazy-mixed-up salad, and strawberries with guilt-free whipped cream.

Shortly after my summertime visit, I received an e-mail from Liz's friend Josephine C. Sherfy, who often assists Liz in her party planning. Liz's latest brainstorm involved a "Kissing Cousins Party" for local relatives, an afternoon party for kids and adults. The menu was to include watermelon, iced tea, lemonade, and a big tray of assorted cookies. Josephine reported that she would soon be haunting craft stores to find red lip stickers to adorn the invitations. And as soon as that party was over, it would be time to plan the next celebration–in honor of Liz's upcoming eighty-eighth birthday.

Lemon-Ginger Chicken Canapés

Jim Manning and I attended Ole Miss at the same time, but never met. It wasn't until later that we crossed paths working for Houston's Acute Catering and discovered that I'd briefly dated one of his roommates. Jim now heads his own business, Jim Manning Catered Affairs, and is one of Houston's top caterers. This recipe is a lot of work, but it's elegant and serves a huge crowd, and most of the labor can be done in advance. It's a great option if you're hosting a large-scale event. Otherwise, the recipe can be cut in half or even in quarters.

Makes about 150 bite-size portions

CHICKEN

2 tablespoons chopped fresh lemongrass

1 tablespoon chopped fresh ginger

1 teaspoon ground turmeric

2 teaspoons grated lemon zest

1 tablespoon freshly squeezed lemon juice
(about half a medium lemon)

1/2 teaspoon kosher salt

1/4 teaspoon freshly ground black pepper

1 1/2 pounds boneless, skinless chicken
breasts, cut into 3/4-inch pieces

1 1/2 cups all-purpose flour

1 1/2 cups cornstarch

1/2 cup vegetable oil, for frying

LEMON-GINGER HONEY

2 1/2 cups simple syrup (see Tips)

1/4 cup fresh ginger juice

1/4 cup freshly squeezed lemon juice
(about 2 medium lemons)

1 1/2 cups honey

BLACK CURRANT MAYONNAISE

3 cups mayonnaise

1/2 cup ginger preserves

1/2 cup black currant jelly or preserves

WONTONS

1 (75-count) package (3 1/2-inch) square
wonton wrappers, halved diagonally with
kitchen scissors

Vegetable oil, for frying

Chopped fresh chives, for garnish

TO MAKE THE CHICKEN: In a large bowl combine the lemongrass, ginger, turmeric, lemon zest, lemon juice, salt, and pepper. Stir in the chicken, cover, and refrigerate overnight. In a large bowl, stir together the flour and cornstarch. Remove the chicken from the marinade, drain, and toss it, 1/2 cup at a time, in the flour mixture to coat. In a large skillet set over medium-high heat, warm 1/4 cup of the vegetable oil. Add the chicken, 1/2 cup at a time, and fry until the pieces are golden brown and cooked through, about 10 minutes; add more oil as needed. Drain the chicken on paper towels.

TO MAKE THE LEMON-GINGER HONEY: In a saucepan set over medium heat, combine the simple syrup, ginger juice, and lemon juice and simmer for 20 minutes. Stir in the honey and cool.

190

TO MAKE THE BLACK CURRANT MAYONNAISE: In a bowl, stir together the mayonnaise, ginger preserves, and black currant jelly.

TO FRY THE WONTONS: In a large skillet or Dutch oven, heat 3 inches of oil over medium heat until it reaches 365°F on a deep-fat thermometer. Fry the wontons in batches until golden and drain on paper towels.

TO ASSEMBLE THE CANAPÉS: In a saucepan over medium-low heat, combine the chicken and the lemon-ginger honey and heat until warm. Arrange the fried wontons on a tray. Spoon about 1/4 teaspoon of the mayonnaise near one of the triangle's tips. Spoon about 1 teaspoon of the chicken mixture in the middle of the wonton and sprinkle with chopped chives. Serve immediately.

DO IT EARLY

The chicken can be fried and refrigerated up to 3 days in advance. The mayonnaise and ginger syrup can also be made in advance and refrigerated. Fry the wontons early the day you plan to serve them. The canapés should be assembled shortly before serving.

TIPS Make your own fresh ginger juice by grating fresh peeled ginger (you'll need about three 4-inch pieces to get the needed 1 cup grated), placing it in a square of cheesecloth, and squeezing it to extract the juice. Discard the leftover ginger solids. Or you can buy it at the grocery store.

To make simple syrup, boil equal parts water and sugar until the sugar is completely dissolved. Stored in a tightly sealed glass jar, simple syrup keeps indefinitely in the refrigerator.

Homemade Potato Chips

These are my downfall—as are french fries, sweet potato fries, or anything else that involves spuds and a deep-fat fryer. I can resist the fudgiest brownies, chewiest cookies, or even the loveliest three-layer cakes, but I cannot walk away from a single salty potato chip. I'm a believer in the golden rule of party giving: Feed your guests as you would like to be fed yourself. No wonder my cocktail parties invariably include potato chips. I often serve them with Chipotle Ketchup (page 254), but sometimes I crave them bare with just a light shower of plain or fancy salt and a large glass of good red wine.

Serves 8

2 pounds baking potatoes, such as russet or
   Yukon Gold (about 2 large)

8 cups vegetable oil

Kosher salt

Fill a large bowl halfway with cold water. Peel the potatoes, or just scrub them well under running water. Using a mandoline or a sharp paring knife, cut the potatoes into ⅛-inch-thick slices and drop them into the bowl of water. Refrigerate the potatoes for about 15 minutes or overnight. (You can skip this step, but it produces crispier potato chips.)

In a stockpot, heat the oil over medium heat until it reaches 350°F on a deep-fat thermometer. While the oil heats, remove the potato slices from the water and drain them on a layer of paper towels. Cover with more towels and pat the slices dry so they don't splatter when they hit the hot fat and spew scalding drops of oil in your general direction. Using a slotted spoon, lower small batches of potato slices into the hot oil and cook until golden brown, or darker, depending on your preference, 3 to 4 minutes. (Monitor the temperature of the oil so it stays

at 350°F or the chips will be greasy.) Remove the chips from the hot oil, sprinkle with salt, and drain on paper towels. Serve warm or at room temperature.

DO IT EARLY

These can be made ahead, but only on the same day you plan to serve them.

VARIATION

If a stockpot filled with hot oil intimidates you, try baked chips. (They won't match the crisp wonderfulness of their deep-fried cousins, but they are healthier and mighty tasty.) Preheat the oven to 400°F. Spread the sliced potatoes in 1 layer on a baking sheet lined with parchment paper or silicone baking liner. Spray or brush good-quality olive oil on both sides of the slices and bake for about 15 minutes, turning once halfway through the baking time, until they are golden. Sprinkle with salt and serve straight out of the oven.

Cheddar Soup Cups

It took my mother years to convince Chef Heinz at the Beaumont Country Club to share his recipe for brandied Cheddar cheese soup. Once she got the recipe, it became one of her favorite party soups. I've tweaked it a little, substituting beer for brandy and omitting the Cheese Whiz (it was the 1960s, after all). Serve it in little bowls, shot glasses, or espresso cups, so friends can pick it up and enjoy this rich, tummy-warming combination in a few sips, without a spoon.

Serves 8

1/2 cup (1 stick) unsalted butter

1 cup finely diced celery (about 3 large stalks)

1 cup finely diced carrots (about 2 medium)

1 cup finely diced yellow onion (about 1 medium)

1 cup thinly sliced green onions, white and green parts

1/2 cup all-purpose flour

3 cups chicken stock

3 cups whole milk

6 ounces Shiner Bock beer (or any dark beer)

1 tablespoon dry mustard

1 teaspoon Tabasco sauce

1 teaspoon kosher salt

2 cups shredded sharp Cheddar cheese (about 8 ounces)

2 cups shredded Monterey Jack cheese (about 8 ounces)

In a large stockpot set over medium heat, melt the butter and add the celery, carrots, and the yellow and green onions. Cook until the onions are soft and translucent, about 3 minutes. Stir in the flour and cook for 1 minute more. Stir in the chicken stock and milk and simmer until the soup has thickened, about 10 minutes. Whisk in the beer, mustard, Tabasco, and salt. Stir in the shredded Cheddar and Jack cheeses and stir over low heat until the cheese is melted.

Serve warm in small sipping cups or glasses.

DO IT EARLY

The soup can be made up to 2 days in advance and refrigerated. For serving, be sure to warm it gradually over low heat or the soup will scorch. If it's too thick after reheating, thin with milk or stock.

VARIATION

For an extra-rich and creamy soup, substitute 1/2 pound of ripe, rind-free Brie for the Cheddar.

Avocado Pancakes with Crème Fraîche and Trout Roe

These delicate, pale-green avocado pancakes come from my former big-city life as executive pastry chef at Anthony's, owned by Tony Vallone, one of Houston's top restaurateurs. The recipe for these savory pancakes was shared by a sous chef there, and I fell in love with them. We served them with crab and pico de gallo. In this version, I top them with homemade crème fraîche and trout caviar, a gorgeous, orange, medium-grained roe. (It is also more reasonably priced than many caviars and sustainably raised.) Incredibly simple, the pancakes must be made at the last minute and served warm.

Makes 25 small pancakes

CRÈME FRAÎCHE

- 1 cup heavy whipping cream
- 1 tablespoon cultured buttermilk

PANCAKES

- 1/4 medium white onion
- 1 ripe avocado, peeled and pitted
- 1 large egg
- 1/2 cup all-purpose flour
- 1/4 teaspoon baking powder
- 3/4 cup whole milk
- 1/2 teaspoon kosher salt
- 1/4 teaspoon ground white pepper

- 2 ounces trout roe

TO MAKE THE CRÈME FRAÎCHE: Pour the cream into a glass container or bowl. Stir in the buttermilk, cover, and let the mixture sit in a warm spot until the mixture thickens to the consistency of sour cream, at least 8 hours and up to 24 hours. Cover and refrigerate.

TO MAKE THE PANCAKES: In the work bowl of a food processor fitted with the metal blade or the jar of a blender, process the onion until pureed.

Add the avocado, egg, flour, baking powder, milk, salt, and pepper, and process until the mixture is creamy and resembles breakfast-pancake batter, about 4 minutes. Set a large, lightly oiled skillet over medium-low heat. Drop the pancake batter by tablespoonfuls about 1 inch apart onto the heated skillet. Cook until the pancakes puff up, deflate slightly, and are lightly browned on both sides, 2 to 2 1/2 minutes per side.

TO ASSEMBLE THE PANCAKES: Top each warm pancake with 1 tablespoon of crème fraîche and 1 teaspoon of trout roe. Serve immediately.

DO IT EARLY

The crème fraîche will keep for 1 week in the refrigerator.

TIPS If you don't feel like making your own crème fraîche, most grocery stores carry it.

Many high-end markets, such as Whole Foods and Central Market, carry trout roe. A number of vendors offer it online as well.

Mary's Crayfish Pies

I fancy myself to be part Cajun, not surprising since I grew up on the Texas-Louisiana border. When entertaining, I often include a little something with Cajun flair. My Shreveport-born friend Mary Cunningham feels the same way. She served these at a recent dinner party in her home and happily shared her recipe (once she figured out what she did and wrote it down, that is). Like many accomplished home cooks I know, Mary rarely measures, cooking by taste and feel. I've adapted her recipe and created a cornbread crust to go with it. Depending on where you live, it may be tough to find crayfish. It can be ordered online, but if necessary, substitute an equal amount of chopped, fresh shrimp.

Makes 2 dozen 3-inch pies

CORNMEAL CRUST

1 cup (2 sticks) chilled unsalted butter, cut crosswise into ¹/₂-inch slices

2 cups all-purpose flour

1 cup cornmeal

¹/₂ teaspoon kosher salt

¹/₂ teaspoon Cajun seasoning

¹/₄ teaspoon cayenne pepper

2 large eggs

2 large egg yolks

2 teaspoons ice water

CRAYFISH FILLING

¹/₂ cup (1 stick) unsalted butter

¹/₂ cup all-purpose flour

¹/₂ cup diced yellow onion

3 green onions, white part only, diced

1 red bell pepper, cored, seeded, and diced

4 ribs celery, diced

1 pound Louisiana crayfish tails (thawed, if frozen)

4 teaspoons minced garlic (about 4 medium cloves)

¹/₃ cup brandy

1¹/₂ cups heavy whipping cream

¹/₄ cup finely chopped, stemmed Italian parsley

2 shakes Tabasco sauce

¹/₂ teaspoon kosher salt

¹/₂ teaspoon Cajun seasoning

TO MAKE THE CRUST: Lightly grease twenty-four 3-inch muffin cups with cooking spray (you may need to prepare the pies in two batches). In the work bowl of a food processor fitted with the metal blade, pulse the 1 cup butter, 2 cups flour, cornmeal, ¹/₂ teaspoon salt, ¹/₂ teaspoon Cajun seasoning, and cayenne until the dough is the size of small peas. Add the eggs, egg yolks, and the 2 teaspoons ice water. Pulse until the dough begins to form a ball. (If you prefer, this can be done in a big bowl with your hands or a pastry cutter: work the butter, flour, cornmeal, salt, Cajun seasoning, and pepper together until they are the size of small peas. Add the eggs, egg yolks, and water and work until the dough forms a ball.) Pat the dough into a disk, cover with plastic wrap, and refrigerate while you make the crayfish filling.

TO MAKE THE CRAYFISH FILLING: In a large, heavy skillet set over medium heat, melt the ¹/₂ cup butter until it bubbles. Slowly sprinkle on the

continued

199

½ cup flour, stirring constantly until the mixture is combined. Add the yellow and green onions, bell pepper, and celery and cook, stirring constantly, for 15 minutes. Stir in the crayfish, garlic, brandy, cream, parsley, Tabasco, ½ teaspoon salt, and ½ teaspoon Cajun seasoning, and cook an additional 5 minutes. Remove from the heat.

To assemble the pies: Preheat the oven to 350°F. Sprinkle a work surface with flour. Pinch off enough cornmeal dough to make 1½-inch balls. Press the dough balls into prepared muffin cups to cover the bottom and up the sides. Spoon the crayfish filling almost to the top of each pie shell. Bake until the filling is hot and the crust is crisp, about 30 minutes.

Serve warm or at room temperature.

DO IT EARLY

Freeze well-wrapped baked and cooled pies up to 3 weeks in advance. Thaw in the refrigerator the night before you plan to serve them. Bake for 15 minutes at 350°F to warm before serving.

TIP These may seem large, especially if you're serving them at a utensil-free cocktail party. (For a first course at a dinner party, I present them on plates with knives and forks.) For cocktail parties, cut them in halves or quarters and set them out on serving dishes so they can be easily picked up and eaten in a bite or two.

The Buddy System

When Kori Green throws a party, she's got built-in entertainment—her husband, country music star Pat Green. If party guests are lucky, Pat will pull out his guitar and say, "Hey, I just wrote a song last night and want you to hear it." Or he'll start on a new song and let friends build on it, adding lines as they go.

Pat and Kori, married since 2000, favor laid-back entertaining at their Fort Worth home, and music is always an essential element. "It just makes people relax and adds to the atmosphere," Kori says. Given that many of Pat and Kori's friends are musicians, it's inevitable that guitars come out at many of their get-togethers. But if they don't, adds Kori, Pat makes "great mixes of the music he likes" and friends often leave the party saying, "I need that list."

Kori, who holds a law degree from University of Texas, grew up in a rural Texas town so small, she says, that when its only stoplight broke they didn't bother to replace it. She hadn't done a lot of entertaining when she first met Pat, but that changed quickly when she became close friends with the couple's wedding planner, Elizabeth Harris, a childhood friend of Pat's. (Incidentally, Elizabeth was the "curly-headed girl back in seventh grade" mentioned in "George's Bar," an early Pat Green song.)

When Elizabeth started dating a musician, she and Kori started The Band Widows Club. "All of our friends were musicians' girlfriends. None of them could cook. They'd come over, I'd cook, and Elizabeth would arrange everything," Kori recalls. "We were a good team."

Kori and Elizabeth lived in Austin then. They hosted so many parties together that when Elizabeth married she bought white china that matched Kori's so they could pool dishes for large celebrations.

Kori says collaborating with Elizabeth taught her the value of entertaining with a buddy—especially one with complementary talents. Kori's are cooking and small-scale events. Elizabeth's are decorating, organizing, and conceptualizing big events—no surprise there, she now runs a successful event design business. Elizabeth's creative flair was apparent when she helped Pat and Kori with a party celebrating their son Kellis's first birthday. On one side the invitation said, "Eat cake with Kellis," on the other, "Drink beer with Pat." Elizabeth also had custom cups made that said "eat cake" on one side and "drink beer" on the other.

Both Elizabeth and Kori have since moved away from Austin—Elizabeth to Fredericksburg, where she runs Elizabeth Harris Event Design, and Kori to Fort Worth and her jewelry-making business, Kori Green Designs. Both continue avidly entertaining, but with two kids apiece, their parties often revolve around the whole family.

In the summertime, Pat and Kori host numerous backyard pool parties, where kids and adults can relax, swim, and eat dinner off the grill. Their children are young now, but Kori knows how quickly they grow up. "I want to appreciate them as long as I can."

Lemongrass-skewered Quail Sausage

Good redneck that he is, John Pennell says he started making sausage out of every critter he hunted. Apparently that wasn't enough, and he turned to making it out of quail purchased from nearby Diamond H Ranch in Bandera, Texas, a leading quail breeder and processor. Soon John's sausage became so popular that he chucked a sixteen-year stint in construction to concentrate on a new business: Uncle John's Quail Sausage. He ships his sausage all over the country and supplies numerous Texas restaurants (mine included) with his delicious quail links. Uncle John's getting pretty well known in these parts, but I'm just as big a fan of his wife, Lanette, leader of Almost Patsy Cline, one of the area's top party bands. A vocalist, songwriter, and bassist, she and fellow vocalist and keyboardist Vicki Gillespie started the band in 2002. The duo got so many requests for covers of country legend Patsy Cline's songs that they named their band after her. As the band's popularity grew, they brought in artists Larry Nolen (guitars, vocals), Bryan Kibbe (guitars, vocals) and Rick Reynolds (drums, vocals), expanding the group's repertoire to include the music of numerous male legends. I'd sure like to have Almost Patsy Cline at my next party. On the menu, of course, would be Uncle John's quail sausage on skewers, making it easy to grab a bite and keep on dancing.

Serves 8 to 12

1 (2-pound) package Uncle John's Quail Sausage, regular or jalapeño

10 fresh lemongrass stalks

Grill or pan-fry the sausage according to package directions. While the sausage cools, wash the lemongrass and remove the outer leaf. Slice each stalk lengthwise into 4 skewers. Cut each cooked sausage crosswise on the diagonal into 6 equal slices. Using a metal or bamboo skewer, drill holes in the sides of the sausage to make it easier to insert the lemongrass. Insert the lemongrass stalks, arrange the sausage skewers on a platter, and serve warm or at room temperature.

DO IT EARLY

The sausage can be cooked early in the day and refrigerated. Warm up the links in a 325°F oven for about 15 minutes, slice, and place on skewers. Serve warm or at room temperature.

TIPS
Sturdy stalks of lemongrass make the best skewers. Look for lemongrass at farmers' markets and Asian markets. I've also found high-quality lemongrass at upscale grocery stores such as Whole Foods and Central Market.

Uncle John's sausage can be found at selected Hill Country farmers' markets or from www.unclejohns quailsausage.com.

Lemon-Chip Cookies

Cookies at Rather Sweet Bakery are very large, and that's how our customers like them. For a dinner or cocktail party, I prefer small cookies. That way guests can indulge in more than one sweet finale. I've found that a dessert tray stocked with a variety of one- or two-bite treats is extremely popular. This recipe is adapted from a sugar cookie recipe given to me years ago by The Austin Chronicle's *food editor, Virginia Wood. Now that I've added fresh lemon juice and chocolate, she probably won't recognize it. (Pictured opposite, bottom right.)*

Makes 2 dozen 2-inch cookies

$1/2$ cup (1 stick) unsalted butter, at room temperature

$1/2$ cup vegetable oil (such as canola)

$1/2$ cup granulated sugar

$1/2$ cup powdered sugar

1 large egg

Grated zest and freshly squeezed juice of 1 medium lemon (about 2 tablespoons juice)

2 cups all-purpose flour

$1/2$ teaspoon baking soda

$1/4$ teaspoon salt

1 (12-ounce) package semisweet chocolate chips

Preheat the oven to 350°F. Line baking sheets with parchment paper or silicone liners or grease generously with butter or cooking spray.

Using an electric mixer fitted with the paddle attachment, beat the butter on medium speed until fluffy, about 1 minute. Add the vegetable oil, granulated and powdered sugars, egg, and lemon zest and juice and beat on medium speed until combined. Add the flour, soda, and salt and beat on low speed just until incorporated. Stir in the chocolate chips. The dough will be very soft. Refrigerate for 1 hour or freeze for 15 minutes to make it easier to scoop.

Using a tablespoon-size scoop, drop mounds of dough about 1 inch apart on the prepared baking sheets. Press the dough evenly with your fingers or palm to slightly flatten the cookies. Bake until the edges turn golden, 8 to 10 minutes. Let the cookies cool on the baking sheet for at least 10 minutes before removing.

DO IT EARLY

The cookies can be baked and stored in an airtight container for up to 3 days, or frozen for up to 3 weeks. Alternatively, make the dough up to a week in advance, and refrigerate in a covered container. Bake a day or two before you plan to serve them.

Chile Crinkle Cookies

Here's an old favorite turned just a little edgy, thanks to the addition of ancho chile powder. Ancho chiles (dried poblanos) have a sweet undertone that combines well with chocolate. For the freshest flavor, grind your own chile powder as directed in the Tip following this recipe. Be advised, though, that some anchos are spicier than others. Taste your ground chiles to check their heat levels and add or subtract the amount added accordingly. (Pictured page 204, bottom left.)

Makes about 4 dozen 3-inch cookies

6 ounces bittersweet chocolate, coarsely chopped

1/2 cup (1 stick) unsalted butter

2 cups granulated sugar

2 teaspoons vanilla extract

4 large eggs

2 cups all-purpose flour

2 teaspoons baking powder

1/2 teaspoon kosher salt

2 tablespoons ancho chile powder

1/8 teaspoon cayenne pepper

1 cup semisweet chocolate chips

1 cup powdered sugar

In a metal bowl set over a saucepan filled with 2 inches of simmering water, melt the chocolate and butter. Stir in the granulated sugar. Remove from the heat and cool for 5 minutes. Using an electric mixer fitted with the paddle attachment, beat the chocolate mixture on medium speed until blended; stir in the vanilla. Beat in the eggs, 1 at a time, scraping down the bowl after each addition. Add the flour, baking powder, salt, and chile powder and beat on low speed just until incorporated. Stir in chips. Refrigerate dough several hours or overnight.

Preheat the oven to 375°F. Line baking sheets with parchment paper or silicone liners or grease generously with butter or cooking spray.

Roll the dough into 1-inch balls, then roll in powdered sugar. Place at least 2 inches apart on the prepared baking sheets. Bake until visible crinkles have formed and the cookies have puffed and spread slightly, 8 to 10 minutes.

DO IT EARLY

The cookies can be baked and stored in an airtight container for up to 3 days. Or freeze for up to 3 weeks. Alternatively, make the dough up to a week in advance and refrigerate in a covered container. Bake them a day or two before you plan to serve them.

TIP To make chile powder from dried chiles, toast the chiles in a 250°F oven for about 3 to 4 minutes, or in a heavy skillet over medium heat until they soften slightly and become fragrant, 3 to 4 minutes. Stem and seed the chiles. Grind to a powder in a blender or food processor fitted with the metal blade. Four ancho chiles makes about 4 tablespoons powder.

Chocolate Mousse Cookies Two Ways

I love a dramatic dessert at a cocktail party, but I also want a pick-up dessert that doesn't need plates and utensils. A deep, dark-chocolate mousse that's piped onto a choice of two very different kinds of cookies fits the bill. Although I like to make both cookie bases and serve them together, you may want to save a little time by choosing to make only one. (Pictured page 204, center and top.)

Makes about 3 dozen tuiles and 16 meringues, with filling

BITTERSWEET CHOCOLATE MOUSSE

12 ounces bittersweet chocolate (70 percent cacao), coarsely chopped

2 tablespoons unsalted butter

5 large egg yolks

$1/2$ cup water

$1/2$ cup sugar

1 tablespoon vanilla extract

$1^1/2$ cups heavy whipping cream, chilled

2 tablespoons amaretto (optional)

ALMOND TUILES

$1/2$ cup (1 stick) unsalted butter

$1/2$ cup sugar

$1^1/4$ cup sliced almonds

$1/2$ cup light corn syrup

$1/4$ cup all-purpose flour

Pinch of kosher salt

MERINGUES

4 large egg whites

$1/2$ teaspoon cream of tartar

Pinch of salt

$1^1/4$ cups sugar

TO MAKE THE MOUSSE: In a large metal bowl set over a saucepan filled with 2 inches of simmering water, melt the chocolate and the 2 table-spoons butter. Set the chocolate mixture aside to cool. Using an electric mixer fitted with the paddle attachment, beat the egg yolks until thick and pale, about 5 minutes; stir in the vanilla.

In a small saucepan, combine the water and sugar and simmer over medium heat until the mixture reaches a soft ball stage, 234°F on a candy thermometer. In a slow, steady stream, add the sugar mixture to the egg yolk mixture, beating on low speed until combined. Increase the speed to medium and beat until thickened and cooled, about 5 minutes.

Using a large rubber spatula, fold the egg yolk mixture into the chocolate mixture, one-third at a time. Using an electric mixer fitted with the whisk attachment, whip the cream at high speed until soft peaks start to form. (If you continue to beat the cream beyond this point, the mousse will get lumpy.) Gently fold the whipped cream and amaretto, if desired, into the chocolate mixture.

TO MAKE THE TUILES: Preheat the oven to 350°F. Line baking sheets with parchment paper or silicone liners or grease generously with butter or cooking spray.

continued

In a saucepan set over medium heat, melt the 1/2 cup butter and stir in the 1/2 cup sugar and almonds until combined. Stir in the corn syrup, flour, and salt; remove from the heat and let cool 15 minutes.

Drop teaspoonfuls of dough at least 2 inches apart onto the prepared baking sheets. Bake until golden, 12 to 15 minutes. Remove from the oven and cool for 2 minutes. Roll the warm cookies into cones. If the cookies get too hard, return to the oven for 1 or 2 minutes. Cool completely and store in airtight containers, with waxed paper between layers.

TO MAKE THE MERINGUES: Preheat the oven to 300°F. Line 2 baking sheets with parchment paper or silicone liners.

Using an electric mixer fitted with the whisk attachment, beat the 4 egg whites, cream of tartar, and pinch of salt on high speed until soft peaks form, about 2 minutes. Add the 1 1/4 cups sugar, 2 tablespoons at a time, and continue beating on high speed until stiff peaks form.

Spoon the meringue into a pastry bag fitted with a medium round tip. Pipe 2-inch rounds onto the prepared baking sheets. Bake the meringues for 1 hour. Turn off the oven and leave them inside the closed oven for 1 hour more, or overnight if that is easier.

TO ASSEMBLE: Spoon the mousse into a pastry bag fitted with a medium star tip. For the tuiles, pipe about 1 tablespoon of mousse into each cone. For the meringue, pipe it on top of each meringue disk.

DO IT EARLY

The mousse must be made the day it is served. Pipe the mousse into the cookies about 2 hours before serving and keep at room temperature. The tuiles and the meringues can be made up to 1 day in advance and kept in airtight containers. (Be sure to separate the tuiles with waxed paper as they tend to stick together.) If the weather is very humid, it is best make both cookies the day you plan to serve them.

Black-and-White Bars

A sensational ending for a dinner party, cocktail party, or just about any event, these rich cheesecake-like bars always draw sighs of pure delight. The recipe comes from my early days as a caterer in Houston. I think they taste best cold, but no matter how they're served, they disappear quickly.

Makes about 2 dozen 1 1/2-inch-square bars

CHOCOLATE WAFER CRUST

- 1/2 cup (1 stick) unsalted butter, melted
- 18 chocolate sandwich cookies

CHEESECAKE FILLING

- 12 ounces dark chocolate (70 percent cacao), coarsely chopped
- 1/2 cup heavy whipping cream

2 (8-ounce) packages cream cheese, at room temperature

1 cup sugar

5 large eggs, separated

1 teaspoon vanilla extract

1/4 cup Kahlúa

Pinch of kosher salt

WHITE CHOCOLATE TOPPING

12 ounces white chocolate, coarsely chopped

1/2 cup heavy whipping cream

1/4 cup white crème de cacao (optional)

TO MAKE THE CHOCOLATE WAFER CRUST: Line the bottom and sides of a 9 by 13-inch baking pan with heavy-duty aluminum foil. Using a pastry brush, lightly coat the foil-lined pan with melted butter. In the work bowl of a food processor fitted with the metal blade, process the chocolate cookies into crumbs (or put the cookies between 2 layers of waxed paper and crush with a rolling pin). Combine the remaining melted butter (you should have at least 7 tablespoons) with the cookie crumbs. Press the crumb mixture evenly over the bottom of the foil-lined pan.

TO MAKE THE CHEESECAKE FILLING: Preheat the oven to 300°F. In a large metal bowl set over a pan filled with 2 inches of simmering water, melt the dark chocolate, stirring occasionally, until smooth. Remove from the heat and stir in the cream. Using an electric mixer fitted with the paddle attachment, beat the cream cheese and the 1 cup sugar on medium speed until smooth. Beat in the egg yolks, 1 at a time, scraping the sides of the bowl frequently with a rubber spatula. Add the chocolate-cream mixture, vanilla, Kahlúa, and salt and beat at medium speed for 2 minutes. Using an electric mixer fitted with the whisk attachment and a clean bowl, whip the egg whites on high speed until firm peaks form. Using a large rubber spatula, gently fold the egg whites into the chocolate-cream cheese mixture. Spoon the filling evenly over the chocolate crumb crust. Bake the bars for 30 minutes; the filling will rise and will be almost set. Turn off the heat and leave the bars in the oven for 30 more minutes. Transfer the baking pan to a wire rack to cool completely.

TO MAKE THE WHITE CHOCOLATE TOPPING: In a large metal bowl set over a pan filled with 2 inches of simmering water, melt the white chocolate, stirring until smooth. Remove from the heat and slowly stir in the cream and the crème de cacao, if you wish. Pour the mixture over the cooled cheesecake. Freeze overnight, making sure you keep the pan level or the white chocolate topping will set unevenly. When ready to serve, lift the foil out of the pan and set on a work surface. Using a long, sharp knife, cut the cake into 1 1/2-inch-square bars. Dip the knife in hot water and wipe it clean between cuts, or the bars lose their perfect black-and-white look.

DO IT EARLY

The uncut cheesecake can be made up to 3 weeks in advance, wrapped, and frozen until ready to cut and serve.

TIP Be sure to use real white chocolate made with cacao butter for the topping. Some products labeled "white chocolate" include other, cheaper, and often unhealthier fats for the cocoa butter. Read labels carefully to ensure you are getting the real thing. I like Green & Black's excellent organic white chocolate bar made with 30 percent cacao butter.

Big-City Cocktails

Friend and champion mixologist David Alan created two cocktails for our big-city cocktail party, both named for landmarks in Houston, the state's most populous city. Skyline takes its name from downtown Houston's Skyline District, famous as the third tallest skyline in the United States. Hermann Park, created in 1914, is a 445-acre urban playground that encompasses an outdoor theater, municipal golf course, Japanese garden, miniature train, and the Houston Zoo.

Each makes 1 drink

Skyline Cocktail

2 sprigs mint

1 teaspoon simple syrup (see Tips, page 191)

1/2 ounce (1 tablespoon) freshly squeezed lime juice

1 1/2 ounces (3 tablespoons) gin

1/2 ounce (1 tablespoon) orange curaçao or Paula's Texas Orange liqueur

1/2 ounce (1 tablespoon) crème de cassis

Ice cubes

Chill a cocktail glass. Using a small wooden spoon or mallet, lightly muddle or press together 1 mint sprig with the simple syrup in the bottom of a mixing glass or cocktail shaker. Add the lime juice, gin, curaçao, and crème de cassis. Shake vigorously with ice to chill; strain into the chilled glass. Garnish with the remaining mint sprig.

Hermann Park Cocktail

Dash of green Chartreuse

1 1/2 ounces (3 tablespoons) white rum

1 ounce (2 tablespoons) Lillet Blanc

3/4 ounce (1 1/2 tablespoons) freshly squeezed lemon juice (about 1 small lemon)

1/2 ounce (1 tablespoon) simple syrup (see Tips, page 191)

Ice cubes

Orange peel twists, for garnish

Chill a cocktail glass. Pour a splash of green Chartreuse into the chilled glass, swirl to coat the inside, and dump what Chartreuse remains. In a mixing glass or cocktail shaker, combine the white rum, Lillet, lemon juice, simple syrup, and ice to chill and shake well. Strain into the chilled, Chartreuse-rinsed cocktail glass. Garnish with an orange twist.

CHAPTER SIX

WEST TEXAS DINNER PARTY

EVERYTHING IS BIG in West Texas—the vistas, the appetites, the distances between towns. Well, maybe not everything. When it comes to population, West Texas—especially the wild Big Bend Country—lags behind the rest of the state. The standard joke about Marfa, the Presidio County seat, is that its population is half its 4,830-foot elevation, and that's no exaggeration.

Tourists can blow through nearby Jefferson Davis County without encountering a single stoplight. County seat Fort Davis (population 2,500) contains fewer residents than Carla Kennedy's Austin high school. Carla and her husband, Steve, moved out to Fort Davis from Austin to open their Old Schoolhouse Bed & Breakfast and to get away from the big city. "We lived in the same house for twenty-five years and didn't know our neighbors," Carla says. "Here your neighbors are your entertainment." And that pretty much sums up why parties in this part of the country are such a big deal. The word *neighbor*, by the way, takes on an expanded meaning in this area of expansive distances. When the local National Public Radio station, headquartered in Marfa, held its first fundraising party, "neighbors" showed up from towns located in three different counties within approximately a seventy-five-mile radius—Fort Davis, Alpine, and even Marathon. This year's event, dubbed the Hamburger Ball, lived up to its name with the erection of an open-fire hamburger pit and a burger bar stocked with all of the traditional fixings, as well as salads, side dishes, and an array of homey desserts, such as lemon squares, peach cobbler, and chocolate brownies.

You might expect such a remote area to be terribly homogeneous, but according to local accounts, that's not so. Artist and Marfa resident Jason Willaford says the area attracts a number of different types. There are artists lured by the legacy left by the late, internationally recognized sculptor Donald Judd, who bought a 45,000-acre ranch on the outskirts of Marfa and transformed it into a permanent contemporary art installation, now run by the Chinati Foundation. In addition, city refugees from all over the country have swarmed to the area in recent years, along with so-called Big Benders, outdoor enthusiasts drawn to the huge national park that extends from the Rio Grande River that delineates the U.S.-Mexican border northward toward Marathon, Marfa, and Alpine. Of course, there are the ranchers, some of the first Anglo-American settlers to populate this wild territory after the completion of the Southern Pacific Railroad in the late 1800s. This unusual mix of people leads to parties that can range from very high-end to very informal, says Jason's wife, Ree, owner of the local Galleri Urbane. And the food that's served often reflects the varied backgrounds of the locals. For example, her husband once flew in boxes of fresh oysters from his native Florida for a party they hosted.

Tammy King, a Fort Davis Realtor and UT graduate, says she's the only person in her extended family to move from her Castroville hometown near San Antonio. "I know what it is like to be without family," she says. At Christmas she hosts a party for one hundred guests and invites whomever she sees in the days leading up to it. She's been known to call up a few friends and invite them over for a martini—with less than an hour's notice! You won't see Gucci purses and country club chic around these parts. Tammy describes the typical West Texas wardrobe as "more function than fashion. What you wear is not important," Tammy says. "It's what you bring to the conversation." At Thursday night garden parties in Fort Davis, friends show up with an appetizer and a glass. Tammy says she delights in the freedom of being in a community far from her roots. What she and her neighbors have in common is an independent streak, a love of art and music, wide-open spaces, fresh air, and a need to be away from big cities, with no pressure to keep up with the Joneses.

"We come here to get rejuvenated. We want to bring friends out here, but we don't necessarily want them to move in."

El Rancho Chopped Salad with Cornbread Croutons and Creamy Poblano Dressing

My dear friend Paula Disbrowe, cookbook author, chef, and general partner in cooking, partying, and eating, created this recipe. She says, "Don't be fooled by the term salad. *This gigantic tumble of ingredients creates an incredibly satisfying meal, with big, bold flavors that will satisfy friends and ranch hands alike. Be sure to remove any wilted or bruised outer leaves from the head of romaine, so you only use the crisp, sweet inner leaves in your salad." This salad calls for jalapeño cornbread croutons (page 241). Bake them up first and let them cool while you prepare the rest of the recipe.*

Serves 8

CREAMY POBLANO DRESSING

- 1 large poblano chile
- 1/2 cup chopped fresh cilantro leaves and tender stems
- 2 tablespoons freshly squeezed lime juice (about 1 medium lime), or more
- 2 green onions, white and green parts, thinly sliced
- 1 clove garlic, coarsely chopped
- 1/2 cup mayonnaise
- 1/2 cup well-shaken buttermilk
- Kosher salt

SALAD

- 2 tablespoons olive oil
- 8 strips thick-sliced applewood-smoked bacon, cut into 1/2-inch pieces
- 8 ears sweet corn, unshucked
- Jalapeño Cornbread with Cheese, Corn, and Arugula (page 241)
- 2 medium heads romaine lettuce, trimmed and thinly sliced
- 2 large ripe avocados, peeled, seeded, and diced

- 1 cup thinly sliced celery hearts (and small leaves, if possible)
- 8 green onions, white and green parts, thinly sliced
- 1 pint yellow or orange currant or grape tomatoes, halved
- 1 cup finely grated Cotija cheese

TO MAKE THE DRESSING: Roast the poblano chile with a kitchen torch, over a gas burner, or under an oven broiler until evenly charred. Using an oven mitt, place the pepper in a bag, close the opening, and let the pepper steam for at least 10 minutes. Remove the pepper from the bag and peel off the skin, which should slide off easily. In the jar of a blender or the work bowl of a food processor fitted with the metal blade, puree the poblano, cilantro, lime juice, green onions, garlic, mayonnaise, and buttermilk until smooth. Season with salt and more lime juice. Refrigerate until ready to use.

continued

217

TO MAKE THE SALAD: Have a plate lined with paper towels ready. Heat a grill or grill pan medium-hot. Heat the olive oil in a skillet (preferably cast-iron) over medium heat. Add the bacon and cook until the fat is rendered and the pieces are browned but still somewhat chewy, 5 to 6 minutes. Use a slotted spoon to transfer the bacon to the prepared plate.

When the grill is hot, grill the corn, turning with tongs for even cooking, until the kernels are tender and just starting to release their milk, about 8 minutes. Remove the husks and trim the kernels from the cob with a paring knife; set aside.

Halve the cornbread. Set half aside. Cut the remaining half into 2 equal pieces and grill them until they are crisp and toasted on both sides, 6 to 7 minutes total; set aside to cool. When the cornbread has cooled, cut into 1½-inch cubes.

Cover the remaining cornbread with plastic wrap and freeze for making croutons the next time you make the salad.

Combine the lettuce, avocado, celery, green onions, tomatoes, bacon, and corn kernels in a large salad bowl. Drizzle the salad with dressing and toss well to evenly coat the ingredients. Garnish the tossed salad with the cornbread croutons and grated Cotija cheese.

DO IT EARLY

The dressing can be made up to 2 days in advance and refrigerated. The cornbread croutons can be made up to 3 days in advance and kept in an airtight container until ready to use. In fact, Paula points out that day-old cornbread makes the best croutons. The salad should be made the day it is to be served. Toss with the dressing just before serving.

Iceberg Wedge with Chunky Blue Cheese Dressing

Once looked down upon as so 1950s, the iceberg wedge with tangy blue cheese dressing has made a comeback, and with good reason. I'm always amazed at the enthusiastic response when I set out these salads—either on a party buffet table, or for a sit-down dinner. Guys especially love it.

Serves 8

BLUE CHEESE DRESSING

2 cups mayonnaise

1 1/2 cups sour cream

1 tablespoon grated white onion

1 teaspoon minced garlic (about 1 medium clove)

1/2 teaspoon celery salt

1 tablespoon freshly squeezed lemon juice (about 1/2 medium lemon)

1 teaspoon Worcestershire sauce

1/4 cup dry white wine

1/4 cup thinly sliced green onions, white and green parts

2 cups good-quality blue cheese, crumbled (about 8 ounces)

1/4 cup finely chopped Mexican or French tarragon leaves (optional)

SALAD

2 heads iceberg lettuce, cored and quartered

1 pint cherry tomatoes, halved

8 slices crisp cooked bacon, crumbled

In a large bowl, whisk together all the dressing ingredients until combined. When ready to serve, set each lettuce wedge on a plate, spoon on about 1/2 cup dressing, and top with a handful of cherry tomato halves and a sprinkling of crumbled bacon.

DO IT EARLY

The dressing and the bacon crumbles can be made up to 2 days in advance and refrigerated. Assemble the salad shortly before serving.

TIPS Mexican tarragon (also called mint marigold) is easily grown throughout Texas and is similar in taste to French tarragon, which literally can't take the Texas heat. If you don't find Mexican tarragon in the grocery store, look for the flowering plants at your local nursery. Little pots of these herbs also make charming party favors.

If you are so inclined, cut the calorie and fat load by using low-fat or nonfat mayonnaise and low-fat or nonfat sour cream instead of the full-fat stuff.

Mary Jane's Bean Pot Soup

Years ago, my dad owned a Honeybee Ham store, which he bought mostly as a tax write-off—until my sister Mary Jane got involved, that is. She took over the kitchen and started making, among other things, her fabulous bean soup for the store's little front-of-the-house café. Business took off. But my father, whose main business was swimming pool contracting, finally sold it. Until he did, for years we had ham for every occasion—parties, family reunions, holidays. After that, I didn't eat ham for a while.

My little sister died suddenly last year, and I recently found her handwritten bean soup recipe in an old notebook. Serve it with my iceberg wedges (page 219) and Sweet Potato Biscuits (page 239), and you've got an easy, fortifying meal fit for a group of friends or family on a cool winter evening. Don't forget that the beans need overnight soaking before cooking.

Serves 8 to 10

2 tablespoons olive oil

1 large yellow onion, diced

3 stalks celery, diced

3 tablespoons minced garlic (about 9 medium cloves)

2 jalapeño chiles, stemmed, seeded, and chopped

4 medium carrots, diced

10 cups water

1 (20-ounce) package 15-bean mix, soaked overnight according to package directions

1 meaty ham bone, or 1 (14-ounce) package smoked sausage, sliced

1 (10-ounce) can Rotel tomatoes (see Tip, page 138)

1 teaspoon ground ginger

2 teaspoons kosher salt

1 teaspoon freshly ground black pepper

Heat the olive oil in a large stockpot set over medium heat; sauté the onion, celery, garlic, jalapeños, and carrots for about 3 minutes. Add the 10 cups water, the soaked and drained beans, ham, tomatoes, ginger, salt, and pepper. Bring the mixture to a boil over high heat, decrease the heat, and simmer, uncovered, until the beans are tender, $2^{1}/_{2}$ to 3 hours.

DO IT EARLY

The soup can be made up to 4 days in advance and refrigerated. It can also be frozen for up to 2 months. To serve, reheat and add water or stock if it has become too thick.

TIP My dad sold ham bones for soups at his Honeybee store, so it is worth asking for bones at your local ham store.

Not Really Son-of-a-Bitch Stew

I'm betting it took a strong stomach to handle what cowboys called son-of-a-bitch stew, a concoction that included cow innards, even, and especially, the guts. "A son-of-a-bitch might not have any brains and no heart, but if he ain't got guts he ain't a son-of-a bitch" is the old cowboy saying. Known as son-of-a-gun stew in polite company, the dish was standard chuck wagon fare and said to include everything from a young calf but "the hair, horns, and holler." According to Come an' Get It: The Story of the Old Cowboy Cook *by the late western folklorist Ramon F. Adams, the real thing did not include any vegetables save perhaps a "skunk egg," cowboy slang for onion.*

I guess the only thing that my stew has in common with the cowboy favorite—and I know I am stretching things here—is my use of venison, just about as accessible to many of us Texans as the calves were to cowboys on the range. Everyone around here shoots deer, and many of my friends have freezers full of venison to prove it. If you don't, feel free to substitute beef stewing meat. You can make this stew up to 3 days in advance, or freeze it for up to 3 weeks.

8 to 10 servings

4 pounds venison stew meat, cut into bite-size cubes

2 (12-ounce) cans cola soda

3 cups all-purpose flour

1 tablespoon kosher salt

1 tablespoon freshly ground black pepper

1 tablespoon Cajun seasoning

2 tablespoons olive oil

1 cup chopped yellow onion

2 tablespoons minced garlic (about 6 medium cloves)

1/2 cup silver tequila

2 cups red wine

4 cups beef stock

1 (14.5-ounce) can diced tomatoes

2 large sweet potatoes, peeled and cubed

5 stalks celery, chopped

6 medium carrots, chopped

1/2 teaspoon ground cinnamon

Place the venison in a large bowl and cover with cola. Cover and refrigerate for at least 2 hours, but no more than 8. In a large bowl, combine the flour, salt, pepper, and Cajun seasoning. Drain the meat and roll the pieces in the seasoned flour to coat. Heat the oil in a large skillet set over medium heat. Brown the venison on all sides, working in batches so as not to crowd the meat. Transfer the browned meat to a large bowl and set aside. In the same skillet used to brown the meat, sauté the onion over medium heat until soft and translucent, about 3 minutes. Stir in the garlic and sauté another minute. Pour in the tequila, stirring up the browned bits that stick to the bottom of the pan. Stir in the venison, wine, stock, tomatoes with juice, potatoes, celery, carrots, and cinnamon. Bring the mixture to a simmer, cover, and cook until the vegetables are tender, about 45 minutes. Serve warm.

Beer-braised Short Ribs

I've yet to meet a man—Texan or otherwise—who can resist these meltingly tender short ribs. (Most women can't either, but they tend not to eat as many.) Serve them over a pile of creamy cornmeal mush and you'll have a party full of satisfied customers. At one gathering, I asked a group of guys how many ribs they thought they'd eat. The majority estimated that three would be plenty. They changed their tunes after taking a few bites and revised the number upward to four or five—and they kept their word. Short ribs come in varying sizes, so I figure about a pound per person, especially if my guest list includes a bunch of guys with big appetites.

Serves 8

SHORT RIBS

2 tablespoons olive oil

8 pounds beef short ribs

Kosher salt and freshly ground black pepper

6 slices applewood-smoked bacon

3 cups coarsely chopped yellow onion

10 cloves crushed garlic

3 (12-ounce) bottles Shiner Bock or other dark beer

1/4 cup reduced-sodium soy sauce

2 tablespoons balsamic vinegar

4 tablespoons Worcestershire sauce

12 medium carrots, coarsely chopped

1 cup tawny port

CORNMEAL MUSH

6 cups whole milk, or more

2 cups fine-grained cornmeal or polenta

1/2 cup (1 stick) unsalted butter

1 1/2 teaspoons kosher salt

1 cup freshly grated Parmesan cheese (about 4 ounces)

Preheat the oven to 325°F. Set a large Dutch oven over medium-high heat; add the olive oil. While the pot is heating, season the short ribs on all sides with salt and pepper. Brown the short ribs over medium-high heat in batches with ample room between them so they brown, not steam (if they start to burn, decrease the heat a little), 2 to 3 minutes per side. Remove from the pot and reserve on a plate.

In the same pot used to brown the ribs, sauté the bacon and onion over medium heat until the onion is soft, about 3 minutes; add the garlic and sauté 1 minute more. Stir in the beer, soy sauce, vinegar, and Worcestershire. Return the browned ribs to the pot, cover, and cook in the oven for 3 hours. Remove the pot from the oven and stir in the carrots and port. Cook until the meat is tender and just about falling off the bone, another 1 1/2 to 2 hours, for a total cooking time of 4 1/2 to 5 hours. After 4 hours of braising, stick a knife in the thickest rib; if the meat is still firm, continue cooking. Remove the pot from the oven; pour the liquid into a large glass measuring cup and let it sit until the fat rises to the top, about 15 minutes. Pour off the fat and return the liquid to the cooking pot.

TO MAKE THE CORNMEAL MUSH: Heat the milk until steaming in a large, heavy saucepan set over medium heat. Slowly pour in the polenta, whisking constantly. Turn the heat to low and continue whisking for 10 to 15 minutes until the mixture thickens. If it seems hard to whisk, thin with an additional $1/4$ cup of milk. The cornmeal should be on the loose side. Whisk in the butter, salt, and Parmesan. Serve immediately topped with short ribs.

DO IT EARLY

The short ribs can be made a day ahead, refrigerated, and reheated just before serving. The cornmeal can be made an hour or so before serving. Reheat over medium heat; add milk in $1/4$-cup increments until the mixture is creamy and smooth.

Blue Javalina Grilled Lamb with Quinoa Pilaf

I met chef Kevin Stewart and his partner, Richard Cordray, at my friend Loncito Cartwright's South Texas ranch. Kevin prepared this dish using Loncito's grass-fed lamb and I asked for the recipe, named after Kevin and Richard's former Marfa restaurant, Blue Javalina. Wild packs of javalinas—compact, coarse-haired, piglike animals with short snouts—roam the high plains of West Texas. Javalinas do not come in blue, nor do they make for great eating. Loncito's lamb is a different story. His grass-fed lamb has a mild taste that appeals to even the most reluctant lamb eater. It is available at select farmers' markets and specialty foods stores throughout Texas.

Serves about 12

LAMB

1 (12-ounce) bottle pomegranate molasses

1/3 cup extra-virgin olive oil

1/4 cup finely chopped fresh ginger root (about a 3-inch piece)

3 or 4 cloves garlic, crushed

3 or 4 whole cinnamon sticks

1 tablespoon freshly ground black pepper

3 to 4 pounds lamb stew meat (leg), cut in strips for grilling

1 tablespoon kosher salt, for grilling

SALSA

6 medium-large fresh ripe peaches, diced (peel only if the skins are tough)

1/2 large purple onion, finely chopped

1/4 cup firmly packed, coarsely chopped fresh cilantro, plus a few sprigs to garnish the finished dish

2 jalapeño chiles, stemmed, seeded, and finely chopped

2 tablespoons freshly squeezed Key lime juice (about 2 Key limes)

1/2 teaspoon kosher salt

1/4 teaspoon freshly ground black pepper

PILAF

6 cups water

1 (12-ounce) box quinoa (preferably Ancient Harvest), pan-toasted

Generous pinch of kosher salt

2 1/2 cups whole pecans (preferably Texas Hill Country nuts)

TO MAKE THE MARINADE: In a large bowl, combine the molasses, olive oil, ginger, garlic, cinnamon sticks, and 1 tablespoon pepper in a bowl. Stir in the lamb to coat; cover and refrigerate for at least 6 hours or overnight.

TO MAKE THE SALSA: In a large bowl, combine the peaches, onion, cilantro, jalapeños, Key lime juice, 1/2 teaspoon salt, and 1/4 teaspoon pepper and let the mixture stand at room temperature for at least 1 hour.

TO MAKE THE PILAF: In a saucepan, bring the 6 cups water to a rapid boil over high heat; add the quinoa and salt and decrease the heat to medium-low. Cover and cook until fluffy and

continued

225

the water has evaporated, about 20 minutes. Set aside. To toast the pecans, heat a skillet over medium-high heat, add the pecans, and keep them moving until they begin to darken slightly and become fragrant, about 6 minutes. Transfer to a bowl to cool. In the work bowl of a food processor fitted with the metal blade, pulse the nuts 6 to 8 times to chop coarsely.

TO GRILL THE LAMB: Prepare an outdoor grill. Remove the lamb from the marinade, pat dry with paper towels (do not skip this step), and season with 1 tablespoon salt. Pour the remaining marinade into a saucepan, bring it to a boil over medium-high heat, and reduce by at least half; set aside. Grill the lamb over medium-high heat to desired doneness. (I like it medium-rare.) Cut the lamb into bite-size pieces.

TO ASSEMBLE THE DISH: In a very large ceramic or glass bowl, combine the salsa (with juices),

quinoa, and toasted pecans. Spoon the lamb over the pilaf or stir it in, drizzle with the marinade reduction, and garnish with cilantro sprigs. Serve warm or at room temperature.

DO IT EARLY

Quinoa pilaf can be made up to 1 day in advance, covered, and refrigerated. The salsa is best made the day it is served. Grill the lamb the day you plan to serve it and add it to the warmed pilaf.

TIP Kevin advises using dried apricots if fresh peaches are not in season. Reconstitute by soaking the apricot halves in hot water for about 1 hour. Quarter or coarsely chop them and add to the salad. You can find pomegranate molasses at Middle Eastern or specialty markets.

Chicken-fried Steak

Tom Perini started as a chuck wagon cook. Ten years later, in 1983, he opened The Perini Ranch Steakhouse on the family spread in Buffalo Gap, not too far from Abilene. After twenty-five years, his business is still going strong.

Tom has cooked all over the country, including the White House, and he still takes his 1850s-vintage chuck wagon to rodeos and other events throughout Texas. Chicken-fried steak is one of my all-time favorites, and I knew exactly where to go for a genuine rendition. Tom gave me permission to adapt this recipe from his book Texas Cowboy Cooking. He says, "Cream gravy is a must with chicken-fried steak." No argument there, so I've included his gravy recipe too.

Serves 8

3 pounds rib-eye or strip steak, cut about
  $^1/_2$-inch thick

$^3/_4$ cup whole milk

1 large egg, beaten

2 teaspoons seasoning salt

$^1/_2$ teaspoon ground white pepper

Flour

Vegetable oil, for frying

CREAM GRAVY

3 heaping tablespoons all-purpose flour

2 cups (about) cold whole milk

Salt and freshly ground black pepper

TO MAKE THE CHICKEN-FRIED STEAK: Flatten the beef out evenly with a mallet. Cut the meat into 8 pieces. In a wide bowl, stir together the milk, egg, seasoning salt, and pepper to make an egg dip. Dip the steaks in the egg dip, then dredge them in the flour; repeat the process. Cover the bottom of a large, heavy-bottomed skillet with about $^1/_2$ inch of oil and heat over medium to medium-high heat. When the oil spatters after you add a few drops of water, put in your steaks. Flip the steaks when the juices begin to surface and the bottom is brown and cook until done, about 10 minutes total.

TO MAKE THE CREAM GRAVY: After frying the steak, let the drippings sit until the excess browned bits settle to the bottom of the skillet. Pour off most of the fat, leaving about $^1/_4$ cup and the browned bits. Add the 3 tablespoons flour, stirring until well mixed. Place the skillet over medium heat and slowly add the cold milk, stirring constantly. Cook until the gravy boils and thickens, about 5 minutes. You may need more or less milk for your desired consistency. Season with salt and pepper. Serve the steaks with the gravy.

DO IT EARLY

Don't. Any cowboy will tell you a chicken-fried steak needs to be fried up and eaten straight off the griddle.

TIP Some like their steaks on the rare side, but apparently no cowboy wanted to see blood on his steak. The late Dallas-born cowboy expert Ramon F. Adams recorded this old cowboy saying, a response to a serving of rare beef: "I've seen cows get well that was hurt worse than that."

Stuffed Bandera Quail
with Pepper Glaze

Stuffed quail sizzling on the grill is a common sight at many a West Texas barbecue. A lot of my friends use a shotgun to bag their quail, but I snag mine on the Internet from The Diamond H Ranch in Bandera, Texas (www.texasgourmetquail.com), where they raise the birds and process them, too. They come vacuum-packed and ready for cooking, with the back, breast, and thigh bones removed. All I have to do is stuff them with a spicy chile-cheese mixture, wrap them up with a piece of bacon, and then put 'em on the grill. I finish them off with a jalapeño jelly glaze just before serving. In all, a mighty nice dinner treat to share with friends.

Serves 8

Kosher salt and freshly ground black pepper

8 semi-boneless quail (back, breast, and thigh bones removed)

2 (8-ounce) packages cream cheese, each cut crosswise into four equal slices

4 fresh jalapeño chiles, stemmed, seeded, and sliced lengthwise into strips

2 to 4 sweet-hot pickled jalapeños, or use homemade (see page 254)

8 strips thick-cut applewood-smoked bacon

2 cups jalapeño pepper jelly

Preheat an outdoor grill. Rub salt and pepper all over the quail to season. Lay the quail on baking sheets, skin side down. Set a slice of cream cheese in the center of each bird and top with 2 strips of fresh jalapeño and 1 or 2 slices of sweet-hot pickled jalapeños. (If you prefer, you can do all fresh chiles—4 strips per bird, or all pickled chiles—3 or 4 slices per bird.) Fold the quail with the cheese and chiles inside and wrap a piece of bacon around each bird to secure. Grill the quail on both sides over medium heat until cooked through, about 30 minutes total, turning the birds with tongs halfway through cooking. A few minutes before the quail are done, heat the jelly in a small saucepan set over medium heat until it liquefies. Set the cooked quail on a serving platter and brush generously with the jelly glaze. Serve the quail immediately.

DO IT EARLY

The quail can be stuffed and wrapped with bacon, securely wrapped in plastic wrap, and refrigerated up to 1 day in advance. Grill just before serving. The chilled quail may need a little extra grilling time.

Green Tomato Macaroni and Cheese

Cowboy nicknames for their cattle-drive cooks—biscuit shooter, dough puncher, and dough belly— suggest how important sourdough biscuits were to hungry, range-riding wranglers. No self-respecting chuck wagon cook traveled without a dough keg for his prized sourdough starter, the fermented yeast needed to make sourdough biscuits.

I covered this macaroni and cheese with a generous blanket of buttered sourdough breadcrumbs in honor of chuck wagon cooks of the past. The rest has little to do with old-time chuck wagon cooking, but I don't know a modern cowboy or anyone else who would turn down a bubbling pan of freshly baked mac and cheese.

Serves 8

1 pound cavatappi (a curly macaroni) or your choice of pasta

$3/4$ cup ($1^1/2$ sticks) unsalted butter

6 tablespoons all-purpose flour

4 cups hot whole milk

2 teaspoons Tabasco sauce

1 tablespoon dry mustard

1 teaspoon kosher salt

$1/2$ teaspoon ground white pepper

2 cups shredded chipotle Cheddar cheese (preferably Cabot), about 8 ounces

3 cups shredded extra-sharp Cheddar cheese (about 12 ounces)

3 cups shredded Monterey Jack cheese (about 12 ounces)

10 green tomatoes (4 to 5 pounds), cored and thinly sliced

2 cups sourdough breadcrumbs (see Tip)

Preheat the oven to 350°F. Grease a 9 by 13-inch pan or casserole dish of similar capacity with cooking spray.

In a large pot, cook the pasta in plenty of hot water according to package directions, but remove it a few minutes earlier than suggested so it doesn't turn mushy when baked later. Drain the cooked pasta in a colander and hold under cold running water to stop it from cooking further. Set aside.

In a large saucepan set over medium heat, melt $1/2$ cup of the butter. Add the flour, stirring constantly until the mixture is smooth and golden brown, about 5 minutes. Slowly pour in the milk, whisking constantly until thick, about 2 minutes. Stir in the Tabasco, dry mustard, salt, and white pepper. Stir in the cheeses and cook until they are completely melted. Spoon half the cooked pasta into the prepared pan. Cover with half the cheese sauce. Arrange a single layer of sliced tomatoes on top. Spoon the remainder of the pasta on top; pour on the remainder of the cheese sauce. Top with a second layer of sliced tomatoes.

In a large skillet set over medium heat, melt the remaining $1/4$ cup butter. Stir in the breadcrumbs

continued

231

and cook until the crumbs are evenly coated with butter. Spoon the crumbs evenly over the top of the tomatoes. Bake for 30 minutes, or until the crumbs have turned golden and the casserole is bubbling. Serve hot.

DO IT EARLY

The casserole can be assembled a day in advance, covered, and refrigerated. Make the breadcrumbs, too, but don't add them to the casserole until ready to bake and serve. Bake just before serving. Add extra baking time if the casserole goes from refrigerator to oven.

TIP It's easy to make homemade breadcrumbs: toast 3 or 4 slices of sourdough bread until golden brown. Let the toast cool for a few minutes. Tear the toast into small pieces and process into crumbs in a food processor or blender.

232

Party Maestro Don Strange

Parties are serious business for Don Strange. From intimate dinners to events for up to ten thousand guests, big-time caterer Don Strange has masterminded parties all over Texas and all the way to the White House, New York's Rockefeller Center, and Hollywood. Along the way, Don has pioneered entertaining ideas that have become a permanent part of the party landscape. His signature style: putting party food preparation front and center, providing delicious sustenance and entertainment value all at once.

His aha! moment happened more than thirty years ago, when he witnessed an intriguing new restaurant trend: dramatic tableside preparations of caesar salad and steak Diane. "Nobody's doing that for parties," Don recalls saying. "Maybe we ought to start with that." Then, during a meeting with a client in Laredo to plan a celebration for a local bank opening, someone suggested he serve fajitas, a local specialty. Never heard of it, Don responded, but he stopped to sample the dish on his way out of town. Soon afterward, grilled-to-order beef fajitas folded into warm tacos and served on the spot became a Don Strange party sensation and led to the widespread popularity of the dish.

Since then Strange and his company have prepared just about everything imaginable smack in the middle of the festivities. They've set up oyster sauté stations, fired up griddles for cooking hand-formed gorditas (corn tortilla cakes), and created a dramatic spectacle by roasting sides of beef over open mesquite fires. Food that pops, sizzles, and browns in front of guests' eyes is just one component of a Don Strange production. Don recognized early on the powerful allure of the "tremendous smoking aroma" that greets guests well before they've entered the party premises.

"You start thirty minutes before guests come and they are going to smell it as soon as they get out of their cars," Don says. Home party givers, take note.

Don's company routinely stages parties at Texas's biggest ranches, including the iconic King Ranch in the Rio Grande valley and ranches throughout the Lone Star State. He made a splash when he catered the hundredth anniversary party at the Y.O. Ranch, a forty-thousand-acre spread known for its longhorns, as well as for its wild and native game hunting. Hundreds of guests poured in from all over the world, invited by the late Charles Schreiner III, grandson of the ranch founder. The 1980 party was such as success that a club formed to make it an annual event. The Y.O. Social Club has staged the event ever since. About one thousand revelers attend for an evening filled with food, drink, and musical entertainment with a little social responsibility thrown in—each year organizers donate a portion of the proceeds to a worthy nonprofit cause.

After more than forty years' experience on the party circuit, Don's fiesta philosophy is grounded in simplicity and common sense. He always dispenses the same advice to would-be hosts and hostesses: Plan your parties to emphasize your personality and the personality of your home, no matter how many guests you're inviting. "I always say if you have 150 people, do it the same as you would for 12 to 15 of your closest friends."

Achiote-seared Chickpeas

Lou Lambert, another one of my chef friends who grew up on a ranch, now owns two Texas restaurants—Lamberts Downtown Barbecue in Austin, and Lambert's steak house in Fort Worth. Lou got the idea for his seared chickpeas when he was a kid growing up on the family ranch near Odessa. "We had a camp cook who would make hominy loaded with chili powder and garlic. I adapted his dish with chickpeas. I originally put this on the menu at the first Lambert's on South Congress, and it has been a mainstay at all the restaurants since." I've been coveting this recipe ever since I first tasted it at Lou's first restaurant. Now that I have it, I know it will become a mainstay for me, too, especially when I have some entertaining to do.

Serves 8 as a side dish or appetizer

ACHIOTE OIL

1 cup olive oil

2 tablespoons achiote paste

ROASTED TOMATOES

3 Roma tomatoes, halved lengthwise

1 tablespoon olive oil

Kosher salt

CHICKPEAS

2 tablespooons olive oil

1 medium red onion, cut into 1-inch dice

2 cloves garlic, coarsely chopped

3 cups cooked chickpeas

2 tablespoons dark chili powder

1/2 teaspoon kosher salt

1/4 teaspoon freshly ground black pepper

2 tablespoons freshly squeezed lemon juice
(about 1 medium lemon)

3 ounces baby arugula

2 teaspoons fresh oregano, stemmed and
coarsely chopped

2 teaspoons fresh Italian parsley, coarsely
chopped

4 ounces goat cheese

Toasted pita bread, brushed with olive oil and
sprinkled with cumin, for serving

TO MAKE THE ACHIOTE OIL: In the jar of a blender, process the oil and achiote paste until smooth. Pour into a small saucepan and heat over medium heat to about 200°F on a candy thermometer, about 2 minutes. Remove from the heat and let steep for at least 30 minutes. Strain the infused oil through a fine strainer, reserving the oil and discarding the achiote.

TO MAKE THE ROASTED TOMATOES: Preheat the oven to 225°F. Lay the tomatoes, cut side up, on a baking pan. Sprinkle the cut sides of the tomatoes with the 1 tablespoon olive oil and salt. Roast until the tomatoes are lightly browned and most of the liquid has evaporated, about 2 hours. Coarsely chop and set aside.

TO MAKE THE CHICKPEAS: In a skillet, heat the 2 tablespoons of olive oil over medium-low heat. Add the onion and cook, stirring occasionally, until caramelized, about 15 to 20 minutes. Set aside. Preheat a large skillet over medium-high heat and add the 1 cup achiote oil. Drop the garlic into the hot oil, swirling the pan. As soon as the garlic browns lightly, which will happen quickly, add the chickpeas and increase the heat to high. Let the chickpeas sear in the hot pan for about 1 minute before stirring, then continue to cook until the peas begin to sizzle and pop. Stir in the chili powder, ¹/₂ teaspoon salt, and black pepper. Add the caramelized onion and the 3 chopped roasted tomatoes and continue to cook until heated through, about 2 minutes. Add the lemon juice and continue to cook for another minute. Remove the pan from the heat and fold in the arugula, oregano, parsley, and half the goat cheese. Transfer the chickpeas to a serving platter and crumble the remaining goat cheese over the top. Serve with the toasted pita bread.

DO IT EARLY

Make the achiote oil and the roasted tomatoes up to 1 week in advance and refrigerate. The chickpeas and toasted pita bread should be made just before serving.

TIP Achiote paste is made from the achiote seed, which comes from the annatto tree. Dark red in color, it's commonly used in Indian, Spanish, and Latin American dishes. Look for it in the Mexican food aisle at most grocery stores.

Butter Beans and Mixed Greens

For Southerners like me, there's not a better meal on the planet than cornbread, beans, and greens cooked with lots of bacon. I know a lot of good old ranch cooks who feel the same. There wasn't much green to eat for cowboys on the range, but beans cooked with salt pork were common. So common, in fact, that cowboy nicknames for beans were many: Mexican strawberries, prairie strawberries, and whistle berries. But the funniest of all, recorded in Ramon F. Adams's book Come an' Get It, *was "deceitful beans 'cause they talk behind yore back."*

Serves 8 to 10

BEANS

- 1 (1-pound) package dried butter beans or large lima beans
- 8 strips thick-sliced applewood-smoked bacon, cut into bite-size pieces
- 1 large yellow onion, coarsely chopped
- 2 stalks celery, chopped
- 6 cloves garlic, minced
- 8 cups chicken stock
- 2 teaspoons kosher salt
- 1/2 teaspoon freshly ground black pepper
- 2 shakes Tabasco sauce
- 1 tablespoon cider vinegar
- 1 large red bell pepper, stemmed, seeded, and coarsely chopped

MIXED GREENS

- 8 slices thick-sliced applewood-smoked bacon, cut into bite-size pieces
- 1/2 large red onion, chopped
- 1 tablespoon plus 2 teaspoons minced garlic (about 5 cloves)
- 2 (12-ounce) packages cut and cleaned greens, such as mustard, collard, or baby spinach
- 1 tablespoon balsamic vinegar
- 1 teaspoon kosher salt
- Jalapeño Cornbread with Cheese, Corn, and Arugula (page 241), for accompaniment

TO MAKE THE BEANS: Rinse the beans and pick through to get rid of any foreign matter. In a large stockpot, cover the beans with water, set the pot over high heat, and bring to a boil. Remove the pot from the heat and let the beans sit for 1 hour to soften. Drain the beans in a colander. Set the stockpot over medium heat and sauté the bacon, onion, celery, and garlic over medium heat, about 3 minutes. Add the chicken stock, drained beans, salt, pepper, Tabasco, and cider vinegar and bring to a boil over high heat. Decrease the heat to medium-low and simmer the beans uncovered until tender, about 1 1/2 hours. For added color, stir in the bell pepper just a few minutes before the beans are done. Serve hot with greens and cornbread.

TO MAKE THE GREENS: In a large stockpot set over medium heat, sauté the bacon, onion, and garlic until the bacon is cooked through, about 15 minutes. Stir in the greens, cover, and cook until the greens are wilted, about 5 to 7 minutes. Stir in the balsamic vinegar and salt. Serve immediately with beans and cornbread.

Sweet Potato Biscuits

Cooked sweet potato adds body and flavor to these biscuits, but they are more savory than sweet—just right for buttering and sopping up gravy of any kind. Try them with Not Really Son-of-a-Bitch Stew (page 221), Tom Perini's Chicken-fried Steak (page 227), or Beer-braised Short Ribs (page 222).

Makes about 10 large biscuits

3 cups all-purpose flour

1 tablespoon baking powder

1 teaspoon salt

1 tablespoon sugar

$^1/_2$ cup (1 stick) chilled unsalted butter, cut into 1-inch pieces

$1^1/_4$ cups mashed cooked sweet potatoes (about 1 medium sweet potato)

$^1/_4$ cup buttermilk

$^1/_4$ cup heavy whipping cream

Butter, at room temperature. for accompaniment

Preheat the oven 400°F. Grease a baking sheet with butter or cooking spray. In a large bowl, mix the flour, baking powder, salt, and sugar until combined. Add the chilled butter and work with your hands or a pastry cutter until the mixture is crumbly with visible bits of butter about the size of baby peas. Lightly work in the sweet potato; add the buttermilk and cream, mixing just until the dough can be formed into a ball. On a floured work surface, lightly press the dough into a disk about $1^1/_4$ inches thick. Using a 3-inch biscuit cutter dipped in flour, cut out biscuits as close together as possible. Mold the scraps into a small disk of the same thickness and cut out the rest. Place on the prepared baking sheet and bake until the biscuits are light golden brown, 12 to 15 minutes. Serve hot with butter.

Bud's Mashed Potato–Creamed Corn Casserole

This casserole is a lot like the man who invented it—larger than life, over the top, and guaranteed to make you happy. Bud's the name behind Royers Round Top Café, a "contemporary comfort food" oasis in, no surprise—Round Top, a $1^1/_2$-hour drive from Austin—that serves up heaping portions and Bud's famous pies. Bud's casserole is a side dish that's hearty enough to qualify as a main course, and a great option if you have vegetarian guests coming for dinner.

Makes 8 to 10

5 pounds russet potatoes, peeled and quartered (about 15 medium potatoes)

$^1/_2$ cup (1 stick) unsalted butter, melted

$^1/_2$ cup sour cream

$^1/_2$ ($^1/_2$-ounce) package ranch dressing mix

1 (1-pound) bag frozen corn

$^1/_2$ cup (1 stick) unsalted butter

1 (16-ounce) can creamed corn

1 (8-ounce) package cream cheese, cut into 1-inch chunks

$^1/_2$ teaspoon kosher salt

$^1/_4$ teaspoon freshly ground black pepper

$^1/_2$ cup diced red onion

1 cup crumbled blue cheese (about 4 ounces)

Preheat the oven to 350°F. Grease a large, deep casserole with butter or cooking spray.

Place the potatoes in a large stockpot, cover with water, and bring to a boil over high heat. Immediately decrease the heat to medium and cook until the potatoes are fork-tender (literally when you stick a fork in a spud, it slides out with ease), about 20 minutes; drain. Return the warm potatoes to the pot and mash with the $^1/_2$ cup melted butter, sour cream, and ranch mix, leaving just a few chunks of potato. Set aside.

In a saucepan set over medium heat, stir together the corn kernels and the remaining $^1/_2$ cup butter until the corn is heated through. Stir in the creamed corn, cream cheese, salt, and pepper and cook until the cream cheese has melted and combined with the rest of the ingredients.

Stir the creamed corn mixture into the potato mixture and turn it out into the prepared casserole. Bake until hot, about 30 minutes. Just before serving, sprinkle the onion and blue cheese over the top of the casserole. Serve immediately.

DO IT EARLY

The casserole can be assembled up to 1 day in advance, covered, and refrigerated. Bake just before serving.

Jalapeño Cornbread with Cheese, Corn, and Arugula

Bob and Nancy Green live on the land Bob's pioneer father settled in 1881 and Bob has been a rancher for most of his life. Now in her eighties, Nancy continues to indulge her lifelong passion for entertaining. She favors groups up to sixteen, because she can seat them all "gracefully" at her table without having to round up chairs from other parts of the house. Nancy keeps her guests happy with a good supply of cornbread, baked in a Texas-shaped skillet.

Serves 8 to 10

6 large eggs

1/2 cup honey

3 cups whole milk

3/4 cup canola oil

3 cups medium-grind cornmeal

1 1/2 cups all-purpose flour

1 1/2 tablespoons baking powder

1 1/2 teaspoons kosher salt

2 tablespoons unsalted butter

3 cups chopped onions

1/2 cup chopped jalapeño chiles
    (about 3 stemmed and seeded chiles)

3 cups fresh corn kernels (about 4 ears)

1 1/2 cups diced red bell peppers

1 (5-ounce) package baby arugula

3 cups shredded Monterey Jack cheese
    (about 12 ounces)

Preheat the oven to 350°F. Grease a 14-inch cast-iron skillet. Heat it in the oven while making the cornbread batter. In a large bowl, whisk together the eggs, honey, milk, and oil. In a bowl, mix the cornmeal, flour, baking powder, and salt until combined. Stir the flour mixture into the egg mixture until combined.

In a large skillet set on medium heat, melt the butter and sauté the onion, jalapeño, corn, and red pepper, about 3 minutes. Stir in the arugula, and cook for 1 minute more, until the greens are wilted. Fold the sautéed vegetables and cheese into the cornbread mixture.

Use a kitchen mitt to remove the heated skillet from the oven. Spoon the batter into the prepared skillet and return it to the oven. Bake until the cornbread is golden around the edges and a toothpick inserted in the middle comes out clean, 35 to 40 minutes. Serve straight from the skillet hot or at room temperature.

DO IT EARLY

You can bake the cornbread in the skillet early in the day and reheat in a 300°F oven before serving. Make croutons a day ahead.

VARIATION

If you are making cornbread croutons for chopped salad (page 217), skip the vegetables and cheese, and bake in a greased 13 by 18-inch pan until golden around the edges and a toothpick inserted comes out clean, about 30 minutes. Let cool and cut into croutons.

Giant Chocolate Cake with Cowboy Coffee Frosting

I named this dense chocolate cake with a mountain of coffee-flavored icing for the 1956 movie Giant. *which put the small West Texas town of Marfa on the map. The stars were Elizabeth Taylor, Rock Hudson, and James Dean in his last movie role before he died in a car accident at age twenty-four. Hotel Paisano, where the cast stayed during the filming, still pays homage to the production with a* Giant *memorabilia room and Jett's Grill, named after Dean's character, oilman Jett Rink.*

Serves 12 to 14

CAKE

- 1 cup (2 sticks) unsalted butter, at room temperature
- $1/2$ pound good-quality bittersweet chocolate, coarsely chopped
- 4 cups granulated sugar
- 1 tablespoon vanilla extract
- 1 tablespoon baking soda
- 1 cup sour cream
- 4 large eggs
- 4 cups all-purpose flour
- 2 cups hot brewed coffee

FROSTING

- 8 tablespoons instant espresso coffee powder
- $1/3$ cup hot brewed coffee
- 2 pounds (8 sticks) unsalted butter, at room temperature
- 4 cups powdered sugar
- 2 teaspoons vanilla bean paste

Fresh strawberries, for garnish (optional)

TO MAKE THE CAKE: Preheat the oven to 350°F. Place 1 oven rack in the top third of the oven and the second in the bottom third. Line three 9-inch round cake pans with parchment paper rounds, grease with butter or cooking spray, dust the pans with flour, and knock out the excess.

Melt the 1 cup butter and chocolate in a metal bowl set over a saucepan with 2 inches of lightly simmering water. Stir constantly until the chocolate is completely melted. Whisk in the granulated sugar and vanilla extract. In a small bowl, stir the baking soda into the sour cream. Whisk the sour cream-soda mixture into the melted butter and chocolate; whisk in the eggs, 1 at a time, then whisk in the flour until thoroughly combined. Add the 2 cups hot coffee and whisk until smooth.

Spoon the batter evenly into the prepared cake pans. (Each cake pan will have about 3 cups of batter.) Set 2 filled pans on 1 oven rack and the remaining pan on the other. Arrange the cake layers on the racks so that no layer is directly over another. Bake until the cake is firm to the touch and a toothpick inserted in the middle comes out clean, 35 to 40 minutes. Monitor the layers carefully for doneness; each one may be done at a different time. Cool the layers in their pans about 10 minutes; unmold onto wire racks to cool completely.

continued

TO MAKE THE FROSTING: Dissolve the espresso powder in the ¹/₃ cup hot brewed coffee. Set aside to cool. Using an electric mixer fitted with the paddle attachment, beat the 2 pounds butter and powdered sugar on medium-high until light and fluffy, about 3 minutes. Add the cooled espresso and vanilla paste and beat on medium-high speed until even lighter and fluffier than before, an additional 4 to 5 minutes.

TO ASSEMBLE THE CAKE: Stack 1 cake layer on a serving plate and spread the top with about 1 cup of the frosting. Repeat with the second cake layer and another 1 cup frosting. Stack the final cake layer on top of the first 2 and generously cover the cake's top and sides with the remainder of the frosting. Garnish with fresh strawberries, if desired.

DO IT EARLY

The cake can be made up to 1 day in advance, frosted, and refrigerated. Take the cake out of the refrigerator about 3 hours before serving. Serve at room temperature.

Sohnne's Mama's Double-Decker Blackberry Cobbler

This recipe is from Laura Emma, the mother of my friend Sohnne Hill. Sohnne says it was one of her mother's favorites. After testing it, I know why. Packed with an abundance of fruit, hiding a tender layer of crust in its midst, and topped with a crisp, golden brown top, it is the ultimate comfort dessert.

8 to 10 servings

CRUST

1 cup plus 1 tablespoon sugar

6 cups all-purpose flour

$^1/_4$ teaspoon kosher salt

$1^1/_4$ cups ($2^1/_2$ sticks) chilled unsalted butter

1 cup shortening (preferably made from nonhydrogenated fat)

$1^1/_4$ cups (about) cold water

FILLING

4 (10-ounce) packages frozen blackberries, or 12 cups fresh blackberries

2 cups sugar

$^1/_3$ cup all-purpose flour

$^1/_2$ cup cold water

2 tablespoons vanilla extract

Vanilla ice cream, for accompaniment

TO MAKE THE CRUST: Grease an 8-inch square baking pan with butter or cooking spray. In a large bowl, stir together the 1 cup sugar, the 6 cups flour, and salt. Cut 1 cup of the butter into $^1/_2$-inch cubes. Add the butter cubes and shortening to the flour mixture and work with your hands until the mixture looks crumbly, with bits of dough the size of baby peas. (The butter and shortening should be evenly distributed.) Add the cold water, $^1/_4$ cup at a time, lightly mixing it in with your hands after each addition. After adding 1 cup of the water, pinch a small bit of dough to see if it holds together. If it is still too dry, add water, 1 tablespoon at a time, until it holds together. Divide the dough in half, then divide 1 of the halves in half again. Gently fashion each hunk of dough into a ball (you'll have 3), cover tightly with plastic wrap, and refrigerate for at least 30 minutes.

TO MAKE THE BERRY FILLING: Combine the berries and sugar in a large saucepan set over medium heat. Heat, stirring occasionally, until the sugar is dissolved and the berries just begin to simmer, about 10 minutes, or a little less if you are using fresh berries. In a small bowl, whisk together the $^1/_3$ cup flour and $^1/_2$ cup cold water, making sure there are no lumps. Add the flour-water mixture to the berries and cook over medium heat until the liquid begins to simmer and the mixture has thickened slightly, about 4 minutes. Stir in the vanilla extract. Remove from the heat.

TO ASSEMBLE THE COBBLER: Preheat the oven to 400°F. Unwrap the largest dough ball and set it on a lightly floured work surface. Roll out into a $^1/_8$-inch-thick square large enough to cover the bottom and sides of the prepared baking pan with about 2 inches to spare on all sides.

continued

To keep the dough from sticking, gently lift it and rotate it periodically as you roll it out, adding more flour underneath if needed. Drape the dough over the bottom of the prepared pan so that it comes up the sides and hangs over the pan's edges evenly. Add half of the berry mixture. Roll out the remaining 2 balls of dough to ⅛ inch thick, making sure that each is about an 8-inch square. Cut the dough into strips about 1½ inches wide. Place a line of parallel strips over the berries in the pan. The strips do not need to touch, but place them close together. Cover with the remaining berries. Arrange the remaining dough strips in a crisscross pattern on top of the berries. Cut the remaining ¼ cup of chilled butter into bits. Dot the dough with bits of butter and sprinkle with the remaining 1 tablespoon of sugar. Bake until the top crust is golden brown and the berry mixture is bubbling, 25 to 35 minutes. Serve warm or at room temperature with vanilla ice cream.

Drunken Brandy-Peach Bread Pudding

A great do-ahead dessert for a large crowd. Although I make it most often with fresh peaches, the recipe works with just about any fruit-nut combo you can dream up, including fresh berries and hazelnuts, fresh pears and almonds, bananas and pecans, or even craisins or raisins and pecans.

Serves 12 to 14 with leftovers

PEACH BREAD PUDDING

2 cups granulated sugar

4 cups half-and-half or heavy whipping cream

1 teaspoon ground cinnamon

3 large eggs

1 loaf challah or French bread, cut or torn into 2-inch chunks

3 cups chopped fresh peaches (about 6 peaches)

1 cup pecan halves

PEACH BRANDY SAUCE

½ cup (1 stick) unsalted butter

1 cup firmly packed golden brown sugar

1 large egg

Pinch of kosher salt

¼ cup peach brandy or liqueur of your choice

TO MAKE THE BREAD PUDDING: Preheat the oven to 350°F. Grease a 9 by 13-inch baking pan with butter or cooking spray. Mix the granulated sugar, half-and-half, and cinnamon in a large saucepan over medium heat. Stir occasionally until the sugar dissolves. (No need to boil the mixture.) Remove the saucepan from the heat.

Whisk the 3 eggs in a bowl until the whites and yolks are combined. Pour about ¼ cup of the hot cream mixture into the eggs, whisking as you pour. (This tempers the eggs, which keeps them from curdling when they are mixed into the hot cream mixture.) Pour the tempered egg mixture into the cream mixture left in the saucepan and whisk until the sauce is smooth.

Gently combine the bread cubes and peaches in a large bowl. Spoon into the prepared pan. Pour the sauce over the peach-bread mixture and let sit for about 30 minutes to let the sauce soak into the bread. Sprinkle the pecans on top.

Bake until the pudding is firm and lightly browned on top, about 1 hour. Cut into squares and serve warm or at room temperature with warm Peach Brandy Sauce.

TO MAKE THE PEACH BRANDY SAUCE: Melt the butter and brown sugar together in a saucepan set over medium heat. Remove the mixture from the heat. In a bowl, whisk the 1 egg with a fork. Temper the egg by adding about 2 tablespoons of the butter-sugar mixture to the egg and whisk constantly until the egg is incorporated. Pour the tempered egg mixture into the saucepan with the remaining sugar-butter mixture and whisk until the sauce is smooth. Add the salt and whisk in the brandy. Keep the sauce warm until ready to serve. Pour it over the bread putting as soon as it comes out of the oven.

DO IT EARLY

The bread pudding can be made up to 12 hours in advance, covered, and refrigerated. Warm in a 300°F oven. The sauce can be made up to 48 hours in advance and refrigerated until ready to use. Reheat it in a heavy saucepan set over low heat until it is warm but not hot; or microwave it on medium power in a microwave-safe container until warm, about 1 to 2 minutes.

Maple-Pecan Butter Thins

Keeping a batch of slice-and-bake cookies in the refrigerator at all times is one of the smartest things a hostess can do. Fire up the oven, slice off as many as you need, bake them off, and you've got dessert in less than 30 minutes. Thanks to my old friend and pastry chef Jeannie Hemwattakit for lending me her recipe for these delicate, buttery cookie thins, which never last long in the refrigerator or on the cookie plate.

Makes about 30 cookies

1 cup chopped pecans

1 pound (4 sticks) unsalted butter, at room temperature

1 cup sugar

2 large egg yolks

$^1/_4$ cup maple syrup

$2^3/_4$ cups all-purpose flour

$^1/_2$ teaspoon kosher salt

1 teaspoon vanilla extract

Preheat the oven to 350°F. Place the pecans on an ungreased baking sheet and toast them until they turn slightly darker and fragrant, about 7 minutes; set aside. Line baking sheets with parchment paper or silicone liners, or generously grease with butter or cooking spray. Using an electric mixer fitted with the paddle attachment, beat the butter and sugar in a large bowl on medium-high speed until light and fluffy, about 4 minutes. Beat in the egg yolks and maple syrup. Add the flour, salt, and vanilla and beat on low speed until just incorporated. Stir in the toasted pecans. The dough will be soft and somewhat sticky. Divide the dough into 2 clumps. Set each on a long sheet of plastic wrap or waxed paper, shape the dough into 2 even logs, and wrap tightly. (I like the look of a square cookie, so I lightly press the logs on 4 sides to flatten.) Refrigerate the dough for at least 2 hours or overnight. If you're really in a hurry, freeze the dough for about 20 minutes, just until they retain their shape when sliced.

When ready to bake, unwrap a log of dough and cut it into $^1/_8$-inch-thick slices. Place them on the prepared cookie sheet and bake until they turn golden around the edges, 10 to 12 minutes.

DO IT EARLY

The cookie dough can be made and rolled into logs up to 1 month in advance and frozen, or up to 1 week in advance and refrigerated. To prepare frozen dough for baking, remove it from the freezer and set it at room temperature 1 hour before baking; or simply transfer the dough from freezer to fridge the night before baking. Refrigerated dough can be sliced and baked straight from the refrigerator. The baked cookies will keep in an airtight container for up to 3 days.

TIP To make rectangular cookies as pictured opposite, form the dough into 1 rectangular-shaped loaf, wrap and refrigerate as directed above, cut into slices lengthwise, and bake.

Top-Shelf Tea

This is mixologist David Alan's grownup version of that old college party favorite Long Island Iced Tea. By using premium spirits in small amounts, David creates a balanced drink that isn't too sweet or too strong, a far cry from the frat boy rendition, where one drink could put you out for the night. David omits the standard sweet-and-sour mix and tops the cocktail with the traditional splash of cola. Incidentally, despite its name, the drink doesn't contain tea, but when all the ingredients are mixed together it sure looks like it.

Makes 1 drink

¹/₂ ounce (1 tablespoon) silver tequila

¹/₂ ounce (1 tablespoon) white rum

¹/₂ ounce (1 tablespoon) vodka

¹/₂ ounce (1 tablespoon) Cointreau

¹/₂ ounce (1 tablespoon) gin

1 ounce (2 tablespoons) freshly squeezed
lemon juice (about 1 medium lemon)

¹/₂ ounce (1 tablespoon) simple syrup
(see Tip, page 191)

4 ounces (¹/₂ cup) cola soda

Lemon twist, for garnish

Combine the tequila, rum, vodka, Cointreau, gin, lemon juice, and simple syrup in a cocktail shaker filled three-quarters of the way with ice. Shake well and strain into a tall glass two-thirds filled with ice. Top with cola and a lemon twist and serve immediately.

TIPS To avoid the overly sweet taste of high fructose corn syrup, use Boylan Cola or Mexican Coca-Cola, which still uses cane syrup as its sweetener.

Use large ice cubes for drinks on the rocks. Big ice keeps the drink cold longer and takes longer to melt, which keeps the drink from becoming a diluted version of its former self before it is finished.

Smoke Old-Fashioned

This is David Alan's take on an old-fashioned that incorporates a smoky flavor from the home-smoked orange juice used as a base. Although smoked juice adds an extra layer of flavor, the drink also tastes good with plain orange juice.

Makes 1 drink

2 sugar cubes

2 dashes Peychaud's Aromatic Bitters

2 ounces (4 tablespoons) rye or bourbon whiskey

$1/2$ ounce (1 tablespoon) Smoked Orange Juice (recipe follows)

1 orange, for the zest garnish

1 lemon, for the zest garnish

In the bottom of a mixing glass, muddle the sugar cubes with the bitters. Add the whiskey and smoked orange juice. Stir with ice to chill; strain onto clean ice in an old-fashioned glass. Using a vegetable peeler, cut a wide piece of zest from the skin of the orange; repeat with the lemon. Hold the orange zest, colored side down, over the cocktail near the edge of the glass and fold it in half to squeeze the essential oils from the citrus skin onto the surface of the cocktail. Repeat with the lemon zest. Drop the orange and lemon zest into the glass for garnish.

Smoked Orange Juice

Makes about 8 ounces (1 cup) juice

3 to 4 medium oranges, halved

Set the orange halves, cut side up, on the rack of a stove-top smoker. Smoke for about 10 minutes over pecan chips or other favorite hardwood. Oranges may also be smoked in a traditional outdoor smoker. Be careful not to over-smoke the fruit, as it will dry out. Squeeze out the juice of the smoked oranges over a strainer set over a bowl or measuring cup. The juice will keep for 3 days in the refrigerator.

Basics and Sources

Basic Recipes

PICKLED REFRIGERATOR JALAPEÑOS
Makes about 4 cups

14 ounces whole jalapeño chiles
(about 4 cups), seeded and sliced

5 cloves garlic

1 cup cider vinegar

1 cup sugar

Put the jalapeños and garlic in a large heatproof bowl. In a saucepan set over medium-high heat, combine the cider vinegar and sugar and bring to a rolling boil. Remove from the heat and pour the liquid over the jalapeños. Let cool for about 30 minutes. Spoon the jalapeños into clean screw-top jars, and cover with the liquid. Refrigerate for at least 24 hours before serving. They will keep for up to 3 months.

CHIPOTLE KETCHUP
Makes about 3 cups

2 tablespoons canola oil

1 medium yellow onion, diced

2 large red bell peppers, seeded and diced

4 cloves garlic, minced

About 5 Roma tomatoes, cored and coarsely
chopped

1/2 teaspoon kosher salt

1/3 cup champagne vinegar

1/3 cup sugar

1/4 cup canned chipotle chiles in adobo sauce

Heat the oil in a large skillet set over medium heat. Add the onion and peppers and sauté until softened, about 5 minutes. Add the garlic, tomatoes, and salt and cook over medium heat for about 25 minutes. Add the vinegar and sugar and cook until the mixture has thickened, another 20 to 25 minutes. Pour the mixture into a blender with the chipotle chiles and blend until smooth. Return the mixture to the heat and simmer until it is about as thick as bottled ketchup, about 30 minutes. Transfer to a container and refrigerate until cold.

TYPICAL RED SAUCE
Makes 3 cups

2 1/2 cups Heinz ketchup

1/4 cup prepared horseradish

6 tablespoons freshly squeezed lemon juice
(about 3 medium lemons)

1 tablespoon Worcestershire sauce

3 shakes Tabasco sauce

In a bowl, stir together all the ingredients. Refrigerate for at least 2 hours before serving.

SPICY REMOULADE
Makes 4 cups

3 cups mayonnaise

3/4 cup Heinz ketchup

1/4 cup freshly squeezed lemon juice
(about 2 medium lemons)

3 tablespoons prepared horseradish

1/4 cup spicy Creole mustard

Tabasco sauce, for seasoning

In a bowl, stir together all the ingredients. Refrigerate for at least 2 hours before serving.

HOMEMADE MAYONNAISE
Makes about 2 1/2 cups

1 large egg

6 large egg yolks

1 tablespoon Dijon mustard

2 tablespoons freshly squeezed lemon juice
(about 1 lemon)

1 teaspoon kosher salt

2 cups canola oil

In the jar of a blender set on medium speed, process the egg, yolks, mustard, lemon juice, and salt until thoroughly mixed. Decrease the speed to low and add the oil in a slow, steady stream—the mayonnaise will thicken as you pour. It is done when it becomes thick and creamy, just after all of the oil has been added. Spoon it into a clean container, cover, and refrigerate immediately. It will keep for about 1 week.

ROASTED GARLIC
Makes 1 head

1 head garlic, unpeeled

Olive oil

Preheat the oven to 375°F. Slice off the top of the garlic head about 1/4-inch of the way down, exposing the inside of the garlic. Set it on a square of aluminum foil, drizzle the top with olive oil, and wrap to cover completely. Bake for about 50 minutes, or until the garlic is soft and caramelized. Store in the refrigerator for up to 1 week and use to enhance the flavor of soups, stews, or salad dressings.)

GUACAMOLE
Serves 8 to 10

4 medium ripe avocados

2 tablespoons freshly squeezed lime juice
(about 1 medium lime)

1 teaspoon kosher salt

Peel and seed the avocado and mash with a fork or potato masher. Stir in the lime and salt. Serve immediately.

Sources

Here are a few of the specialty ingredients I've called for in this book, and where to get them online.

Pickled Jalapenos

The Original Bread 'N' Butter Jalapeño
www.peppertraders.com

Cutter's Cross Sweet Hot Jalapeños
www.cutterscross.com

Smoke-dried Tomatoes

Boggy Creek Farm
www.boggycreekfarm.com.

Venison

Broken Arrow Ranch
www.brokenarrowranch.com
Free range, humanely slaughtered

Quail and Quail Sausage

Diamond H Ranch
www.texasgourmetquail.com

Uncle John's Quail Sausage
www.unclejohnsquailsausage.com

Acknowledgments

I GREW UP around parties—thanks to four gifted Texas hostesses who never seemed to tire of throwing them—my mother Tommye Wood and friends Ann Herrington, June Ohmstede, and Ann Ohmstede. They imbued in me a lifelong love of parties, which provided the inspiration for this book. I'm grateful to them all.

I could not have written this book without the help of many others. Sincerest thanks go to:

Rancher Loncito Cartwright for his consistent wise counsel and for introducing us to so many wonderful Texas hosts and hostesses; Carol Hicks Bolton and her husband, Tim, for lending us their lovely Gulf Coast home; Cindy Grieves for her cheerful, nonstop help with logistics during the Gulf Coast photo shoot; Sara and Sam Bell Steves for allowing us into their beautiful San Antonio home; Stuart Rosenberg for sharing his chic Houston condo; Armando Palacios for opening up his eponymous restaurant's kitchen as we prepared for our Houston photo shoot; Cinda Ward and her daughter, Allie, for their invaluable help with the Houston photo shoot; Liz Carpenter and Josephine C. Sherfy for so generously giving of their time; Cibolo Creek Ranch owner John Poindexter, and general manager Ron Hulsey, for providing a stunning location for the West Texas photo shoot; Castle Heep of Fredericksburg's Root for providing clothes for my daughter Frances; Sue Porter of Fredericksburg's Rawhide for dressing me for the West Texas chapter and more; Martha Pincoffs for her invaluable cooking assistance on several photo shoots; Yvonne Bowdon for supporting my efforts throughout the writing of this book as recipe tester, kitchen assistant, and general helpmate (she says I put five pounds on her); the entire staff at Rather Sweet Bakery for putting up with the usual book-writing craziness, especially Jasper, Katie, Shelton, Marsela, Tomas, Rosa, Betty, Romelia, Blanca, and Aurelio; Patricia and Donald Oresman for offering up their New York City kitchen for recipe testing; Ruth Stanton of Houston for testing several recipes; Carolyn Wood for sharing her Bolivar beach house; Barbara Gordon McNeill for generously sharing the story of her family's historic Bolivar residence; my business partner Dan Kamp for his support; Nancy, Matthew, Kezzie, and John Kamp for help with the Big City photo shoot; friends Mary and Marshall Cunningham, Kay Oxford, Margie French, Jim Manning, and Donna Bevil; Callie Wilson for her energetic and invaluable assistance during the Big City and San Antonio shoots; and my daughter, Frances, for making quesadillas and for continuing to be a really good sport throughout the writing of three Pastry Queen books.

Special thanks to our extraordinary photographer, Laurie Smith; our endlessly creative food stylist, Erica McNeish, who also went the extra mile to expertly test many recipes; our clever, tireless, and patient editor, Clancy Drake; our gifted art director, Toni Tajima; our steadfast and multitalented agent, Doe Coover; and our stalwart publisher, Aaron Wehner, for his enduring support of what turned out to be a more ambitious and complicated enterprise than any of us anticipated. **RR**

Beyond all of those mentioned above, I'd like to thank my Seattle-area support team, friends and family who kept me going throughout the writing of this book: Kathleen Hunt, Emily Anderson, Courtni Billow, Danielle Cuvillier, Ernie Davis, Kyoko Harrison, Marcie Spahi, Marcia Houdek Jimenez, Stan Mandell, Cathy Lindsay, Colleen Willoughby, Carla Lewis, Rhoda Altom (and all the rest of my colleagues at Washington Women's Foundation), Sarah Peter, Kit Young, Jane Dudley, Kathryn Ramquist, and the Wednesday night meditation group, and Yaffa Maritz and the Tuesday night meditation group. My husband, Warren, kept his sense of humor, a positive attitude, and a willingness to listen to endless talk of Texas parties during the long weeks of writing on deadline, when I was too busy to accompany him to a single party, make dinner, or even go to the grocery store. My son, Danny, provided his usual perceptive palate as a recipe taster; my daughter, Callie, lent her calm and cool persona, hard work, and incredible organizational skills to our five-day photo shoot in San Antonio and Houston; my brother, Tom Oresman, offered his medical expertise at a critical moment (thanks, too, to his wife, Julie, who gracefully endures an endless stream of calls to Tom from his relatives seeking free medical advice); my brother Craig Oresman and wife, Sandra, road-tested several recipes at parties in their New Mexico home; my niece, Amy Oresman, offered her usual spot-on makeup advice; and my parents, Patricia and Donald Oresman, have continued to be ardent supporters of my work in myriad ways. I feel deeply grateful to have all of you in my life. **AO**

257

Index